Academic Irregularities

This book evaluates cultural and discursive changes within UK universities which have evolved within an era influenced by neoliberal governmentality from 1981 to the present. The authors make connections between economic and political developments in society and the changes to conditions of labour and values operating in (largely) Western universities. The original contribution of the research presented in this book is to bring the tools offered by applied linguistics to the analysis of the discourses emerging from the marketised, managerial academy where the nature of academic identities and the role of the university in society are being contested. Using some of the tools of applied linguistics (specifically corpus linguistics, critical discourse analysis and appraisal analysis), the authors uncover the power relations and contradictions experienced by those working and studying in UK universities. Morrish and Sauntson argue that there is presently a massive reorientation of universities away from their previous mission as serving the public good, as repositories of knowledge, as a refuge from the discipline of the market and capitalism and governed by the pursuit of knowledge for its own sake. The discourse analysed throughout the book is more than just a reflection of these changes – it is arguably constitutive of ideological change and of a new kind of neoliberal, self-managing, subordinate subject. This important work is a key resource for students and scholars in applied linguistics, critical discourse analysis, sociology, business and management studies, education and cultural studies.

Liz Morrish is an independent scholar. For over 30 years, she taught linguistics at Nottingham Trent University.

Helen Sauntson is Professor of English Language and Linguistics at York St John University.

Routledge Critical Studies in Discourse

Edited by Michelle M. Lazar
National University of Singapore

Analysing Fascist Discourse
European Fascism in Talk and Text
Edited by Ruth Wodak and John E. Richardson

Discourse and Democracy
Critical Analysis of the Language of Government
Michael Farrelly

Language and Masculinities
Performances, Intersections, Dislocations
Edited by Tommaso M. Milani

Discourses of Ideology and Identity
Social Media and the Iranian Election Protests
Chris Featherman

The Discourse Strategies of Imperialist Writing
The German Colonial Idea and Africa, 1848–1945
Felicity Rash

Discourses of Denial
The Rhetoric of American Academic Labor
Thomas A. Discenna

Discourses of (De)Legitimization
Participatory Culture in Digital Contexts
Edited by Andrew S. Ross and Damian J. Rivers

Academic Irregularities
Language and Neoliberalism in Higher Education
Liz Morrish and Helen Sauntson

For more information about this series, please visit: www.routledge.com/Routledge-Critical-Studies-in-Discourse/book-series/CDA

Academic Irregularities

Language and Neoliberalism in Higher Education

Liz Morrish and Helen Sauntson

Routledge
Taylor & Francis Group
LONDON AND NEW YORK

First published 2020 by Routledge

2 Park Square, Milton Park, Abingdon, Oxon, OX14 4RN
605 Third Avenue, New York, NY 10017

Routledge is an imprint of the Taylor & Francis Group, an informa business

First issued in paperback 2020

Library of Congress Cataloging-in-Publication Data
A catalog record for this book has been requested

ISBN: 978-1-138-67395-3 (hbk)
ISBN: 978-0-367-78415-7 (pbk)

Typeset in Sabon
by Apex CoVantage, LLC

For Kathleen O'Mara and Peter Sauntson

Contents

Tables

Figures

Acknowledgements

During the course of this project, Helen and Liz have both faced professional upheaval. This resulted in Helen changing jobs (and earning promotion to professor) and Liz leaving academia. In completing this book, we have been sustained by colleagues both personal and virtual too numerous to mention. Special mentions must go to our spouses: Caroline Sauntson and Kathleen (K.O.) O'Mara who have patiently buoyed us with their belief that our work is worthwhile.

We have valued encouragement from and the opportunity for discussion with Thomas Docherty, Justin Cruickshank, Eva Bendix Petersen, Kate Bowles, Richard Hall, Aidan Byrne, Derek Sayer, Yoke Sum Wong, Craig Brandist, Eric Royal Lybeck, Nicky Priaulx, Nick Megoran, Raksha Pande, Rosie Miles, Filip Vostal, Jana Bacevic, Mark Carrigan, Sarah Amsler, Annabelle Mooney, Emilie Whitaker, Veronika Koller, Erika Darics, Kerry Dobson Clukas, Joanne Hollows, Patrick O'Connor, Lisa Clughen, Richard Bromhall, Catherine Adams, Steve Jones, Jean-Pierre Boule, Nic Dunlop, Monica Franco-Santos, Louise Mullany, Martin McQuillan, Charlotte Walker and Robert Compton. There are also a few university pro vice chancellors and registrars who might wish to remain anonymous. We are fortunate to have been writing in an age of social media when there are blogs, Twitter accounts and Facebook groups for like-minded scholars which have offered support and information.

We mourn the untimely loss of Judith Baxter and Joyce Canaan whose work has enlightened us and their insights have informed each chapter of this book.

Colleagues from universities across the world have shared their stories, examples of discourse and dissatisfaction with the neoliberal academy. Whilst a reorientation of universities from a focus on knowledge creation to a focus on the student consumer has subdued the enthusiasm of many for academic life, these changes have, nevertheless, provided an endless source of data for our enquiry.

And, lastly, we owe sincere thanks to the managers, without whose opaque and hyperbolic discourse in strategy documents, policies, training courses and all-school messages, this book could not have been written. You have been an inspiration.

Introduction

Critical university studies is a newly identified field (Petrina and Ross 2014) and one which is flourishing. Since the mid-2000s there has been a surge in higher education research focusing on 'the neoliberal academy', 'the marketised academy' and 'the student as consumer'. In this climate, we seek to make connections between economic and political developments in society, and the changes to conditions of labour and values operating in (largely) Western universities. The original contribution of the research presented in this book is to bring the tools offered by applied linguistics to the analysis of the discourses emerging from the marketised, managerial academy where the nature of academic identities and the role of the university in society are being contested. As yet, the existing body of research on critical university studies has not drawn on the tools of applied linguistics despite its concern with 'discourses'. This book redresses this obvious research gap.

The book evaluates cultural and discursive changes within UK universities which have evolved within an era influenced by neoliberal governmentality from 1981 to the present. Neoliberalism in its various forms celebrates the free market and, significantly, the value system that flows from that. In this culture, all public institutions feel obliged to cast themselves as simulacra of profit-making organisations. What has taken shape in universities is a culture of the 'corporate boast', with markets and competition as priorities, distorting the internal priorities of universities.

In the UK, there has been much interest and debate generated since *The Browne Review* (or *Independent Review of Higher Education Funding and Student Finance*) published its findings in October 2010 (Department for Business, Innovation and Skills 2010). The explicit purpose nominated by Cable and Willetts in their white paper *Putting Students at the Heart of Higher Education*[1] was to introduce a potential for a new dynamic between academic staff and students – one of students as consumer of higher education. In the wake of the report came a flurry of critical work weighing the benefits and limitations of the shifting new axis in universities. An additional unforeseen result of these changes was that students have simultaneously become positioned as saleable 'products' of universities, and this tension in discursive positioning of students is a key issue which will be evidenced and explored throughout this book.

Since the 2010 *Browne Review*, the market has become more than metaphor, and universities now see themselves as competing for students (Williams 2013). There is a consensus, and concern, about the changing ethos and values of UK universities (Barnett 2013; Bousquet 2008; Collini 2012; Molesworth *et al* 2011; Williams 2013; Wright and Shore 2017). Our research analyses the discourse which communicates these changes. In UK universities, it is common to encounter two 'communities of practice' – managers and academics. Inevitably, we have seen a degree of panic arising when the corporate discourse and values of the former do not align with, and impede, the self-evident purpose of universities as critical spaces for contestation, learning and the creation of knowledge.

Similarly, despite universities' claims to be driven by consumer demands, the institutional discourse functions precisely to set limits on those demands. We offer case studies that indicate students' unions (SU), once sites of antagonism to corporate identities and hierarchies, are now fully compliant with neoliberal governmentality. Since 2014, we have seen universities (Sussex, Birmingham, UCL, University of London) subdue student protest with disciplinary procedures, and threatened (or actual) suspensions. What has been apparent is a struggle over discourse, values and power. Strategies for resisting discourse are less obvious than those for resisting policy. However, the tools of applied linguistics to critically analyse discourses in university contexts offer a valuable way forward (Sealey 2014).

In this book, we examine key sites of transmission of the discourse and institutionally ratified values of universities focusing on case studies of institutional discourse. We use some of the tools of applied linguistics (specifically corpus linguistics, critical discourse analysis [CDA] and APPRAISAL[2] analysis) to uncover the power relations and contradictions experienced by those working and studying in UK universities. Specific research questions addressed in the book are as follows:

1. What does a critical linguistic analysis of managerial discourse reveal about academic values and identities?
2. How can the tools of applied linguistics be used to enhance knowledge and understanding about critical university studies?
3. What can critical linguistic analysis reveal about the role of discourse in formulating resistance to the managerial project?

In each of the following chapters, we consider a key issue in relation to language and critical university studies. Each chapter starts by introducing the issue, considering the issue in relation to the current higher education context and briefly reviewing any existing relevant literature. We then examine each issue in a series of case studies. The case studies use specific frameworks of linguistic analysis to analyse the language used in a range of written data taken from HE environments in order to enhance understanding of each issue. The application of linguistic frameworks of analysis enables us to examine not just *what* the discourses are, but *how* they emerge and are manifested in texts. This use of systematic linguistic frameworks is a key point of originality in the book and the research ultimately aims to enhance understanding of the discourses currently circulating in universities and some of their effects on those who work and study in them. The remainder of this introductory chapter introduces the tools of critical applied linguistics which are drawn on throughout the book. Chapter 1 then elaborates on key issues in the higher education context briefly introduced earlier.

Analytical framework: critical applied linguistics

Throughout the book, we use an overarching critical applied linguistics (CAL) approach. CAL has been defined as 'the practice of applied linguistics grounded in a concern for addressing and resolving problems of inequality' (Hall *et al* 2017: 18). According to Hall *et al*, critical applied linguistics is an approach to language study which addresses a specific problem for the benefit of a defined set of 'clients' or end-users.

> First and foremost, applied linguistics is concerned with individuals' and groups' language-related *needs* [. . .] Applied linguistics is, above all, a problem-solving discipline, and while any project in applied linguistics may *begin* with a description or empirical investigation of the role of language in a real-world problem, it should aim to *end* with the planning, testing and evaluation of a potential solution.
>
> (Hall *et al* 2017: 17)

They argue that the identification of a 'real-world' problem should be informed by the people who experience it. This approach, therefore, lends itself well to investigating the problematic issues identified by those working within academia.

Critical applied linguistics is closely aligned with CDA (Fairclough 2001), an approach which conceptualises language as a form of social practice and sees any 'text' as both reflecting and affecting the social and interactional contexts in which it is produced and received. This differs from more 'traditional' forms of discourse analysis in which analysis can be quite de-contextualised. Fairclough (2001) argues that exploring the relationship between texts, interactions and contexts is a key principle of CDA, with a specific focus on how power is enacted and reflected through language. Ideologies which prevail in the wider social context in which texts circulate become inscribed in texts, often in subtle ways. Thus, CDA may be used to uncover ideologies about education, academic identity, equality and other pertinent issues which are embedded in written documents which circulate in university environments. Although individual CDA-based studies may differ in their focus and in terms of the specific language features analysed, what they generally have in common is an emancipatory goal. CDA and CAL-based studies tend to work towards social justice – they often focus on identifying the ways in which particular groups in society are vulnerable, exploited or relatively disempowered and, through uncovering how this happens discursively, aim to use their findings as a pre-requisite for social change. This is precisely why we situate our work within a critical applied approach.

There is a growing tradition in applied linguistics of combining different methods and approaches in order to provide a more detailed and nuanced analysis of texts in particular contexts. Rampton *et al* (2002: 373) note that applied linguistics involves a lot of 'hybrid interdisciplinarity'. Both CDA and CAL have historically drawn on various linguistic analytic frameworks and have focussed on a range of linguistic features. Throughout this book, within the overarching CAL approach, we follow this tradition of deploying a hybrid approach to linguistic analysis by using a combination of the methods of corpus linguistics (specifically keyword analysis), multimodal critical discourse analysis (MCDA), the CDA of 'strategically deployable shifters' (or SDS) (Urcioli 2000) and their main presuppositions, the analysis of evaluative language using an APPRAISAL framework and an analysis of the key metaphors used throughout the texts. Employing these frameworks of analysis enables us to identify the key linguistic means by which the discourses of corporatisation and neoliberal governmentality are achieved in the documents analysed throughout the volume. Depending on the data set/s used in the case study, differing emphases may be placed on the application of the different analytical frameworks, which we go on to explain next.

We advocate the use of some quantitative methods within a broader critical discourse framework. Baker (2008), in his discussion of the use of corpus linguistics within CDA, argues that 'numbers count' in the sense that the frequencies with which speakers use particular linguistic features can be used to uncover the 'cumulative effects of language' (2008: 77):

> A single word or phrase might just suggest the existence of a discourse. But other than relying on our intuition [. . .] it can sometimes be difficult to ascertain whether such a discourse is hegemonic, mainstream, resistant or marginal. It is only by collecting numerous supporting examples of similar linguistic phenomena, that we can start to witness the cumulative contribution of specific linguistic items to a given discourse.
>
> (Baker 2008: 76)

In this book, we use a similar combination of quantitative and qualitative approaches to linguistic analysis in order to explore how repeated discourse patterns (identified through the application of the specific frameworks of corpus linguistics and APPRAISAL) can contribute to the cumulative effects of discourse in university contexts. The deployment of this combination of approaches to linguistic analysis provides a rigorous means of showing *how* neoliberal discourses in higher education are affected. Because the approaches reveal the subtle ways in which neoliberal discourse is manifested linguistically, they can also point to what makes such discourses difficult to resist and challenge.

Within the scope of a single book, the choice of analytic frameworks is necessarily selective. The motivation behind our selection of particular frameworks comes from our experience and expertise in using these methods in linguistic research. Secondly, the data we analyse in the book lends itself well to being analysed using these frameworks. Many of the texts we examine (e.g. prospectuses mission statements) are fairly formulaic and therefore are potentially interesting to examine in terms of linguistic patterns which emerge. Corpus linguistics and APPRAISAL are well-suited to identifying linguistic patterns across collections of texts. Some of the texts also contain a lot of evaluative language which inscribes values and judgements and, therefore, lends itself well to being analysed using critical metaphor analysis and APPRAISAL frameworks. Indeed, one of the primary purposes of the entire book is to investigate how the values of an institution, and the groups and individuals who work within them, are embedded in the texts which circulate within universities. In this sense, APPRAISAL as a framework which explicitly sets out to examine the language of evaluation is suitable for applying to the analysis of texts such as mission and diversity statements. Texts such as SU websites are highly visual and so lend themselves well to being analysed using MCDA. All of the document sets examined in this project are full of metaphors and SDS, therefore we use SDS and critical metaphor analysis in a number of the case studies. Each framework will now be explained in more detail.

Corpus linguistics

Sinclair (1991: 171) defines a corpus as 'a collection of naturally-occurring language text, chosen to characterise a state or variety of a language'. Corpus linguistics is a largely quantitative method which involves using a computer-held body of naturalised texts, and a range of computerised methods, to explore aspects of language and language use. A main advantage of using corpus linguistics is that it enables us to make observations about language use which go beyond intuition, and, because it is computer-based, it allows the exploration of patterns of language use which are not observable to the human eye. The majority of work in corpus linguistics has involved building large corpora, consisting of examples of language taken from a range of text types and contexts, in order to make generalised observations about the way a whole language (e.g. English) is used. However, it is acknowledged that the use of smaller and more specialised corpora can make useful contributions to understanding the language use of specific groups of people or the language patterns found in particular text types. Specialised corpora are usually designed with very specific research projects in mind. In the chapters that follow, we present analyses of a number of specialised corpora which we have built from the data sets listed in Table II.

The kind of linguistic analysis used at a descriptive level within an overarching CAL approach also needs to be systematic and able to identify repeated patterns across stretches of text. It is only through repetition that particular ideologies become naturalised through discourse. The more quantitative methods of corpus linguistics are well-placed to identify these kinds of repeated patterns across large stretches of interactional text. Indeed, a concern which has been levelled at critical approaches to language analysis such as CDA is that the analysis can be biased. If analysts set out to find evidence of particular kinds of discrimination or inequality in texts, this potentially leaves the analyst open to the criticism that they will simply find what they are looking for and will make the analysis fit their own political agenda. Analysts may also be selective in terms of only presenting texts which support and illustrate the kinds of inequality they have been focusing on – it may be the case that many similar texts are not discursively imbued with the inequality but can be conveniently ignored by the analyst. Baker *et al* (2013) suggest that one way of reducing this potential bias is to combine CDA with more 'objective' methods of analysis and this is the primary rationale for incorporating some corpus-based analysis within a broader critical approach in this book. Baker (2008) has argued that corpus linguistics and CDA can be used productively together and that using a combined approach can go a long way to addressing some of the criticisms which have been levelled at both approaches when they are used in isolation. These points are supported by Mautner (2009) who provides a comprehensive discussion of the mutual benefits of combining corpus linguistics with CDA.

In the case studies presented throughout this book, the specific corpus techniques used are keywords and concordance analyses, available using the software Wordsmith Tools (Scott 2014). Corpus analysis often starts with an analysis of keywords across the corpus. Scott (2014) defines a 'keyword' as a word that occurs in a corpus more often than would normally be expected when compared to another corpus. A keyword list is a useful starting point for word-based corpus analysis as it can begin to reveal information about themes and discursive priorities within the texts comprising the corpus. This can then provide a basis for further analysis. Stubbs (2001: 48), cited in Mautner (2005: 100) defines keywords as 'nodes around which ideological battles are fought'. Keywords, then, are very revealing in terms of the more unusual meanings and trends presented in the corpus. A keyword analysis requires the corpus under scrutiny to be compared with a 'reference corpus' which is a larger and more general corpus. In this case, the keywords lists were generated by comparing each document set with a word frequency list from the British National Corpus (www.natcorp.ox.ac.uk/). It is standard practice in corpus linguistics to remove the grammatical words from a keyword list so that the words presented are the lexical, or content, words. Therefore, in the keyword lists presented throughout this book, only the lexical words are included.

A next stage commonly used in corpus analysis, and one which we employ in the data analysis chapters, is to consider the semantic environment of some lexical items. Examining a word's concordances (a specified number of words to the left and right of the search term) can help to build up a semantic profile of that word which can contribute to revealing any underlying discourses and ideologies in the corpus. Using keyword and concordance analysis together can provide a fairly good overview of the main themes, discourses and ideologies prevalent in the corpus.

In sum, corpus linguistics can be used to enhance and support the claims made through the application of the more qualitative analytical tools of CDA (e.g. SDS analysis and critical metaphor analysis). The combination of these approaches also facilitates a critical analysis of large amounts of text and therefore enables a critical analysis of language *patterns* to be conducted. Baker (2008) and Baker *et al* (2013) have written extensively on the combination of corpus linguistics and CDA and have examined in detail how corpus linguistics can be used to enhance and support the claims made through the application of CDA. Stubbs (1996) also argues that the semantic patternings revealed by these techniques can contribute to the production of certain discourses in the corpus and he defines a discourse as 'recurrent phrases and conventional ways of talking, which circulate in the social world, and which form a constellation of repeated meanings' (Stubbs 1996: 158). Corpus linguistics, therefore, is a helpful way of revealing particular neoliberal discourses as they are embodied in written texts which circulate in university contexts. The corpus tools of keyword and concordance analysis are used in all of the case studies except for Case Study 1.

SDS analysis

Fairclough (1995: 91) recognises that regimes coerce via a 'technologisation of discourse', which he defines as the use of discourse to regulate others and control access to power. Chiefly, in university managerial discourse, and therefore in the texts scrutinised throughout this book, we see the employment of abstract nouns with shape-shifting definitions.

These have been termed by Urcioli as Strategically Deployable Shifters (SDS). Urcioli (2000: 4) defines SDS as follows:

> A lexical item or expression deployed in different discursive fields so that, in effect, people using term X in a referring expression in field A are engaged in a different pragmatic activity from those using the formally identified term X in a referring expression in field B. The salient interpretation of the term depends on the relation of its user to its audience and so shifts with context

Urcioli provides an example focusing on the use of the term *skills* in academic-institutional discursive fields. In the field of technical, engineering or production work, she observes that *skills* denotes specific techniques or procedures that can be learned through training. But in the field of academic performance, *skills* shifts to denote the capacity to read, write and do other academic tasks well. However, for those operating in each distinct field, the meaning of *skills* is perceived to be presupposed, unproblematic and *not* semantically slippery. Similar examples occur in the data analysed throughout this book. For instance, in Chapter 2, we identify *satisfaction* as an SDS. In the context of student surveys, *satisfaction* is taken to be an indicator of quality when used in relation to student satisfaction. However, when the same lexeme is used in undergraduate prospectuses, its meaning shifts to that of being a 'pass/fail' measure in relation to admissions requirements such as Disclosure and Barring Service (DBS) checks and health checks and declarations. We note that what emerges from the use of satisfaction as a SDS is a dual system whereby academic staff and the courses they teach are being judged as 'satisfactory' or not by students, and, at the same time, students are being assessed as to whether they 'satisfactorily' meet the requirements for being admitted to and passing courses. Through a process of 'pragmatic sedimentation' (Urcioli 2000: 4), SDS become naturalised into different fields which makes their meanings transparent to users within, but not across, fields.

Because SDS are multi-functional and polysemic, they are not always the sites of overt struggle. Many of the university documents analysed throughout this book are (sometimes almost entirely) made up of slippery, semantically vague usages e.g. *quality*, *excellence*, *leading*. As we focus on an analysis of SDS in the case studies, we will see how various lexical items appear to have been co-opted for managerial purposes on the force of their polysemicity. In particular, we will show through the SDS analysis how there is slippage between managerial and academic discourses, a significant damaging effect of which is academic struggle to find self-worth by measuring achievement in terms set by the institution. SDS analysis is used in Case Studies, 2, 5, 6, 7 and 8.

Critical metaphor analysis

Metaphor analysis is a fairly standard component of CDA more broadly. In their seminal work *Metaphors We Live By* (1980), Lakoff and Johnson define metaphors as the main means through which we understand abstract concepts and engage in abstract reasoning. According to Lakoff and Johnson (1980: 3), metaphors shape the way we interact with and think about the world, and our conceptual system thus plays a central role in defining what we understand as everyday realities. In what has become termed conceptual metaphor theory, they posit that we are not usually conscious of the workings of our conceptual system and are, therefore, unaware of how everyday metaphors may shape our thinking and perceptions of the world. What made this work groundbreaking was that metaphors came to be understood not just as a linguistic device for enriching linguistic description, but as a central means of understanding and creating social realities. As Lakoff and Johnson (1980: 146) themselves posit:

> Metaphors [. . .] are among our principal vehicles for understanding. And they play a central role in the construction of social and political reality.

In other words, most of our conceptual system is actually metaphorical – thought and action are largely structured through metaphorical thought. In Lakoff and Johnson's conceptual theory of metaphor, they propose that we use the understanding of one familiar concept (source domain) in order to understand another less familiar and more abstract concept (target domain). The sources domains are often physical and experiential whereas the target domains are more often abstract and cerebral.

Gatti and Catalano (2015) provide the example of the LIFE IS A JOURNEY[3] metaphor in which certain elements of the journey (source) domain are mapped onto the more abstract concept of 'life' (target domain). So specific elements of the LIFE IS A JOURNEY metaphor may include the following:

Source	*Target*
Traveller	Person leading a life
Destination	Purpose of life
Obstacles	Difficulties in life
Distance covered	Progress made

Source: Adapted from Gatti and Catalano 2015: 150

Examples from our own data include: UNIVERSITY AS MILITARY UNIT; UNIVERSITY AS ATHLETE/SPORTS TEAM; KNOWLEDGE AS A BUILDING. Gibbs (2017) observes that war metaphors are common in political, business and health discourse. It is therefore interesting to note that we also find that they are common in the higher education discourse scrutinised throughout this book. War metaphors are also identified as a common feature in political discourse by Charteris-Black (2004). Taking the UNIVERSITY IS AN ATHLETE/SPORTS TEAM metaphor as an example, the way that these metaphors work in terms of mapping source and target domains is shown next.

UNIVERSITY IS AN ATHLETE/SPORTS TEAM:

Source	*Target*
Track record	Past achievements of the university
Baseline	Minimum requirements of a university
Tackling	University competes with other universities
Goals	What the university needs to do to be better other universities
Set a high bar	University aspires to be better than other universities
Champion	What the university becomes when it is better than other universities
Gaming 'metrics'	Universities try to cheat and manipulate
Level the playing field	Universities have to act fairly

Charteris-Black (2004) writes about sports metaphors and their prevalent use in political discourse. He notes that a key element of sports metaphors is that there are 'teams', 'winners' and 'losers'. In this sense, sports metaphors are related to a higher order conceptual key of sport as a struggle for survival. If these associations are applied to a university context, then the reality that is constructed is that universities are places of struggle where it is human survival that is at stake. Charteris-Black goes on to argue that sport, war and survival are, in fact, all conceptually related. Semino (2008) has also written about the extensive use of sports metaphors in politics, arguing that their relative simplicity (they are based on a simple conceptual opposition between winning and losing) functions to obscure the ideological and ethical complexities of their target domain. Stored in our conceptual frame for sport is the fact that there are winners and losers, and the activity is competitive, it is difficult and requires practice and training, there are rules and punitive consequences (penalties) if the rules are not followed. When readers are prompted to conceptualise the target domain of academic work in these terms, we can immediately see how the meanings become restricted and obscure other possibilities of how academic work could be (and is) conceptualised (e.g. collegial, cyclical, noncompetitive, no clear rules). We see this process occurring repeatedly in the texts examined through this book, as we discuss in greater detail in later chapters.

What is significant about metaphorical mapping processes is that they 'preserve the cognitive typology [. . .] of the source domain, in a way consistent with the inherent structure of the target domain' (Lakoff 1993: 203). This puts constraints on the mappings that can occur. As Charteris-Black (2004: 14) explains:

> Mappings therefore involve a set of relations rather than single attributes so that what is transferred is a knowledge of a set of properties, their behaviour and interrelationships as they are known in the source domain.

It is for these reasons that, although rooted in cognitive linguistics, metaphors have more recently proved useful and revealing foci of investigation in CDA. A number of writers (e.g. Cameron 2003; Goatly 1997; Semino 2008) have argued that there should also be a pragmatic discourse dimension in the study of metaphor with a consideration of the social and political contexts in which they are deployed. This pragmatic dimension is important for CDA. Put simply, in particular contexts of use, metaphors can 'privilege one understanding of reality over others' (Chilton 1996: 74). Metaphors can be used strategically by text-producers to prioritise particular ideas and value through the deliberate selection of particular source domains over others. This has prompted a number of extended studies of metaphor use in political discourse in recent years (e.g. Charteris-Black 2014; Chilton 2004; Hart 2008; Musolff 2004, 2012; Semino 2008). Other studies have focussed on educational contexts (e.g. Gatti and Catalano 2014; Offstein and Neck 2003; Semino 2008), although these have mainly focussed on classroom interaction and the verbalised experiences of teachers. We contend that the texts circulating in HE provided another rich source for analysing how metaphors are used to promote particular ideologies and values and to subsequently construct versions of reality which ultimately suit the personal and economic needs of university managers rather than upholding the academic identities and values held by most students and staff.

Charteris-Black (2004) was the first to synthesise conceptual metaphor theory with CDA in his formulation of critical metaphor analysis. A primary aim of CDA is to make explicit ideological motivations and socio-political values that would otherwise be implicit or obscured. Through emphasising the pragmatic dimension of metaphors alongside the cognitive dimension, Charteris-Black proposed that critical metaphor analysis is useful for exploring how metaphors function as linguistic evidence of particular ideologies being embedded into texts.

> Critical explanation of a metaphor involves working out exactly what the metaphor brings to our attention and what is obscures. [. . .]

> Critical metaphor analysis seeks to identify both what is implied and the other point of view concealed by the metaphor.
>
> (Charteris-Black 2014: 200)

Because we are not aware of metaphors (because they mainly function as part of our unconscious conceptual system), this makes them difficult to identify and easy to ignore. Charteris-Black extends the work of Lakoff and Johnson by arguing that conceptual metaphors are not just a function of the semantic system. Rather they are 'matters of speaker choice' (2004: 10) and, thus, related to the pragmatic dimension of metaphor. Charteris-Black argues that metaphor is always inherently evaluative because it is about speaker/writer choice involves an imposition of a set of values. When values are imposed by metaphorical choices in texts, it can affect the way the reader/hearer conceptualises and understands the target domain of the metaphor.

Musolff (2012) elaborates further by explaining that the selected source domain in a metaphor carries with it a set of social, emotional and aesthetic values which are carried over, or mapped, onto the target domain, this influencing how it is received and understood by the audience. Metaphors have a rhetorical function of arousing certain emotions in the reader/hearer. Charteris-Black (2014) refers to these as semantic 'entailments'. Metaphors evoke concepts and feelings that arise from cognitive schemas that are activated by the use of particular metaphorical source domains. War, for instance, can be a cognitive trigger for fear. So, for text-producers, the mapping of source domain elements onto a target domain is deliberate, and not arbitrary. The use of specific metaphors in discourse is *strategic*. In our data, for example, the mapping of the military unit source domain onto the university target domain is strategic in that it associates the university with being constantly under threat, vulnerable and needing to engage in hostile, and possibly, violent acts in order to survive. It is easy to see how such metaphors contribute to creating an environment in which academics feel insecure, destabilised, under threat and feel as though they have to be ever vigilant and ready to respond to the caprices of university leaders.

Furthermore, Semino (2008) points out that when metaphors become a dominant way of thinking about a phenomenon, it becomes difficult to challenge the metaphors used to describe it because those metaphors, over time, have become the most common-sense or naturalised way of understanding the phenomenon in question. Such metaphors have become so familiar to use that they often go unnoticed. And they bring with them particular associated attributes or qualities which foreground some things and conceal others. We see this with the prevalence of sport, war and building metaphors which are repeatedly recycled in all of the documents examined throughout this book.

Throughout the case studies presented in this book, we apply a systematic critical metaphor analysis to the texts in order to understand how metaphors are selected to prioritise and promote particular values and ideologies. Following Cameron (2003), we identify metaphors in the texts we analyse by looking for phrases and lexical items which appear to be incongruous with the situation in which they are being used (e.g. the use of *capstone* is normally associated with buildings so it appears incongruous when it appears in the context of education-focussed texts with 'knowledge' as its main referent). After this initial stage, Charteris-Black suggests that linguistic metaphors are then grouped together on the basis of their source domains – so, for example, all words relating to sport are grouped together, all words relating to buildings are grouped together, and so on. A conceptual metaphor can then be inferred from each grouping, so if lots of building terms are used to refer to academic knowledge, then the conceptual metaphor is KNOWLEDGE IS A BUILDING. This method for critically analysing metaphor is applied to the data in Case Studies 2, 5, 6, 7 and 8.

Multimodal Critical Discourse Analysis (MCDA)

MCDA is used to analyse the SU's website data in Case Study 1 (Chapter 2). Rogers (2011) notes that discourse can be understood as a multimodal practice which reflects and constructs the social world through different communicative modes. Machin and Mayr (2012) also observe that meaning is communicated through other semiotic modes as well as language. Language is just one amongst many resources for meaning making. Other resources include music, gesture, still or moving images, and three-dimensional objects. Different semiotic modes, with language, can all be drawn into a coherent meaning-making whole. Kress and Van Leeuwen (2001: 20) define 'multimodality', therefore, as 'the use of several semiotic modes in the design of a semiotic product or event, together with the particular way in which these modes are combined'.

Taking a critical approach to the analysis of multimodal texts, then, involves analysing the multimodal features in order to uncover the values and ideologies underlying the multimodal choices made by the text producer. Kress and Van Leeuwen (2006) and Kress (2011) have done extensive work on applying CDA to semiotic modes of communication other than language. Kress and Van Leeuwen (2006) develop a detailed and systematic descriptive framework, informed by a social semiotic theory of representation, that can be used as a tool for visual analysis. This work has also been developed by O'Halloran (2004) who specifically explores how systemic functional linguistics can inform the multimodal analysis of a range of texts. Machin and Mayr (2012) go on to explain:

> Both text and image can be thought of as being composed of communicative choices by authors that seek to do certain kinds of work for them. The job of Multimodal Critical Discourse Analysis is to

> identify and reveal these choices [. . .] Texts will use linguistic and visual strategies that appear normal or neutral on the surface, but which may in fact be ideological and seek to shape the representation of events and persons for particular ends.
>
> (Machin and Mayr 2012: 9–10)

MCDA, then, seeks to 'denaturalise' representations as they are manifested through a range of modes of communication. It is interested in examining the ideological motivations behind particular semiotic choices, and how those choices communicate power relations. Wodak and Meyer (2009) suggest that any form of CDA including MCDA, can take into account features such as how texts are designed, their use of statistics, photographs and pictures, as well as the layout and the use of symbols alongside the linguistic elements of texts. They also encourage attention to be paid to any topics which are conspicuous by their absence.

In Case Study 1, we draw on the analytical framework of MCDA for analysing the visual and linguistic elements in a sample of university SU websites. Websites are multimodal texts consisting of linguistic and visual elements. Using MCDA, we examine the values and ideologies conveyed through the semiotic choices made in the website texts, and the ways in which these choices signal power relations circulating in the wider HE context.

Appraisal

The university mission statement and diversity statement data sets in Case Studies 3 and 4 (Chapter 3) are analysed using APPRAISAL (Martin 2000; Martin and White 2005) as well as corpus linguistics. APPRAISAL is a specific type of discourse analysis which focuses upon categorising evaluative language. APPRAISAL provides a framework for analysing and describing evaluative language and categorising the ways that feelings, emotions, attitudes, judgements, valuations, social relationships and experiences are encoded in language. Martin (2000: 145) defines APPRAISAL as:

> the semantic resources used to negotiate emotions, judgements, and valuations, alongside resources for amplifying and engaging with these evaluations.

A key strength of the APPRAISAL framework is that it is systematic and detailed. It can also be applied quantitatively as numbers of occurrences of each category of APPRAISAL can be counted up to provide an overall picture of which evaluative elements may be predominating in a particular data set (and which ones may be markedly absent or lower in number). The framework is applied in Case Studies 3 and 4 specifically because the texts comprising these data sets are highly saturated with explicitly evaluative language. Unlike many of the other texts analysed throughout the book, the language of the mission statements and diversity statements makes little use of metaphor but, instead, uses other instantiations of evaluative language in order to subtly convey the values and ideologies of the institutions which produce them. This makes APPRAISAL a particularly appropriate framework for analysing these data sets.

APPRAISAL consists of the systems of ATTITUDE, GRADUATION and ENGAGEMENT. It is the system of ATTITUDE which is of most interest in this book. Martin identifies three broad subsystems of attitudinal positioning within the APPRAISAL system:

AFFECT, which refers to the linguistic resources deployed for construing the individual's emotional responses;
JUDGEMENT – the linguistic resources deployed for construing moral or social evaluations of behaviour; and
APPRECIATION – the linguistic resources deployed for construing the 'aesthetic' qualities of processes and natural phenomena.

Some examples are included next (appraising items are underlined).

AFFECT – [Our students] will be <u>inspired</u> to acquire the knowledge, skills and confidence; and
JUDGEMENT – [A university] *dedicated* to academic achievement
APPRECIATION – *one of the world's leading* research and teaching universities.

Each of the categories can have a positive or a negative value (all examples found in our corpora were positive). These values work on a sliding scale of GRADUATION, where evaluations may be intensified, played down and where comparisons may be drawn for amplifying effect. APPRAISAL categories are mainly distinguished semantically, and are realised primarily through the lexico-grammar of a text. Further degrees of delicacy, addressed by Martin (2000) are summarised in Figure I, which provides an overview of the system of ATTITUDE.

AFFECT is primarily concerned with the semantic resources deployed for construing emotions and feelings. Martin (2000) and Martin and White (2005) sub-divide AFFECT into four subsystems to add delicacy to the framework. Table I shows the AFFECT sub-categories which work on a sliding scale of positive and negative dimensions.

JUDGEMENT enables a speaker/writer to evaluate behaviour as conforming or not conforming to a particular set of social/cultural norms. This is the aspect that deals with social evaluations of behaviour and social practice, and it is these aspects of evaluative language that position the individual within a broader social and cultural system. Like all

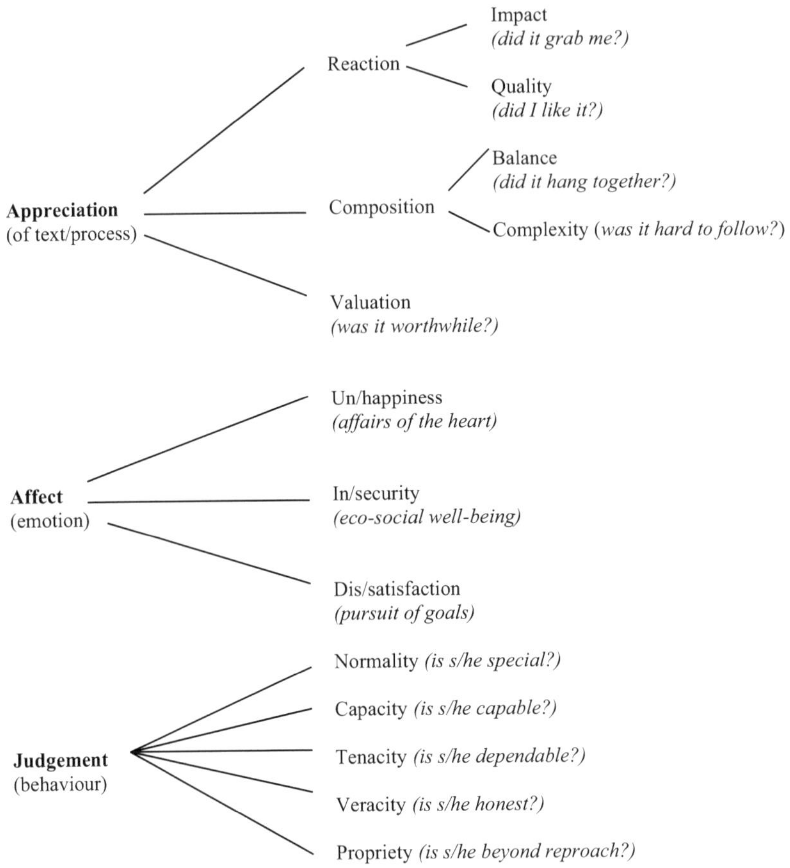

Figure I Attitudinal APPRAISAL framework

Source: Adapted from Eggins and Slade 1997

Table I Attitudinal system of AFFECT

Negative AFFECT	*Positive* AFFECT	*Example from Chapter 3 data*
DISINCLINATION (expresses feelings of fear)	INCLINATION (expresses feelings of desire)	Harassment is unwanted conduct [DISINCLINATION]
UNHAPPINESS (expresses feelings of misery and antipathy)	HAPPINESS (expresses feelings of cheerfulness and affection)	It encourages staff and students to enjoy and celebrate its diverse culture [HAPPINESS]
INSECURITY (expresses feelings of disquiet and surprise)	SECURITY (expresses feelings of confidence and trust)	Confident in its place as a leading international research university [SECURITY]
DISSATISFACTION (expresses feelings of ennui and displeasure)	SATISFACTION (expresses feelings of interest and admiration)	We take a great pride in [SATISFACTION]

Source: Adapted from Martin 2000

APPRAISAL categories, JUDGEMENT works on a sliding scale of positive and negative dimensions and can be subdivided into two broad areas (examples are taken from the mission statement and diversity statement data in Chapter 3):

Social esteem – assesses institutions, individuals and behaviours in terms of their:

NORMALITY (how usual/unusual they are)
Unconventional, risk-taking, experimental, radical, responsive [- NORMALITY[4]]
CAPACITY (how capable they are)
Provision of effective and efficient customer-focussed services in all aspects of our work [+ CAPACITY]
TENACITY (how determined or resolute they are)
We will strive to be an inclusive community [+ TENACITY]

Social esteem markers provide evaluations of how behaviour conforms or does not conform to socially desirable standards in any given culture.

Social sanction – assesses institutions, individuals and behaviours in terms of:

VERACITY (how truthful they are)
We seek and are inspired by truth [+ VERACITY]
PROPRIETY (how ethical they are)
We will act ethically to minimise our impact on the environment [+ PROPRIETY]

Social sanction provides evaluative markers which indicate whether a behaviour is seen as right or wrong in any given culture.

(Adapted from Martin 2000)

Figure II summarises the JUDGEMENT system.

APPRECIATION is the subsystem of ATTITUDE that expresses positive and negative evaluations of texts, processes and phenomena. According to Martin (2000), the APPRECIATION subsystem is organised around three variables – REACTION (the degree to which the text/process/phenomena in question captures our attention and the emotional impact it has on us), COMPOSITION (our perceptions of proportionality [BALANCE] and detail [COMPLEXITY] of the text/process/phenomena) and VALUATION (assessment of the social significance of the text/process/phenomena). Examples of each APPRECIATION sub-category are included below:

REACTION:

Made an impact on people's lives [+ REACTION]

COMPOSITION:

Coherent portfolio of specialist courses [+ COMPOSITION]

VALUATION:

We combine inspirational teaching, world-class research [+ VALUATION]

Martin argues that both JUDGEMENT and APPRECIATION are, to a certain degree, 'institutionalisations of feeling' in that they both encode feelings. Martin (2000: 147) proposes that affect is the basic system of ATTITUDE, which is then institutionalised into JUDGEMENT and APPRECIATION so that 'JUDGEMENT institutionalises feelings as proposals (about behaviour), whereas APPRECIATION institutionalises feelings as propositions (about things)'. For example, if a university environment is evaluated as *exciting*, the appraising item *exciting* is labelled as +APPRECIATION: REACTION because it is a phenomenon (environment) that is being evaluated. But describing an environment as *exciting* implies that I feel excited; therefore, the evaluation contains an element of AFFECT at its most basic level which is then institutionalised into an evaluation of something as exciting.

Additionally, what counts as APPRAISAL is often dependent on the field of discourse in question. APPRAISAL requires the analyst to be sensitive to, and explicit about, the particular context and text type they are examining. In order to identify APPRAISAL markers in a text, it is necessary for the analyst to have an understanding of the institutional practices involved in the texts under scrutiny, and to be aware of the attitudes that readers are expected to have towards those practices. For ease of reference, we have simply 'double-coded' the relevant examples.

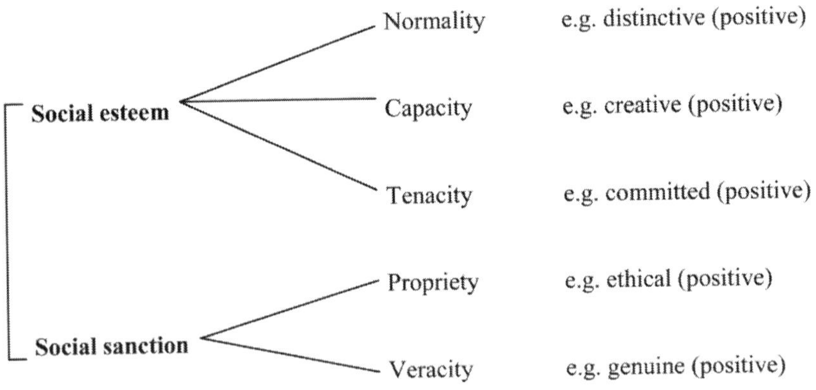

Figure II JUDGEMENT categories

Source: Based on Martin 2000

Some markers of ATTITUDE are often dependent on a referent which is situated elsewhere in the co-text. Where possible, we will try to justify the analysis if it is not immediately evident in the example cited.

Structure of this book

In sum, the combination of corpus tools and the critical discourse analytical tools of SDS analysis, critical metaphor analysis, MCDA and APPRAISAL facilitate a systematic analysis of large amounts of text and therefore enable a critical analysis of language *patterns* to be conducted. These tools are applied to various data sets within an overarching CAL approach which takes as its starting point the 'problem' of a loss of ethical values across the HE section in the UK and US.

Table II provides an overview of the structure of the book, summarises the data sets used within the case studies, and clarifies the accompanying linguistic frameworks which were used to analyse them.

Table II Summary of data sets and analytical frameworks used within the CAL approach

Chapter	*Case study*	*Data set*	*Analytical framework/s*
CAL			
Chapter 2: The Student as Consumer and Commodity	1	SU websites	• MCDA
	2	Online prospectuses and recruitment websites	• Corpus linguistics • SDS analysis • Critical metaphor analysis
Chapter 3: Marketing the Goods	3	Mission statements	• Corpus linguistics • Appraisal
	4	Diversity statements	• Corpus linguistics • Appraisal
Chapter 4: Language and Audit Culture 1	5	Research Excellence Framework (REF) documents	• Corpus linguistics • SDS analysis • Critical metaphor analysis
	6	Performance management documents	• Corpus linguistics • SDS analysis • Critical metaphor analysis
Chapter 5: Language and Audit Culture 2	7	Teaching Excellence Framework white paper – *Success as Knowledge Economy*	• Corpus linguistics • SDS analysis • Critical metaphor analysis

(*Continued*)

Table II (Continued)

Chapter	*Case study*	*Data set*	*Analytical framework/s*
Chapter 6: Colonising the Corporate Academic	8	Staff training documents on • Change management • Gold standard customer service • Leading high performing teams • Personal Development and Contribution Review (PDCR) • Succession planning	• Corpus linguistics • SDS analysis • Critical metaphor analysis

Source: More detail about the content of each data set is provided in its respective chapter.

Before presenting the case studies, Chapter 1 introduces the key issues and aspects of neoliberal discourse to be explored in the subsequent case studies presented in Chapters 2–6. The data chapters all comprise the same structure: a context-setting section, presentation of the case study/ies and a discussion section.

This book is a timely contribution to a wide conversation about recent changes in higher education globally. We hope that the approach we have taken will enable these themes to be recognised and discussed further, with evidence. As we have argued, this book makes use of the latest frameworks of discourse analysis. In the next chapter, we outline how we deploy another set of principles situated in the emerging multidisciplinary field of critical university studies.

Notes

1. www.gov.uk/government/news/putting-students-at-the-heart-of-higher-education
2. All terms used in the APPRAISAL framework are presented using SMALL CAPS.
3. In conceptual metaphor theory and critical metaphor analysis, conceptual metaphors are indicated using CAPITALISATION.
4. The '+' and '-' are, respectively, used to indicate positive and negative instantiations of JUDGEMENT and APPRECIATION.

References

Baker, P. 2008. 'Eligible' bachelors and 'frustrated' spinsters: Corpus linguistics, gender and language. In K. Harrington, L. Litosseliti, H. Sauntson and J. Sunderland, eds. Gender and Language Research Methodologies. Basingstoke: Palgrave. 73–84.

Baker, P., Gabrielatos, C. and McEnery, T. 2013. *Discourse Analysis and Media Attitudes: The Representation of Islam in the British Press*. Cambridge: Cambridge University Press.

Barnett, R. 2013. *Imagining the University*. London: Routledge.

Bousquet, M. 2008. *How the University Works*. New York: New York University Press.

Cameron, L. 2003. *Metaphor in Educational Discourse*. London: Continuum.

Charteris-Black, J. 2004. *Corpus Approaches to Critical Metaphor Analysis*. Basingstoke: Palgrave.

Charteris-Black, J. 2014. *Analysing Political Speeches: Rhetoric, Discourse and Metaphor*. Basingstoke: Palgrave.

Chilton, P. 1996. *Security Metaphors: Cold War Discourse from Containment to Common House*. New York: Peter Lang.

Chilton, P. 2004. *Analysing Political Discourse: Theory and Practice*. London: Routledge.

Collini, S. 2012. *What are Universities For?* London: Penguin.

Department for Business, Innovation and Skills. 2010. *The Browne Report: Securing a Sustainable Future for Higher Education: An Independent Review of Higher Education Funding and Student Finance*.www.gov.uk/government/publications/the-browne-report-higher-education-funding-and-student-finance (Accessed 1 September 2017).

Eggins, S. and Slade, D. 1997. *Analysing Casual Conversation*. London: Cassell.

Fairclough, N. 1995. *Critical Discourse Analysis*. London: Longman.

Fairclough, N. 2001. *Language and Power* (2nd edition). London: Longman.

Gatti, L. and Catalano, T. 2014. The business of learning to teach: A critical metaphor analysis of one teacher's journey. *Teaching and Teacher Education* 45: 149–160.

Gibbs, R. 2017. *Metaphor Wars: Conceptual Metaphors in Human Life*. Cambridge: Cambridge University Press.

Goatly, A. 1997. *The Language of Metaphors*. London: Routledge.

Hall, C., Smith, P. and Wicaksono, R. 2017. *Mapping Applied Linguistics: A Guide for Students and Practitioners* (2nd edition). London: Routledge.

Hart, C. 2008. Critical discourse analysis and metaphor: Toward a theoretical framework. *Critical Discourse Studies* 5 (2): 91–106.

Kress, G. 2011. Discourse analysis and education: A multimodal semiotic approach. In R. Rogers, ed. *Critical Discourse Analysis in Education* (2nd edition). London: Routledge.

Kress, G. and Van Leeuwen, T. 2001. *Multimodal Discourse: The Modes and Media of Contemporary Communication*. London: Arnold.

Kress, G. and Van Leeuwen, T. 2006. *Reading Images: The Grammar of Visual Design* (2nd edition). London: Routledge.

Lakoff, G. 1993. The contemporary theory of metaphor. In A. Ortony, ed. *Metaphor and Thought* (2nd edition). Cambridge: Cambridge University Press. 202–251.

Lakoff, G. and Johnson, M. 1980. *Metaphors We Live By*. Chicago: University of Chicago Press.

Machin, D. and Mayr, A. 2012. *How to Do Critical Discourse Analysis*. London: Sage.

Martin, J. 2000. Beyond exchange: Appraisal systems in English. In S. Hunston and G. Thompson, eds. *Evaluation in Text: Authorial Stance and the Construction of Discourse*. Oxford: Oxford University Press. 142–175.

Martin, J. and White, P. 2005. *The Language of Evaluation: Appraisal in English*. Basingstoke: Palgrave.
Mautner, G. 2005. The entrepreneurial university: A discursive profile of a higher education buzzword. *Critical Discourse Studies* 2 (2): 95–120.
Mautner, G. 2009. Checks and balances: How corpus linguistics can contribute to CDA. In R. Wodak and M. Meyer, eds. *Methods of Critical Discourse Analysis* (2nd edition). London: Sage. 122–143.
Molesworth, M., Nixon, E. and Scullion, R. eds. 2011. *The Marketisation of UK Higher Education and the Student as Consumer*. London: Routledge.
Musolff, A. 2004. *Metaphor and Political Discourse: Analogical Reasoning in Debates About Europe*. Basingstoke: Palgrave.
Musolff, A. 2012. The study of metaphor as part of critical discourse analysis. *Critical Discourse Studies* 9 (3): 301–310.
Offstein, E. and Neck, C. 2003. From 'acing the test' to 'touching base': The sports metaphor in the classroom. *Business Communication Quarterly* 66 (4): 23–35.
O'Halloran, K. ed. 2004. *Multimodal Discourse Analysis: Systemic Functional Perspectives*. London: Continuum.
Petrina, S. and Ross, W. 2014. Critical university studies: Workplace, milestones, crossroads, respect, truth. *Workplace: A Journal for Academic Labor* 23: 62–71.
Rampton, B., Roberts, C., Leung, C. and Harris, R. 2002. Methodology in the analysis of classroom discourse. *Applied Linguistics* 23 (3): 373–392.
Rogers, R. ed. 2011. *Critical Discourse Analysis in Education* (2nd edition). London: Routledge.
Scott, M. 2014. *WordSmith Tools*. Liverpool: Lexical Analysis Software.
Sealey, A. 2014. The neoliberal university: Agency and responsibility. Paper presented at *Neoliberalism, Education and Applied Linguistics Symposium*, Institute of Education, 27–28 June.
Semino, E. 2008. *Metaphor in Discourse*. Cambridge: Cambridge University Press.
Sinclair, J. 1991. *Corpus Concordance Collocation*. Oxford: Oxford University Press.
Stubbs, M. 1996. *Text and Corpus Analysis*. Oxford: Blackwell.
Stubbs, M. 2001. *Words and Phrases: Corpus Studies of Lexical Semantics*. Oxford: Blackwell.
Urcioli, B. 2000. Strategically deployable shifters in college marketing, or just what do they mean by 'skills: And 'leadership' and 'multiculturalism'? *Language and Culture Symposium* 6, Binghampton University. http://language-culture.binghamton.edu/symposia/6/index.html (Accessed 20 June 2018).
Williams, J. 2013. *Consuming Higher Education: Why Learning Can't Be Bought*. London: Bloomsbury.
Wodak, R. and Meyer, M. eds. 2009. *Methods of Critical Discourse Analysis* (2nd edition). London: Sage.
Wright, S. and Shore, C. eds. 2017. *Death of the Public University? Uncertain Futures for Higher Education in the Knowledge Economy*. Oxford: Berghahn.

1 Critical university studies

Defining a field

Introduction

> The SMT initiative on Employability is providing OOB with an opportunity to consider enhanced management in the School through use of JOW resource and will therefore extend beyond that specific role to a proposal relating to all transversal management roles in the School.
>
> (Initials changed)

For those who work in a university in a UK university, this kind of language is as familiar as it is incomprehensible. A key element of this book is essentially a discussion about how managerial discourse has contributed to universities losing their distinctive character (Collini 2012) and offers an analysis of the contexts, meanings and functions of this discourse and proposes some means of resistance.

The problem we identify is that, in universities, the conflict between managerial and academic values is primarily a struggle over discourse and the symbolic. It works by forcing the academic to cite discourse which redefines their subjectivity in terms of managerial values. In the past, the university was conceived of as a refuge from market values in its tolerance of risk and failure, because these are commonly seen to be essential characteristics of knowledge-building. Now, universities welcome only entrepreneurial, self-governing and competitive subjects, who are happy to function within the limits and discourse set for them by the managerial project.

It is important to outline the relationship between managerialism, which applies to institutions, and neoliberalism, the political and economic framework within which it sits (Klikauer 2013: 5). Since the late 1970s, neoliberalism has overtaken 'embedded liberalism' or interventionist Keynesian economics where entrepreneurial and corporate activities were regulated and constrained (Harvey 2005: 11). Since the 1990s, though, the principles of neoliberal thought have spread beyond economics and penetrated the political sphere (Brown 2015), the social sphere, and has now imposed its logic on the individual, demanding that we all live our lives as 'enterprise' (Scarff 2015). Brown (2015: 10) writes:

> [N]eoliberalism transmogrifies every human domain and endeavour, along with humans themselves, according to a specific image of the economic. All conduct is economic conduct; all spheres of existence are framed and measured by economic terms and metrics, even when these spheres are not directly monetized.

Neoliberalism is an ideology, then, which demands that all institutions, experiences and cultures are subordinated to the discipline of the market, and the value system that flows from that. Harvey (2005: 2) defines it thus:

> Neoliberalism is in the first instance a theory of political economic practices that proposes that human well-being can be best advanced by liberating individual entrepreneurial freedoms and skills within an institutional framework characterized by strong private property rights, free markets and free trade.

It is the role of the state in neoliberal economies that is controversial or even paradoxical. Most adherents of neoliberal politics espouse a smaller state and decry government intervention in the rule of the market. Despite this, as Rose (1999) points out, neoliberalism does indeed require the hand of government in ensuring the totality of its reach. It achieves this by assuming a 'there is no alternative' (TINA) approach to its tenets, and presenting them as general principles of good government. As well as market fundamentalism, essential characteristics of neoliberal thought are the upward redistribution of resources (Duggan 2003: ix), an emphasis on personal responsibility so that citizens are urged to be self-managing, self-enterprising individuals in health, professions and education (Ong 2006: 14), and an emphasis on the ideals of self-interest and competitiveness (Steger and Roy 2010: 12). Rose describes these as 'regimes of truth' (1999: 19) which govern the choices of self-managing, enterprising individuals, who all the time believe themselves to be free. These market-based 'truths' infiltrate into the domain, not just into the government of states, but are also absorbed into the conduct and value systems of institutions. This process results in 'neoliberal governmentality' (a Foucauldian term) which denotes modes of governance based on particular premises, logics and power relations (Steger and Roy 2010).

The term 'governmentality' has its origin in Foucault's notion of *biopower*, 'a series of regulatory controls exerted on the population and on individuals in order to harness and extract life forces' (Ong 2007: 13). If neoliberalism and its market-driven principles are accepted as everyday logic for guidance of all forms of human endeavour, then they can be taken to be acting not just on bodies, but also on subjectivities – how social actors conceive of themselves and their roles in the world. Thus, a number of strategies have proliferated amongst both state and corporate actors in codifying, rationalising and extending the logic of the market as a governing principle.

The 1980s saw new techniques of management in the public sector in the UK, known as New Public Management (NPM) and its close relative New Managerialism (NM) (Deem *et al* 2007: 3). Neoliberalism has provided the political context in which managerialism, with its shared ethos of competitiveness and anti-state/pro-market, anti-provider/pro-consumer, could flourish. Managerialism is often described as management to excess so that management becomes an end in itself: 'An ideology which holds that not only can all aspects of organizational life be controlled but that they should be controlled' (Hoyle and Wallace 2005:68). The theory dictates that techniques of management are not domain specific – they are generalisable. The training (often received on MBA courses, and similar tailored training courses), assumes the exclusive possession of managerial knowledge is necessary to efficiently run corporations and societies (Klikauer 2013: 2).

In universities, managerialism looked very different from traditional leadership and management. Until the 1980s, leading roles, such as dean or head of department, had been occupied by somewhat reluctant managers whose fixed-term positions were rotating and offered the prospect of a return to teaching and research (Deem *et al* 2007: 35). What new forms of managerialism appeared to offer were 'unremitting organisational restructuring, sharpening of incentives, and expansion in number, power, and remuneration of senior managers, with a corresponding downgrading of the role of skilled workers' (Klikauer 2013: 7). This last feature, particularly, has been keenly felt in universities. Whereas formerly, academic seniority had conferred considerable status upon the incumbents, what now emerged entailed 'the enhanced instrumental/ market rationality which gnaws away at professional autonomy and control' (Deem *et al* 2007: 22). In the US and UK, these influences have also manifested themselves in more formalised stratification of hierarchies in universities, and. It is not only hierarchies that have been formalised; this has enabled those in power to intensify the scrutiny and performance measurement of those who labour in universities. Morrissey notes that the 'science of management' brings about 'implicit surrendering to an increasingly accepted rationale for effectively governing academics in what could perhaps be best described as the "managerial" or "bureaucratic" university' (Morrissey 2013: 801). These changes are often presented to the workforce as necessary efficiencies which, nevertheless, offered personalisation, customisation, empowerment (Deem *et al* 2007: 10).

It is interesting to note that in their 1997 pioneering work *Academic Capitalism*, Slaughter and Rhoades refer neither to neoliberalism nor managerialism. These two constructs were not yet part of the authors' critical vocabulary. The term neoliberalism has become much more ubiquitous since the 2008 banking crises, which, it was thought, had brought the theory into disrepute (Block *et al* 2012). Indeed, some critics have levelled a charge of a promiscuous application of the term (Clarke 2008).

In 2019, we no longer debate whether this ethic has inflected managerial values in the academy; the takeover has been complete. In order to make sure that notions of efficiency take centre stage for academics, structures of neoliberal govermentality have been implemented to control access to resources. Universities have been obliged to reposition themselves as simulacra of business and to adopt practices traditionally associated with profit-making organisations, such as annual appraisals, audits of teaching hours, transparency reviews of work practices, peer teaching evaluation and teaching and research audits. Many of those who work within these new structures have perceived a degree of alienation and an evacuation of academic values. This new climate has been explored in a number of works (e.g. Canaan and Shumar 2008; Evans 2005).

Harvey (2005) points out that neoliberal institutions open up new fields for capital accumulation. Over the last decade across the UK higher education sector, we have seen the privatisation and commodification of staff and student services. Academic values have been transformed by a strategic manipulation of discourse (Davies and Bendix Petersen 2005). Fairclough (1995) provides one of the first critical studies of this new discourse in universities, referring to a concept he calls 'the technologisation of discourse' (1995: 102). This he defines as:

> a process of intervention in the sphere of discourse practices with the objective of constructing a new hegemony in the order of discourse in the institution or organization concerned, as part of a more general struggle to impose restructured hegemonies in institutional practices and culture.

In a later article, Chiapello and Fairclough (2002) argue that neoliberal practices and values are instilled in individuals by forceful repetition. Since the profit motive has been seen as the only priority, economies inevitably fall on practices that attract income – the teaching and research functions of the university (Davies and Bendix Petersen 2005: 88). Management and 'customer service' are enhanced and funding is shifted to administrators who have an auditing rather than a support function. Mulderrig (2011) notes how these new managerialist discourses have become increasingly evident in UK education policy documents. The extent to which academics may resist inhabiting a neoliberal subjectivity, whilst still compelled to cite its norms, forms the crux of our conclusion.

This book uncovers and critiques the discourses of managerialism circulating in 21st-century universities in the UK and US (a situation also relevant to other international HE contexts such as Ireland and Australia). It is essential to move beyond polemic if academics, and significantly, managers are to be persuaded of the argument. To this end, the book will move the debate to new ground anchored in linguistic evidence. We have a database of texts taken from UK and US universities which originated within managerial functions of audit, marketing and 'customer service'.

In order to frame our theoretical orientation, we turn to three concepts originating with Foucault: discourse, subjectivity and governmentality (Foucault 1994). For Foucault, discourse is critical for allowing the individual to make sense of experiences. Discourses about certain subjects circulate and structure, even limit, our understandings. In the context of this volume, we outline in Chapter 6 how discourses around *change* indicate it is something to be managed and controlled. This is what Foucault would recognise as a 'discursive formation'. These discursive formations are internalised and act to structure the actions and beliefs of those who labour within them. In this way, new subjectivities are constructed, and the discourses render those subjects governable.

'Governmentality' was a concept developed by Foucault in a series of lectures in the late 1970s, and is most often associated with the term 'neoliberal'. In the case of neoliberal societies, the concepts of the market and competition become a kind of common sense which then allows that govermentality to work on labouring subjects. This assumption about the rule of the market can be thought of as a new form of totalitarianism.

The project of neoliberal governmentality in universities is for the institution to produce its ideal employee (Morrissey 2013). The new subject formation works through a destabilisation of established academic practices, and a superseding of existing values of cooperation, collective governance and democracy. In this way, and via the new terms of the discourse, managers hope to produce the ideal employee of the neoliberal university. No longer are knowledge, ideas and intellectual agility the most highly valued gifts in the academy, nor are they seen as the characteristics of 'promotable' academics. The only aspiration viewed as legitimate is that of 'managing'. Indeed, as Docherty (2014a) points out, managers frequently conflate their own status with 'the university'. Morrish (2014) argues that university management is like a Ponzi Scheme which fraudulently endows investors with riches, not on the basis of enhancing productivity, rather the flow of money is only guaranteed when new investors are persuaded to join the scheme. Charles Ponzi, after whom the scheme was named, realised that all new investors need to have a relationship with the central figure, not with underlings. This exceeds mere audit culture – it is the forcible citation of a discourse which inaugurates a new kind of subject.

Our starting point is that discourse is not merely something which is found in texts and contexts; it also structures those contexts and constrains behaviours and identities within them. Differences in discourse reveal different sets of values, and it can sometimes seem as if academics and managers are occupying different universes entirely. Managerial priorities are reflected in the pervasive audit culture which has in many institutions subordinated academic endeavour. It is as if the real academic work of questioning, debate and contest has to take place in subterfuge, and Docherty (2011) writes of the retreat of many academics to an imaginary 'clandestine university'.[1] In the terms of our analytical frameworks, this indicates that there are two different communities of practice, situated in a hierarchical relationship, and this is reflected in the discursive resources and linguistic signifiers adopted by the two camps.

The case studies in subsequent chapters are based on real data of managerial discourse in universities, and the analysis proceeds using the CAL frameworks outlined in the Introduction. There are two principles which guide us: first, the examples we use from the data are familiar to our readership; all academics encounter managerial discourse on a daily basis. Second, our analysis, notwithstanding the application of linguistic rigour, is intended to be accessible. We wish to illuminate our subject so that the critique can be available to readers who are not linguists. It is time to offer an analysis, and a way forward to resist the discourse which nullifies academic values and de-legitimates academic work. Although this work is a critique of managerialism, it will be unique in that it will offer the manager some prospect for remediation. Critiquing and resisting the discourse they are required to cite is one strategy towards that ideal.

The remainder of this chapter introduces the scope of the volume. We discuss the historical context of changes to public service management over the last 30 years. Many critics would say that management has become an end in itself, with US universities expanding the complement of managers and administrators by 85% between 1975 and 2005. During the same time period, the teaching staff increased by 50% (Ginsberg 2011: 25). A report in *The Guardian* (Tahir 2010) also reports a rise of 33% in the number of managers in UK universities. At the same time, UK universities have increased their spend on marketing by 33% since 2010, with a collective spend of £36 million on student marketing (Sandler Clarke 2014). In part, this has been a defensive response in a climate of uncertainty for university funding, and increased competition for student numbers.

Competition, though, has become an autonomous leitmotif of the neoliberal university, forcing academics to prove their competence with publications, accompanying metrics and 'research analytics', citation indices, grant 'capture', PhD completions and student satisfaction ratings. All of this – and much more – must be measured and tracked for each academic, and the resulting 'audit culture' (Strathern 2000) has become another accepted change to the academic working environment. Academics who are successful in these terms may still find their performance deemed inadequate. The culture of management recognises success only in those who join its ranks, and there are many training schemes in universities designed to bring new postulants to the cult of managerialism. Those who have most easily learned to inhabit the corporate culture are most likely to achieve advancement.

Our project is to respond to calls to bring applied linguistics to bear on the discourse and culture of managerialism (Cook 2012; Holborrow 2013). For too long, linguists have been silent in the face of compulsory citation of managerial mantras of 'performance', 'change' and 'excellence'. We aim to join scholars from other disciplines in inaugurating a new field of critical university studies.

New managerialism and corporatisation

It is important to include some relevant history which gives context for how universities got to this point. Universities arguably exist to address and find solutions to constantly changing problems with a view to enhancing all aspects of life. In the last 20 years of the 20th century, societies in the Western world began to question the role of universities in a way that had not been encountered before. For some five centuries, universities had been viewed as an unproblematic space for debate and enquiry, and for the development of knowledge and understanding of the world, but now there were new functions being laid at their doors: a role in professional training for high-rent employability, regeneration of the economy via 'entrepreneurship', as well as universities themselves being charged with maintaining solvency and even profitability. There were more questions too, arising from concerns about diminishing social equality, opportunity and a wish for 'diversity': Who should belong in the academy? Who should determine standards? What knowledge should be imparted within its walls? What are universities for? These questions, and demands for universities to render themselves accountable, resonated particularly in the US, the UK, Australia and Canada. But there was a backlash from conservative sources who declared universities, and particularly the humanities, to have lost their way. In the 1990s, this rupture of trust came about in response to a new focus within the arts and humanities which seemed to emerge from new concerns about social justice and representations of 'other' perspectives than those of privileged white men. If resistance to the impact of new curricula came from supposed white male elites within the academy, at least the humanities departments offered islands of receptivity and a culture which supported new paradigms of research. In the US, new departments of black studies were inaugurated, along with women's studies, whilst in the UK, critical humanities which placed class, race, gender and sexuality more centrally into the university curriculum, were located largely within departments of cultural studies.

In the early 21st century, there are again questions of relevance, and from some quarters, rigour, to be answered by humanities scholars. *Higher Education under Fire* (1995) by Berubé and Nelson was one of the first books to announce a crisis for the humanities in universities. The volume can be considered a response to Bloom's *The Closing of the American Mind* (1987) – the first salvo in what became known as the culture wars. In this, Bloom criticises the new advances in the curriculum as leading students away from 'truth' towards relativism and, indeed, self-centredness. The contributors to the Berubé and Nelson volume struck back with perspectives critiquing charges of 'political correctness' and a dumbing down of the curriculum in order to reach minority students. With chapters entitled 'They're Taking Over! And Other Myths about Race on Campus' and 'Going Public: Political Discourse and the Faculty Voice', we see clear fault lines emerging in the culture wars. The resulting discussion inspired books by others, including D'Souza (1991), on the political right, and a further rejoinder from the political left from Fish (1994). The academy in the US became more politically polarised than at any point since the 1960s.

This climate, though divisive and toxic in some respects, created a setting for productive critique of universities. The debates in the UK were swiftly smoothed, especially by the introduction of another set of issues emerging from the context of a financial squeeze on higher education in the 1980s and 1990s. Universities were obliged to offer new justifications of their collective and individual roles in society, and a consequence was the imposition of 'the skills agenda'. All university courses were obliged to formulate sets of transferable skills, not so much as an accompaniment to knowledge, but almost as the ultimate justification of a university education. Not all academics were in agreement with the new priorities, seeing this as a new anti-intellectual and entirely instrumentalist development. One could argue that such chaotic polarisation as had befallen the US academy was prevented in the UK by a more rapid move towards centralised managerial control of universities.

The results of the neoliberal revolution that took place in UK universities became apparent in the 1990s but had been set in train by the reforms inaugurated by Thatcher's government in 1981. Holborrow (2013: 234) defines neoliberalism as 'policies which consider the capitalist market as the optimal way of organising all social exchanges, including the delivery of education and research'. As we lay out next, various reports and reforms since 1981 have taken us progressively closer to the market revolution envisaged by Thatcher. Of primary interest to us as authors is the way an injection of neoliberal values has been mirrored by a growth of managerialism, especially 'new managerialism' (Deem *et al* 2007).

Certainly, in terms of NPM and new managerialism in universities and governance structures which exclude the academic voice, we recognise the familiar situation of the abject *subaltern* excluded from power structures and decision making. There is a paradox emerging in academia – in institutions which teach about democracy, so little of it is practised within their own walls. Neoliberal institutions, as Harvey points out (2005: 66), are hostile to democracy. It is seen as an unaffordable luxury, kept at bay by the imagined state of constant crisis and financial exigency.[2] We see democratic structures of accountability like university senate committees dissolved in favour of top-down management and autocracy. There is no explicit debate taking place between business-oriented managers and academics who teach and research, but nevertheless, a fault line has opened up over academic values and the purpose of a university.

These conditions have been illuminated by some of the critical tools developed in the social sciences and literary studies (critical theory) and linguistics (CDA). The approach we expound here has much in common with critical approaches in other disciplines which aim to disrupt and contest received wisdom and disciplinary assumptions, and also interrogate, especially within institutions, issues of power, control and inequality (Butler and Spoelstra 2014).

It would be naïve to claim that there was ever a golden era for the autonomy of universities. However, their purpose and remit has been reconceived several times during the expansion of higher education in the late 20th century. In the UK, we note two milestones: the *Robbins Report* (1963) and *the Dearing Report* (1997). Both reports worked to broaden access to universities and address their purpose in UK society. Robbins saw the role of universities as a balance of 'promoting the general powers of the mind' and 'instruction in skills for employment'. Dearing conceived of universities as increasing 'knowledge and understanding for their own sake', and playing a part in 'shaping a democratic, civilised, inclusive society' (cited in Williams 2013: 46–47). However, in three of the four stated purposes, the benefit to the economy and the world of work are emphasised. And so the link between university education as serving the needs of employment was introduced and strengthened in the latter half of the 20th century – a new entrepreneurial university (Barnett 2013), with a focus on internal markets which inscribes both the institution and its members as entrepreneurs. What has also escalated in the last five years in the UK has been a new emphasis on university education as a private good, leading to personal financial gain. Even Universities UK, styling themselves as 'the definitive voice for universities in the UK' (www.universitiesuk.ac.uk), routinely makes the case for universities as a driver of economic growth, but rarely on the basis of academic value. This stands in contrast to the understanding during the Robbins/Dearing eras that universities underpinned the public good. Despite this, strong arguments continue to be made for this latter stance (Barnett 2011; Collini 2012; Docherty 2014b; McGettigan 2013).

Since the 1990s, there has been huge pressure on UK universities to generate 'third stream income', i.e. research and consultancy in partnership with and funded by industry. This has forced universities to become more instrumental in their research strategy, and some critics have seen this as 'short-termism'. This entrepreneurial turn for the academy motivated critics to seek connections between economic and political developments, and the changes to conditions of labour and values operating in (largely) Western universities. Since the mid-2000s there has been a surge of interest in 'the neoliberal academy' and 'the marketized academy', where degrees are seen as the product, not the process, of a university education (Morrish and Sauntson 2013). A number of volumes have documented this trend and offered new arguments and forged routes of resistance. In the UK, this trend has escalated since *The Browne Review* (2010). With its recommendations of a huge increase in tuition fees, and an end to public funding for the humanities, this was taken to inaugurate a new era in higher education. For the first time, students were paying for the whole of their studies, albeit eligible for student loans. These changes set the scene for the managerial and corporate trends that have become sedimented into British and American universities in the last 30 years.

Student as consumer

The *Browne Review* of 2010 in the UK introduced tuition fees of £9,000 per year, and with it arrived a new, transactional quality to higher education. The potential for a new dynamic between academic staff and students arose – one of student as consumer (Molesworth *et al* 2011). In its wake came a flurry of critical work about the context of higher education (Barnett 2013; Collini 2012; Williams 2013) weighing the benefits and limitations (mostly limitations) of the shifting new axis in universities. Most UK universities now, as evidenced by their websites and mission statements, display a preoccupation with branding, fundraising, corporate posturing and league tables. Molesworth *et al* (2011) produced an edited volume whose chapters form a coherent critique of all the manifestations of the marketised university in a neoliberal political climate. The editors outline the subtle ways in which a focus on consumerism, 'managing' student demand and 'student satisfaction' distorts the educational process and the opportunities afforded by a university education in a more unfettered setting. They argue that this is a context which will create more dependent, conservative learners who resist being transformed into creators of knowledge.

Williams (2013) develops the idea that it is consumption itself which is being taught in British universities. Universities have fostered this impression by offering students a 'diet' of modules rather than a coherent overview of subject content and have replaced intellectual challenge with 'satisfaction' (2013: 63). With new instruments of consumer research, such as the National Student Survey, persistent module/ lecturer evaluations, and slogans such as 'You said. We did', universities enslave themselves to the vicissitudes of the nation's 18-year-olds. Organic curriculum development driven by research and innovation is eclipsed in favour of 'enhancing the student experience' and 'student demand'. Indeed, we might predict that lecturers will be increasingly reluctant to teach the more challenging topics and courses, fearing that their course evaluations will take a nosedive, rendering them vulnerable to 'performance management'.

At the same time as students are being ostensibly indulged as customers who drive the institution's priorities, they are also subject to capitalist exploitation. The university presents student as consumer, but acts on student-as-unit-of-revenue. Students pay market, or even inflated, rates for campus accommodation, in campus shops, for graduation, and foot the bill for upgraded sports and teaching facilities (Slaughter and Rhoades 2000).

Marketisation of universities

Another facet of neoliberalism is the impetus to reduce dependency of public services on state subsidy/investment. The *Browne Review* removed the previous teaching grant to universities, and universities were then primarily financed by students enrolling with loans to cover tuition fees. Students, then, became units of revenue to be maximised alongside private sources of funding from business. Universities have relied on corporate funding for many decades (Washburn 2005), and in this sense, marketisation and relations with business and the economy is nothing new. This vision was first raised by E.P. Thompson (1970) who foresaw the corruption of academia by its proximity to business interests. It is perhaps the balance of this activity that is changing, and with it, argues Washburn, the danger that commercial forces will transform every aspect of academic life. This probability has emerged more recently with the publication of the *Wilson Report* (2012), and its recommendations for 'industry-university collaboration' and 'developing enterprise skills' which can be read as an appeal for universities to refashion themselves as training schools for industry. As the 'entrepreneurial university' (Barnett 2013; Clark 1998) takes hold, corporate identification hardens into an entire identity. It is not just students who have succumbed to the demands of the market; individuals are now required to promote their own 'brands'. Mautner argues that when 'people are no longer humans, they are products, commodities that need to be created, promoted and sold in the labour market' (2005: 187). And, of course, it is incumbent upon the individual to be successful in this area; they are responsible for the creation and the reception of the commodified self. As Mooney (2014) points out, it is not uncommon for a corporation to become personified – it is endowed with views, and a characteristic discourse. In Chapter 2, we examine the discourse of university branding and marketisation, with its new emphasis on 'employability' and the discursive positioning of students as both products for sale and consumers.

Higher education, as well as being marketised, has become monetised. We have seen good quality, informed, evidenced critiques marshalled against: privatisation of university finance and student loans (McGettigan 2013); audit culture and REF (Sayer 2014); and academic freedom (Docherty 2014b). Universities, degrees and research are all assessed in terms of (short-term) value for money to the economy and the individual.

Since the *Browne Review*, the market has become more than metaphor, and universities now see themselves as competing for students, especially international students (Williams 2013). Brown and Carasso (2013) do not immediately dismiss the notion of a market in universities – it can reduce costs and weaken monopolies, but also introduces negative forces into the provision of higher education. The book cites arguments that rather than improving academic standards, these might, in contrast, be compromised if institutions feel obliged to retain students with unsatisfactory performance. Additionally, cutting access to student financial aid has meant that more students need to work during term time, and, as a consequence, reduce their hours of study.

The competition for students has made universities re-order their priorities from promoting knowledge to the promotion of self and 'brand' and universities have increased their focus on marketing accordingly.[3] Fairclough (1995) details how post-1990 prospectuses contain a personalisation of the university 'we' and a direct address to the prospective student 'you'. By contrast, any responsibility and obligation of the student have been removed with the deletion of certain modal auxiliaries like *must*. The university, though, boldly states its promissory contract to the student with the modal *will*.

Several linguists have used corpus linguistics methods to track the penetration of the new managerial lexicon in various domains within academia (Mautner 2005; Sanigar 2013; Sauntson and Morrish 2010). Sanigar examined the language of university websites and what she analyses as a dialectical relationship between language and a marketised society. She finds a more covert kind of market-oriented discourse, using the strategic placement of positive, but semantically malleable, evaluative adjectives (e.g. *quality, world-class*) collocating with lexical items like *research*. This is what Moriarty (2014) has termed 'the vacuity of excellence'. Mautner traced the semantic prosodies and distribution of the buzzwords *enterprise* and *entrepreneurial* and found them to be overwhelmingly positive which makes a virtue out of corporate dependency, constructing these as university 'partnerships' (2005: 105). Sauntson and Morrish (2010), similarly, found universities recycling the same lexical resources in order to promote their brand and 'unique selling points'. They favour what Whyte calls 'hooray words' (Whyte 2003, cited in Cook 2012: 40) – words whose specificity is so lacking that anyone might agree with the aims presented: *freedom*, *democracy*, *equality* and, latterly, *sustainability*. This work found that commodification is apparent both in the promotional materials of universities and in their mission statements. Both students and education are portrayed as products to be consumed (Sauntson and Morrish 2010). Burrows (2012), though, argues that the market in higher education is more than transactional, and that the nature of markets in higher education is a form of simulation. Constant audit of metrics, designed to further regimes of accountability, have mimicked the market by transforming universities into unlikely sites of competition. We contend that the function of the market has more of an ideological than practical justification. As Burrows notes, it is the 'structures of feeling', or changes of ethos, that are sedimented by these regimes. This will be further examined in Chapters 3, 4 and 5.

There is a depressing consensus about the changing ethos and values of UK and US universities. A visit to any university website will inform the reader about graduate employment statistics, as well as links between the university and local enterprise. A mission oriented towards the transformation of human potential can sometimes seem far from the forefront of 21st-century universities. Some universities do allude to social and moral values, but these are the exception. And, just as they have felt obliged to justify themselves in terms of economic benefit to the country and region, universities may also shortly be required to account for individual earning potential or even the default rates of their graduates' loan repayments.[4]

Audit culture

Chapters 4 and 5 address the intensifying turn to scrutiny and metrics in order to achieve compliance and 'accountability' for public money (or even private fee money) spent on teaching and research. As competition has become more pervasive in universities, so has the imperative to become more 'efficient and effective' (*Universities UK* report, 26 February 2015). This has justified more intensive scrutiny of working practices and performance. Every academic recognises that the demands of audit, 'performance management' and accountability have intruded into their workplace to the extent they have become its central organising principle. Strathern (2000) has named this 'audit culture', which she recognises has 'broken loose from its moorings in accounting and finance' to infiltrate the academy' (2000: 2). Shore (2007: 278) writes that, 'Calculative practices including "performance indicators" and "benchmarking" are increasingly being used to measure and reform public sector organizations and improve the productivity and conduct of individuals across a range of professions'.

With performance management techniques, a 'competitive, productive and ultimately accountable' institution aims to 'get the best out of everybody' (Morrissey 2013: 800). Morrissey argues that competitiveness, productivity and accountability are distinct measures, linked only as collocates in neoliberal discourse, not as preconditional requirements. In fact, the discourse, and the managerial structures function outside of any valid strategy for improvement; they serve principally to set the limits of academic subjectivity, and 'the endgame is the making of governable subjects' (2013: 799). As Sayer (2014) points out, the REF has lent itself to becoming a tool of performance management. In an era of Big Data, we find that this offers the possibility of ever closer surveillance and assessment. Vice-chancellors maintain 'tools' and 'dashboards' of key performance indicators (KPIs) via which academics are micro-managed, thus ensuring their own, their discipline's or their students' priorities are eclipsed. New scholars are already schooled in citing these norms by the time they start applying for academic posts. Docherty (2014a) presents this view of the REF:

> A graver hazard is that it will not be research selectivity and competition which is delivered, but a new selective and competitive academic will be formed, whose research trajectory is entirely determined by a regime peripheral to their own intellectual curiosity and academic judgement.

It is perhaps unfortunate that academics never previously felt called to defend their values, or even to specify them, as any shared organising principles have been derailed in the name of accountability, transparency, and value for money. In place of principle and autonomy, universities have the REF which distorts research priorities towards a resulting 'impact', rather than an illumination of a research question. On the teaching front, all roads lead to measure of 'quality' such that it rivals 'excellence' for vacuity (Moriarty 2014).

Audit culture has engendered a constant state of anxiety which Hall (2014) has called 'a micropolitics of little fears'. Hall summarises this dialectic:

> I am performance managed to the point where I willingly internalise the question 'am I productive enough?' which aligns with 'am I a good academic?', which aligns with 'am I working hard enough', which risks becoming a projection onto those around me of 'are you working/producing enough?' My example is potentially toxic because being good enough in this productive space is never enough. My culturally acceptable self-harming activities militate against solidarity and co-operation that is beyond value. The defining, status-driven impulse is to increase my value as an entrepreneur, and to demonstrate that through the traces I leave in publications, or managing a team, or in leading research bids, or in blogging and emailing

> at all hours. And the toxicity reduces my/our immunity and leaves us addicted to our status as all that we have. And all that we have is a reified, anxiety-infused identity.[5]

Perhaps the most insidious and time-consuming audit trail of all in the UK has been the requirement to separately cost teaching and research, for fear that they might somehow cross-subsidise each other and upset funding calculations. This has led to TRAC (TRansparent Approach to Costing) and FEC (Full Economic Costing) and associated spreadsheets that academics must fill in when accounting for time spent just doing their jobs. Holmwood's (2011) blog captures this morass in all its absurdity.[6]

The argument that academics must become accountable for the taxpayers' money they spend is always revisited whenever there is a complaint about the imposition of audit. Of course, in institutional management, it is always difficult to challenge hyper-scrupulosity. We would agree with the argument posed by Bendix Petersen and Davies that opposition is blunted when the discourse we are compelled to cite forestalls resistance (Bendix Petersen and Davies 2010). However, the demands for self-audit have become so extensive that we no longer require a system of staff appraisal to serve up public accountability. We have become victims of what Lupton (2013) calls 'the academic quantified self'. In Chapter 4, we analyse documents associated with REF, as well as performance appraisal documents to reveal the many ways in which academics are called to account. In Chapter 5, we examine discourses in which teaching and learning are formulated in the TEF white paper.

Managerialism: colonising the corporate academic

If corporate culture is to successfully eclipse more traditional academic values of collegiality, cooperation and shared governance, there must be 'buy in' from amongst academics. This is achieved by what Fairclough has termed 'technologisation of discourse' – a 'calculated intervention to shift discursive practices as part of the engineering of social change' (Fairclough 1995: 3). In Chapter 6, we present the argument, and exemplify with data taken from university managerial training courses, that neoliberal governmentality works within universities to destabilise established academic practices and to construct the ideal entrepreneurial, self-governing, responsibilised academic (Morrish 2014). The primary strategy to achieve this has been by a calculated intervention to shift the discourse towards the new language of managerialism, marketisation and corporatisation.

Although the effects of the new managerial culture are visible within academia, sometimes less clear are the particular formations through which they work. Morrissey (2013) looks at the tools of contemporary university management and views these strategies through the lens of

Foucauldian governmentality. There has been, in his view, a neoliberal intervention towards a new political economy which has engendered a new kind of subject formation in universities.

As Sealey (2014) makes clear, it is discourse which is central to the project of redefining of subjectivities. The interplay between structure, culture, agency and semantics means that new formations of academic labour are relational. So, for example, when students are customers, the subjectivity of academics is shifted – they become service providers. In this way, academic identities are forcibly reshaped within the discursive paradigms of their managers.

Managers themselves are experiencing an evolution of their identities (Deem *et al* 2007). Deem *et al* (2007) detail changing management structures and identities sourced from a database of interviews with managerial tier staff. The most recent manifestation of this is termed 'New Public Management'. The book offers one of the few cogent definitions of the term managerialism: 'Managerialism insists that "managing" and "management" are, respectively, socio-technical practices and the collective agents and institutions responsible for their enactment that are universally required in a modern and technologically advanced society' (2007: 6). We would go further, and, in fact, the thesis of this book is that the project of managerialism is to make managing and control of labour the institutional objective itself.

Slaughter and Rhoades (2000) identify two key facts to the neoliberal regime in universities. The first is academic capitalism, and the imposition of market-like behaviours; the second is an expansion of 'managed professionals' whose brief is largely to exert increased managerial control of faculty (2000: 4). A picture of professionalisation of the managerial tier emerges (Ginsberg 2011). The new university manager is one who seems relatively at ease with a widening gulf between himself (and there is a preponderance of men in management which is why we deliberately use the pronoun *he* in this instance) and the academic workforce, ready to join an overpaid, expanding cadre of 'deanlets'. Graeber (2013) views this expansion as begetting 'bullshit jobs' characterised by a focus on pointless administration. These are roles which nobody would miss if they were not filled. But nevertheless, there are new technologies of management, an array of courses preparing staff for the career change into those roles – courses which reshape the values (such as 'succession planning') and identities of those who inhabit them (Morrish 2014). These findings are also echoed in work by Shepherd (2014; 2017). Deem *et al* (2007: 190) conclude that preservation of a public service ethos in higher education is incompatible with current managerial technologies of privatisation and performance indicators – 'The future of public higher education does not lie in the over-managed institutionalised mistrust that bedevils it'.

In response to the corporatisation of universities, their staffing resource has been restructured. Starting in the UK with Thatcher's assault on tenure in the 1980s, the workforce has been progressively rendered compliant through insecurity. With the advent of the REF and additional pressures to research and win grant income, more and more academics have been placed under threat of redundancy. There is a growing recognition that the instability and insecurity that is characteristic of the managerialised academy rapidly engenders an environment in which the ambitions of a university cannot flourish.

It is not entirely a function of the 'technologisation of discourse' that managerial power has extended its reach. There is also restructuring of another, more concrete kind. Eagleton (2015) identifies the slow death of humane critique in universities across the world. In the UK we have seen the closure of departments of languages, linguistics, philosophy, sociology, cultural studies – and some have even predicted the eventual disappearance of humanities disciplines. If you decimate the very crucible of critical study, the corporate/managerial project can proceed with no one to prick its conscience. And with no legitimate space for humanities, the potential effects on wider society are devastating.

Framing resistance to managerial discourse

The perception that corporatisation and marketisation have displaced the values that academics have traditionally espoused is widespread. One need only follow a number of academics' blogs, or the electronic comments following *THE* or *Chronicle of Higher Education* articles to confirm this. Our argument is that resistance is more than making demands or counting administrators. If universities are to maintain their distinctive role of nurturing thinking and creativity, then the challenge is one over values and discourse. The discourse of management, then, must be undermined, subverted and returned to the academy. In concert with our use of critical applied linguistics, we share this political position and it drives our analysis.

At this point, we outline our approach to ideology. Following van Dijk (1997, 1998) we propose that ideologies are primarily social, and they define groups. Within these groups, ideologies further serve to facilitate the coordination of acts and practices. A neo-Marxist approach would assume that ideology brings about the domination of privileged and powerful groups (van Dijk 1998: 3), but this ignores the possibility that dominated groups might articulate their own oppositional ideologies. Our interest is the role of discourse in reproducing managerial ideologies, and in the possibilities of articulating and promoting resistant discourses. In the conclusion (Chapter 7), we offer some ideas for resisting the discourse of managerialism.

In a timely intervention, Van Dijk (2013) has charged that there has been a failure to engage in resistance on behalf of academics. With the exception of academics in Spain and New York, there has been little visible direct political action.[7] In the UK, there have been several occupations.[8] In Europe, there have been significant protests in Spain, and occupation in Amsterdam.[9] Van Dijk also adds that it is remarkable that there has been so little work from a discourse point of view, in terms of critique of the academy. Fairclough (1995) set the lead in offering a revealing analysis of the inroads already made by the discourse of marketisation and promotion. Using CDA, he links this to wider social changes, including a migration of authority from the institution (as represented by academics) towards the consumer.

It has taken 20 years for other linguists to join the pushback. But however late to the party, linguists have at last realised that whilst discourse can channel resistance, it also requires huge sensitivity to linguistic choices. Applied linguistics offers the appropriate tools to plot the infiltration of neoliberal values in universities by tracking discursive trends. However, some critics have charged that a focus on discourse marginalises more central issues of materiality and power. It is because of this that Holborrow eschews a classical Fairclough CDA analysis of neoliberal discourse, as she feels that the framework is not well equipped to deal with the wider repercussions of capitalism. Instead, she prefers to identify keywords, such as *knowledge economy, innovative, competitive, human capital*, which she finds relate better to questions of structure and agency, but perhaps also better reflect unstable expressions of ideology. Such words are embedded in a social and political context, and may shift their meaning as hegemony itself shifts its axis. Although we would dispute any outweighing advantage for keywords over a more rigorous CDA analysis, Holborrow demonstrates that it is (key)words which we as listeners respond to, are offended by, and may form the crux of resistance-on-the-ground in universities.

Cook (2012) chides the community of applied linguists for allowing the discourse of managerialism and marketisation to go unchallenged within the academy. He writes that we must expose and resist the means of manipulation and manufacture of consent, which characterise the language of PR with 'its blandness, its vagueness, its omission of evidence, its one-sidedness, and its implicit corporate ideology' (2012: 37). There is a role for a critique of institutional discourse, but this needs to start first in the academy. Evidently, the responsibility lies with applied linguists to do this, otherwise, who else will educate managers?

As we wrote this book, a tragic case came to light which lends particular urgency to the message we are trying to convey to the academic community. A professor of toxicology at Imperial College London, Stefan Grimm, took his own life after he was placed on 'performance management'. Professor Grimm was a well-published leader in his field and had submitted his work to the REF. He had been successful in bringing in money to support his research, but had not been awarded what his managers called 'a large program grant'. This was enough to deem him a failure in their eyes. His rank, his output, his reputation counted for nothing and clearly, neither did his self-esteem. It is the tragic terminus of Neoliberal U, audit culture, markets and competition. It is a managerial discourse that redesignated Professor Grimm's research as inadequate, against all obvious measures of success. That discourse weighed in and constructed Stefan Grimm as an unproductive academic. This is evil, and this is why we must identify, and then fight, this damaging, insidious discourse that strips academics of their autonomy and purpose. This is why we write – precisely because so many academics and, increasingly, managers, recognise this brutalising of management-academic relations as their reality.

Inaugurating a new discipline: critical university studies

A number of critiques have been forthcoming over the last few years, including an edited volume by Bailey and Freedman (2011) which proposes a manifesto for change in UK universities: scrapping of the REF, lowering of staff-student ratios and democratic systems of university governance amongst its demands. We also note campaigning organisations outside of the collective bargaining of recognised trade unions, such as *Campaign for the Public University*, and the *Campaign for the Defence of British Universities*. Many blogs have emerged which have these concerns as central, amongst them *Critical Education* (Andrew Mcgettigan), *The Plashing Vole* (anon) and *Music for Deckchairs* (Kate Bowles). As well as the work cited earlier, we see new platforms – online journals and social media outlets – which bear witness to academic alienation and managerial advancement. Petrina and Ross (2014) portray the proletarianisation and casualisation of the faculty, assaults on tenure in Canada and threats to academic freedom, sometimes enacted through 'respect at work' agendas.

Academics are organising around these central concerns of funding, corporatisation, marketisation, academic capitalism, audit culture, academic governance and citizenship, and it is from this groundswell of concern that critical university studies has emerged. This field of study enjoys kinship with critical management studies and critical legal studies which similarly contest power, control and inequality at work. The shared tenets of these critical approaches are non-performativity (a refusal to adopt corporate and managerial stances), denaturalisation (refusal to adopt managerial narratives at face value, but to seek to expose the ideological underpinnings) and reflexivity (reflection on epistemological, methodological and ideological assumptions) (Butler and Spoelstra 2014; Fournier and Grey 2000). Deem and Brehony (2005) debate whether language is merely performative or constitutive of reality. We argue that managerialism is largely achieved and sustained through discourse. By submitting real-world data to discourse analysis, we will demonstrate that there has been a calculated shift of discourse in order to restructure the values, perceptions and behaviours of academics. This discourse is constitutive of a new kind of academic, and sets limits on what kind of work can be done. Indeed, it circumscribes what even counts as academic work, particularly in terms of research.

It is time to push back and do the intellectual work of fathoming ways to resist the discourse, assumption and strategies of the neoliberal takeover. Petrina and Ross urge academics to 'a new politics of truth' (2014: 67) and to engage in 'remaking the critical and the university'. This book places discourse at the centre of the project to mobilise resistance, and answers calls to show that applied linguistics and discourse analysis are central to critical university studies.

Notes

1. Evidence of this comes, for example, from some universities' increased use of 'writing retreats' which moves what academics perceive to be core research activity away from the physical site of the university. (See, for example, www.yorksj.ac.uk/add/research/events/writing-retreats/)
2. To date, no university has gone bankrupt despite the imagined financial crises. In fact, some VC's excessively high salaries are widely publicised in the public domain which suggests that universities are prosperous. (For example, www.channel4.com/programmes/dispatches/on-demand/66548-005)
3. www.timeshighereducation.co.uk/news/marketing-spend-up-but-applications-fail-to-follow-suit/2012107.article
4. www.theguardian.com/education/2015/feb/09/facebook-friends-student-loan-finance-earnings
5. www.richard-hall.org/2014/07/10/notes-on-the-university-as-anxiety-machine/
6. http://exquisitelife.researchresearch.com/exquisite_life/2011/03/tracked-and-fecked-how-audits-undermine-the-arts-humanities-and-social-sciences.html
7. For further information, see the following online articles: 'Spanish students and academics protest against Higher Education cuts' (www.reuters.com/article/2013/10/24/us-spain-education-idUSBRE99N1GP20131024) and 'US adjunct professors protest against low pay and job insecurity' (www.huffingtonpost.com/2015/02/25/adjunct-walk-out-day_n_6746586.html).
8. http://occupylse.tumblr.com/post/113914552450/why-we-are-occupying
9. www.theguardian.com/higher-education-network/2015/mar/17/dutch-student-protests-ignite-movement-against-management-of-universities

References

Bailey, M. and Freedman, D. eds. 2011. *The Assault on Universities: A Manifesto for Resistance*. London: Pluto Press.

Barnett, R. 2011. The marketised university: Defending the indefensible. In M. Molesworth, E. Nixon, and R. Scullion, eds. *The Marketisation of UK Higher Education and the Student as Consumer*. London: Routledge. 39–51.

Barnett, R. 2013. *Imagining the University*. London: Routledge.
Bendix Petersen, E. and Davies, B. 2010. In/difference in the neoliberalised university. *Learning and Teaching in the Social Sciences* 3 (2): 92–109.
Berubé, M. and Nelson, C. eds. 1995. *Higher Education Under Fire*. New York: Routledge.
Block, D., Gray, J. and Holborrow, M. 2012. *Neoliberalism and Applied Linguistics*. London: Routledge.
Bloom, A. 1987. *The Closing of the American Mind*. London: Penguin.
Brown, R. and Carasso, H. 2013. *Everything for Sale: The Marketisation of UK Higher Education*. London: Routledge.
Brown, W. 2015. *Undoing the Demos: Neoliberalism's Stealth Revolution*. New York: Zone Books.
Burrows, R. 2012. Living with the h-Index? Metric assemblages in the contemporary academy. *The Sociological Review* 60 (2): 355–372.
Butler, N. and Spoelstra, S. 2014. The regime of excellence and the erosion of ethos in critical management studies. *British Journal of Management* 25: 538–550.
Canaan, J. and Shumar, W. eds. 2008. *Structure and Agency in the Neoliberal University*. London: Routledge.
Chiapello, E. and Fairclough, N. 2002. Understanding the new management ideology: A transdisciplinary contribution from critical discourse analysis and new sociology of capitalism. *Discourse and Society* 13 (2): 185–208.
Clark, B. 1998. *Creating Entrepreneurial Universities: Organizational Pathways of Transformation*. Bingley: Emerald Group Publishing.
Clarke, J. 2008. Living with/in and without neo-liberalism. *Focaal* 5: 135–147.
Collini, S. 2012. *What Are Universities For?* London: Penguin.
Cook, G. 2012. Impacts of and impacts on. *Applied Linguistics Review* 3 (1): 25–45.
Davies, B. and Bendix Petersen, E. 2005. Neo-liberal discourse in the academy: The forestalling of (collective) resistance. *Learning and Teaching in the Social Sciences* 2 (2): 77–98.
Dearing Report. 1997. *Higher Education in the Learning Society*. London: HMSO. www.educationengland.org.uk/documents/dearing1997/dearing1997.html
Deem, R. and Brehony, K. 2005. Management as ideology: The case of 'new managerialsim' in higher education. *Oxford Review of Education* 31 (2): 217–335.
Deem, R., Hillyard, S. and Reed, M. 2007. *Knowledge, Higher Education and the New Managerialism: The Changing Management of UK Universities*. Oxford: Oxford University Press.
Docherty, T. 2011. The unseen academy. *Times Higher Education*. www.timeshighereducation.co.uk/418076.article (Accessed 5 May 2015).
Docherty, T. 2014a. *Universities at War*. London: Sage.
Docherty, T. 2014b. Hostile takeover. *Times HigherEducation*. (Accessed 5 May 2015).
D'Souza, D. 1991. *Illiberal Education*. New York: Vintage.
Duggan, L. 2003. *The Twilight of Equality*. Boston, MA: Beacon Press.
Eagleton, T. 2015. The slow death of the university. https://michel-foucault.com/2015/04/17/terry-eagleton-the-slow-death-of-the-university-2015/ (Accessed 14 September 2018).

Evans, M. 2005. *Killing Thinking: The Death of the Universities*. London: Continuum.
Fairclough, N. 1995 [2010]. *Critical Discourse Analysis*. Harlow: Longman.
Fish, S. 1994. *There's No Such Thing as Free Speech*. Oxford: Oxford University Press.
Foucault, M. 1994. The subject and power. In J. Faubion, ed. *Michel Foucault: Power*. New York: New Press.
Fournier, V. and Grey, C. 2000. At the critical moment: Conditions and prospects for critical management studies. *Human Relations* 53: 7–32.
Ginsberg, B. 2011. *The Fall of the Faculty*. Oxford: Oxford University Press.
Graeber, D. 2013. On the phenomenon of bullshit jobs. *Strike Magazine*. http://strikemag.org/bullshit-jobs/ (Accessed 30 March 2015).
Hall, R. 2014. Notes on the university as anxiety machine. www.richard-hall.org/2014/07/10/notes-on-the-university-as-anxiety-machine/) (Accessed 18 May 2015).
Harvey, D. 2005. *A Brief History of Neoliberalism*. Oxford: Oxford University Press.
Holborrow, M. 2013. Applied Linguistics in the neoliberal university: Ideological keywords and social agency. *Applied Linguistics Review* 4 (2): 229–257.
Holmwood, J. 2011. TRACked and FECked: How audits undermine the arts, humanities and social sciences. *Exquisite Lives Research* blogs. http://exquisitelife.researchresearch.com/exquisite_life/2011/03/tracked-and-fecked-how-audits-undermine-the-arts-humanities-and-social-sciences.html (Accessed 18 May 2015).
Hoyle, E. and Wallace, M. 2005. *Educational Leadership: Ambiguity, Professionals and Managerialism*. London: Sage.
Klikauer, T. 2013. *Managerialism: A Critique of an Ideology*. Basingstoke: Palgrave.
Lupton, D. 2013. The academic quantified self. https://simplysociology.wordpress.com/2013/10/14/the-academic-quantified-self/ (Accessed 18 May 2015).
Mautner, G. 2005. The entrepreneurial university: A discursive profile of a higher education buzzword. *Critical Discourse Studies* 2 (2): 95–120.
McGettigan, A. 2013. *The Great University Gamble: Money, Markets and the Future of Higher Education*. London: Pluto Press.
Molesworth, M., Nixon, E. and Scullion, R. eds. 2011. *The Marketisation of UK Higher Education and the Student as Consumer*. London: Routledge.
Mooney, A. 2014. *Human Rights and the Body*. Farnham: Ashgate.
Moriarty, P. 2014. The vacuity of excellence. http://physicsfocus.org/philip-moriarty-vacuity-excellence/ (Accessed 18 May 2015).
Morrish, L. 2014. Institutional discourse and the cult(ure) of managerialism. *Discover Society*. www.discoversociety.org/2014/05/06/institutional-discourse-and-the-culture-of-managerialism/ (Accessed 18 May 2015).
Morrish, L. and Sauntson, H. 2013. 'Business-facing motors for economic development': An appraisal analysis of visions and values in the marketised UK university. *Critical Discourse Studies* 10 (1): 1–20.
Morrissey, J. 2013. Governing the academic subject: Foucault, governmentality and the performing university. *Oxford Review of Education* 39 (6): 797–810.
Mulderrig, J. 2011. The grammar of governance. *Critical Discourse Studies* 8 (1): 45–68.

Ong, A. 2006. *Neoliberalism as Exception: Mutations in Citizenship and Sovereignty*. Durham, NC: Duke University Press.
Ong, A. 2007. *Neoliberalism as Exception*. Durham, NC: Duke University Press.
Petrina, S. and Ross, W. 2014. Critical university studies: Workplace, milestones, crossroads, respect, truth. *Workplace: A Journal for Academic Labor* 23: 62–71.
Robbins Report. 1963. *Higher Education: Report of the Committee Appointed by the Prime Minister Under the Chairmanship of Lord Robbins*. London: Her Majesty's Stationery Office. www.educationengland.org.uk/documents/robbins/robbins1963.html (Accessed 18 May 2015).
Rose, N. 1999. *Powers of Freedom: Reframing Political Thought*. New York: Cambridge University Press.
Sandler, C.J. 2014. Marketing spend up, but applications fail to follow suit. *Times Higher Education*. www.timeshighereducation.co.uk/news/marketing-spend-up-but-applications-fail-to-follow-suit/2012107.article 20 March 2014 (Accessed 18 May 2015).
Sanigar, M. 2013. Selling an education. Universities as commercial entities: A corpus-based study of university websites as self-promotion. *Leeds Working Papers in Linguistics and Phonetics* 18: 85–114.
Sauntson, H. and Morrish, L. 2010. Vision, values and international excellence: The 'products' that university mission statements sell to students. In M. Molesworth, E. Nixon and R. Scullion, eds. *The Marketisation of UK Higher Education and the Student as Consumer*. London: Routledge. 73–85.
Sayer, D. 2014. *Rank Hypocrisies: The Insult of the REF*. London: Sage.
Scarff, L. 2015. Ten ways through which neoliberalism is experienced on an emotional level. *LSE Impact blog*. http://blogs.lse.ac.uk/politicsandpolicy/the-psychic-life-of-neoliberalism/?utm_content=bufferb5340andutm_medium=socialandutm_source=twitter.comandutm_campaign=buffer (Accessed 1 December 2015).
Sealey, A. 2014. The neoliberal university: Agency and responsibility. Paper presented at *Neoliberalism, Education and Applied Linguistics Symposium*, Institute of Education, June.
Shepherd, S. 2014. The changing role of PVC. www.wonkhe.com/blogs/the-changing-role-of-pvc/ (Accessed 18 May 2015).
Shepherd, S. 2017. Managerialism: An ideal type. *Studies in Higher Education* 43 (9): 1668–1678.
Shore, C. 2007. Audit culture and illiberal governance: Universities and the politics of accountability. *Anthropological Theory* 8 (3): 278–298.
Slaughter, S. and Rhoades, G. 1997. *Academic Capitalism and the New Economy: Markets, State, and Higher Education*. Baltimore: John Hopkins University Press.
Slaughter, S. and Rhoades, G. 2000. The neoliberal university. *New Labour Forum* 6: 73–79.
Steger, M. and Roy, R. 2010. *Neoliberalism: A Very Short Introduction*. Oxford: Oxford University Press.
Strathern, M. ed. 2000. *Audit Cultures: Anthropological Studies in Accountability, Ethics and the Academy*. London: Routledge.
Tahir, T. 2010. The irresistible rise of academic bureaucracy. www.theguardian.com/education/2010/mar/30/academic-bureaucracy-rise-managers-higher-education (Accessed 26 February 2015).

Thompson, E.P. 1970. *Warwick University Ltd: Industry, Management and the Universities*. London: Penguin.
Van Dijk, T. ed. 1997. *Discourse as Social Action*. London: Sage.
Van Dijk, T. 1998. *Ideology: A Multidisciplinary Approach*. London: Sage.
Van Dijk, T. 2013. Interview with Teun Van Dijk. In Z. Pinto-Coelho and A. Carvalho, eds. *Academics Responding to Discourses of Crisis in Higher Education and Research*. Braga, Portugal: Communication and Society Research Centre. 79.
Washburn, J. 2005. University Inc.: The Corporate Corruption of Higher Education. New York: Basic Books.
Williams, J. 2013. *Consuming Higher Education: Why Learning Can't Be Bought*. London: Bloomsbury.
Wilson, T. 2012. *A Review of Business – University Collaboration. Department for Business, Innovation and Skills*. www.bis.gov.uk (Accessed 18 May 2015).
Whyte, J. 2003. *Bad Thoughts*. London: Corvo.

2 The student as consumer and commodity

Context

In this chapter, we discuss the context of the growth of consumerism in HE in the UK (and, to a lesser extent, the US) and consider how this produces evidence of neoliberal discourse in 'student-facing' texts that circulate in the HE environment. After outlining the context, the first linguistic case study focuses on a critical analysis of a sample of the SU websites which are primarily, although not exclusively, targeted at the existing student population. The second case study incorporates elements of corpus linguistics along with a critical analysis of a selection of university undergraduate prospectus and recruitment texts. Texts in this case study are primarily marketing documents targeted at prospective students. In both case studies, we find extensive linguistic evidence of neoliberal discourses permeating the HE context and repeatedly constructing students not as learners but as consumers of university products, and also, importantly, as commodities of the university as a corporation. The linguistic evidence reveals the extent of these discursive positionings in ways that have not been shown before.

As critical university studies requires us to reflect on power structures within the university, one aspect of this has been a changing dynamic between academics teaching in universities and their students. Students, it is felt, have become more demanding. This shift has not been so marked in the US where students have always paid tuition fees for undergraduate education. Ironically, those who benefitted from a free university education in the 1960s–1990s felt sorry for American counterparts graduating with a debt whose first payment was due the month after graduation; we now look across the Atlantic with envy at the range of bursaries and loans available to US students.

The first signs of a student as consumer ethos in the UK could be detected as soon as tuition fees were imposed in 1998 in response to the *Dearing Report* (1997). The low fees charged then by universities were soon tripled in a move known as 'top-up fees'. A white paper issued in response to the *Browne Review* (2010) tripled fees again to £9,000 in

2012.[1] The recommendations ended public funding for the humanities, and for the first time, students were paying for the whole of their studies, albeit able to borrow funds from a state-backed source, the Student Loans Company. This ushered in a new era in which students were canvassed on their opinion of their university education as 'value for money'. Unsurprisingly, dissatisfaction with perceived value began to make itself heard in the media, via reports such as the 2017 *HEPI/ HEA Student Academic Experience Report*, and the 2017 *National Audit Office Report* on the higher education market.

However, there was another, more explicit purpose nominated by Cable and David, the authors of *Putting Students at the Heart of Higher Education* (2012). This ensured that the new dynamic between academic staff and students – of student as consumer (Molesworth *et al* 2011) – figured much more prominently for universities. In its wake came a flurry of critical work about the context of higher education weighing the impact of the shifting axis in universities (Barnett 2013; Bousquet 2008; Collini 2012; Williams 2011, 2013).

After student protests of the 1960s, the more visible manifestation of authoritarianism within universities has given way to more collaborative and student-friendly organisations. In solidarity with the student movement, some lecturers appointed during the 1960s and 1970s rejected the old hierarchies. However, new and, to some, unwelcome, changes attached themselves to the more egalitarian ideals, as the idea of the student as consumer became normalised, leaving some academics conflicted with regard to the prominence of the student voice.

The concept of normalisation in discourse and ideology was one associated with Fairclough whose prescient discussion of the discourse of consumerism in universities appeared in 1995. Twenty years on, the British government's Behavioural Insights Team, otherwise known as the Nudge Unit, has worked to bring about a situation whereby universities are gradually and consistently incentivised and persuaded into competing with each other for students, and thus funding. The result has been more transparent appeals to the student as consumer. The competition, though, has led to a very destabilised sector which finds planning compromised by uncertainty.

In a rigged market perpetually tweaked by government regulation (for example, the introduction of very high tuition fees in England in 2012, together with the removal of the student numbers^), all universities are driven to position themselves in more marketetised terms. As Fairclough contends, 'language is always simultaneously constitutive of (i) social identities, (ii) social relations and (iii) systems of knowledge and belief' (1995: 131). What he identified in the 1990s has escalated and is now almost an uninterrogated orthodoxy. There has been massive investment in universities of personnel trained in marketing (*THE* 2014), but also in large numbers of others devoted to 'the student experience', retention, and managing student 'satisfaction' (which is, itself, a contested SDS as we discuss later). In this chapter, we hope to point out that what is not captured in this social practice of marketisation, is how the hegemony is discursively facilitated and maintained, and how new social relations might be redrawn.

The role of the Competition and Markets Authority

The fact that universities are compelled to advertise in the competition for the highest-achieving students has led to some potential pitfalls. In November 2017, a graduate of the University of Oxford sued the university for £1 million in lost earnings. His case alleged that 'appallingly bad' and 'boring' teaching had led to his failure to get a first-class honours degree, and consequently impeded his aspirations to become an international commercial lawyer. The case had several surprising aspects, not least that it was brought 16 years after graduation from the university.[2] Many readers familiar with the traditional hierarchy of prestige amongst universities will find it hard to believe that a 2.1 from Oxford was insufficient to secure the graduate his chosen career in law. Similarly implausible is the fact his claim is based on receiving a poor mark in just one module during a three-year degree. The university contested Siddiqui's contention that missing a first has resulted in unemployment 16 years later. Indeed, for most students, their degree classification has little impact on their career development a decade after graduation.

Nevertheless, this was a case which all UK universities were watching closely as it will have implications not just for their defence of courses and academics exposed to harsh student evaluations, but also, it transpires, the problem of substituting courses advertised in the prospectus. This puts universities in a double-bind following clarification of the law in the *Consumer Rights Act* (2015) and delegation of powers to the Office for Students (OfS) to hold universities to its requirements. The Competition and Markets Authority (CMA) has insisted that a contractual relationship should apply between universities and students, based on 'transparent and accurate information' provided by the former, in view of the 'one-off' nature of the student's 'purchase'. Universities are also encouraged to offer research-led courses at upper levels of undergraduate degree programmes. Universities must ensure compliance with the CRA and obligations include providing appropriate information to students at the point of application and continuing as the student enrols. This can enter problematic territory when, for example, a student claims that the key factor in choosing a course at university X was a final-year module. For very good reasons, the module might not be available; universities encourage such modules to be led by academics whose research reflects the module content. Researchers with expertise in a particular area are not interchangeable, and so retirement, relocation and research leave can easily mean that a course of study does not run as expected. Universities which nurture specialist research and teaching may find it to be a riskier option than running more generalist courses which can be taught by a range of teaching staff.

There is a growing likelihood of more cases coming before the CMA, now that the UK government, with the proposals detailed in the white paper (*Department for Business, Innovation and Skills*, May 2016, which became the *Higher Education and Research Act* 2017), has promised to strengthen the student voice. This assurance can be granted by virtue of the wealth of data now available to government and institutions, and universities are being obliged to release it to prospective student consumers. The OfS announces itself as 'a consumer-focussed market regulator with new statutory powers', and universities will need to ensure that the possibility of unforeseen exigencies is signalled to students so that they do not constitute a breach of consumer law or 'terms and conditions'.[3]

The unfurling of the umbrella of consumer law over universities is perhaps predictable in an era when students are paying tuition fees upwards of £9,000 per year in England. Chapter 5 discusses the evolving discourse of 'value for money' emerging from the *Higher Education and Research Act*, which also introduced the Teaching Excellence Framework (TEF). This new emphasis has focussed media and political attention on the size of vice-chancellors' and other managerial staff salaries, the graduate premium on salaries, graduate employability and employment, teaching quality and intensity and the issue of whether teaching subsidises research.[4]

It has also legitimated greater government interest, perhaps already leaning towards government interference, in universities. In 2018 in the UK, a new regulatory framework in the form of the OfS, another construct of HERA, is about to tack sharply towards a more punitive regime of threats of de-registration and 'market exit' as the chair of OfS flexes muscles granted by the new legislation. Teaching excellence, student satisfaction, supposed grade inflation, freedom of speech and executive salaries were all swiftly added appropriately within its remit.

Needing to consider value for money, student satisfaction and concomitant interest and threats by government ministers are all relatively recent experiences for university leaders and academics. The extent to which this new culture has been mobilised to threaten the reputation of universities by students, media and consumer organisations and politicians has been unprecedented. The student, it seems, is being persuaded to view themselves as a consumer who is buying a one-off product from a provider whose reliability cannot be trusted, despite several centuries of reliable track record. By contrast, the new legislation invites untested private providers, known as 'challenger' institutions, to offer degrees immediately upon registration, with no probationary period. These private providers are expected to cherry-pick courses which are cheap to teach, such as business or law, and which offer the promise of direct routes into employment. As Maringe (2011: 144) argues, it is an approach which prioritises the instrumental value of education ahead of every other consideration, and, certainly, the discourse constitutes a social identity which urges the student to demand more. But more of what?

Personalised learning, ed-tech and learning analytics

All universities wish to enhance their students' satisfaction in the realisation that this will strengthen retention and progression figures (Maringe 2011: 145). To this end, some universities seek to be perceived as offering unique provision and prospects for students. Sometimes this desire is expressed via an enthusiastic pursuit of eye-catching novelties such as climbing walls, or lazy rivers in an effort to fulfil the constructed fantasies of student consumers (Haywood *et al* 2011).[5] Other universities have sought ways to address the rising incidence of mental health issues amongst students, especially at exam time. Nottingham Trent University has brought in piglets to defuse tension, whilst at the University of Bristol they have funded a puppy room. Meanwhile, students at Bath Spa University have access to a petting zoo.[6]

In addition to the frivolities, universities are trying to edge ahead of the competition in terms of retention and progression of students. Accordingly, a new field of academic analytics is emerging. This encompasses the use of student data, for example, information on prior attainment, demographics and choice of courses, all of which can then inform targeted advertising, curricular provision, recruitment and branding strategies. This is sometimes referred to as 'data-veillance' (e.g. Geesin 2016) to emphasise its primary aim of surveilling learners for commodification purposes. In a parallel development, universities are also concerned to use data to optimise the learning environments for students, and so learning analytics has assumed a place of significance in university budgets. Learning analytics is explained thus:

> Every time a student interacts with their university – be that going to the library, logging into their virtual learning environment or submitting assessments online – they leave behind a digital footprint. Learning analytics is the process of using this data to improve learning and teaching.
>
> (Sclater *et al* 2016: 4)

The fact that progression, recruitment and graduation may be used to evaluate universities in league tables and the TEF (Turnbull 2018) (and see Chapter 5) has provided an incentive to facilitate students' success by focussing more closely on their individual needs. So rapidly has 'personalisation' captured the imagination of universities that it has become a 'buzzword' which seemed to carry weight with the 2017 TEF panel, especially if repeated often enough.[7]

The personalisation agenda has arisen in concert with the growth of 'ed-tech' – educational technology. Online learning has established itself in universities, and students will usually encounter it via a virtual learning environment (VLE) which offers access to lecture materials, syllabus and also online feedback. VLEs often support 'blended learning' in which independent and directed learning are delivered electronically so that students may access learning resources at their own pace and in their own time.

Unsurprisingly, universities find that the extent to which a student engages with such a facility will often predict their relative success on the course of study. This is where the waters become muddied because, as well as learning analytics, some institutions work with a related concept, 'predictive analytics' in which the student's digital footprint is correlated with later measures of success. This surveillance data may be collated and commercialised in the form of dashboards, which allow tutors to check particular metrics (VLE logons, library borrowings, card swipes to access buildings, etc.) and so infer academic engagement by these proxies. A case study of a student data dashboard at Nottingham Trent University is reported by Sclater *et al* (2016):

> The NTU Student Dashboard measures students' engagement with their course; the University has found engagement to be a stronger predictor of success than background characteristics. Engagement scores are calculated from VLE access, library usage, card swipes and assignment submissions [. . .] The Dashboard is having positive impacts on behaviour.

These are strong claims for the technology, although very little evidence is assembled to substantiate them.[8]

We must maintain caution since 'predictive' is not synonymous with 'facilitative' and the dashboards advertised to students as 'personalisation', and whose calculations are deemed to reflect 'engagement', in reality comprise impersonal algorithms generated in respect of cohort norms, rather than the intuition of academics who teach them.

Some other commentators have suggested that the popularity of learning analytics has been furthered by some key propositions which are untested. As Prinsloo (2017) points out in his blog, commercial interests have colonised online learning for higher education to the extent that delivery, feedback, attendance and timetabling may be circumscribed by whatever limitations and assumptions the commercial VLE espouses. Further dangers are that the algorithmic nature of these products may over-determine the nature of the educational experience, 'shaping our understanding of learning according to their beliefs, what can be measured, and what is valued'.

Another view is that personalised learning (PL) allows cash-strapped universities to secretly harvest data which has been shared in good faith by students to commercialised dashboard platforms. This can then be analysed to determine which graduates to approach for donations, and by which means. Thus, learning can be opened up to capital exploitation in two ways. Firstly, the sale of learning platforms, and subsequently the capture of student data which can then be made available in other market domains. For example, the student participating in a sports team (dashboard record – extracurricular activities) may be persuaded to fund the new swimming pool whilst the student primary classroom volunteer may wish to participate in mentoring or outreach activities.

There are some who produce more generalised critiques of the 'technological fix' approach to learning (Doxdator 2017; France 2018). These commentaries point out flaws such as restricting the content accessible to the learner and prescribing the order in which it is encountered. France writes of the PL movement, 'It's simply a more sophisticated version of an industrialized model for education', which Doxdator, writing on his blog about US kindergarten–18 schooling, has this to say:

> While we would all like our learning to be personally tailored to us, PL signifies something quite narrow: the use of digital technologies and platforms to monitor and track student progress through prescribed curriculum content, and then displaying student data on a dashboard for teachers, administrators, and parents.[9]

In sum, it is becoming increasingly apparent that the primary purpose of some innovations in ed-tech is motivated by the impulse towards surveillance and monitoring, not the educational support and development of the learner.

Constructing a new kind of student

Perhaps we can hypothesise that one of the outcomes of personalisation, regardless of its debatable pedagogic benefits, is the construction of a student who demands to be front and centre of the university. By contrast, students of earlier generations might have felt somewhat alienated by the empty corridors and hushed libraries. We were aware that important work was taking place behind closed doors, and that students were an unwelcome intrusion. This was evidently antithetical to discovering opportunities for face-to-face learning. But the student as consumer ethos can lead to some unintended consequences as well. Molesworth *et al* (2011) offer several analyses of the subtle ways in which a focus on consumerism, 'managing' student demand and 'student satisfaction' disturbs the educational process and the opportunities afforded by a university education in a more unfettered setting. The chapters form a coherent critique of all the manifestations of the marketised university in a neoliberal political climate, with its preoccupation with branding, mission statements and league tables. In fact, the editors argue this is a context which will create more dependent, conservative learners who resist being transformed into creators of knowledge. Instead, '[Students] understand HE primarily as a commodity they must possess to access a consumer life by obtaining a well-paid job' (Molesworth *et al* 2009: 2).

Extending this critique, Nixon *et al* (2016) look beyond the notion of student as consumer to examine how market ideology sets in place the reproduction of a subjectivity of narcissism, writing, 'student satisfaction and dissatisfaction appear as profoundly narcissistic in character' (2016: 16) and suggesting that catering to this inflicts damage to pedagogy:

> In the post-NSS era, signifiers of the student's sovereign status as 'chooser' are abundant. Many HE institutions now engage in fierce competition for students, expend large promotional and marketing budgets, erect iconic buildings for aesthetic pleasure and exhibit an insatiable desire for growth in student numbers.
>
> (Nixon et al 2016: 3)

Whilst this analysis, and the suggestion of a refusal to address legitimate students concerns about their experience of higher education, may seem harsh in its invocation of narcissism; nevertheless, it should be recognised that the neoliberal turn has centred on the needs of the individual student rather than on those of the collective. This has been reflected in the 'personalisation' agenda discussed earlier, which isolates the student from the community of scholars.

However, at least students can depend on the collective voice in the form of their SU – but even that may also be in retreat. Academic staff have perceived a shift in the stance of SU representatives from embodying an opposition towards university management, to acting as if their interests are conjoined with those of the latter. This has provided a useful 'wedge' for management to exploit on the occasion of labour disputes and industrial action. For example, the email in Figure 2.1 was received from an SU official at a UK university in response to a request for support for a petition from the academic staff union taking strike action. It echoes almost completely the university's response to the notification of strike action.

In order to manage a culture where students are much more likely to raise complaints and claims for recompense, deans of students have been transmogrified into 'Student Experience Managers' (Sabri 2013) lest any temporary issue jeopardise the National Student Survey (NSS) scores. Sabri (2011) writes, '"The student experience" homogenises students

> Thank you for your email. This has been on our radar!
>
> Just to let you know, the University is working with us to ensure that the current strike action does not adversely impact students' academic progress. The number of staff participating in strike related activity at NTU has decreased steadily throughout the period of the dispute and they are making appropriate arrangements should a small number of staff decide to engage in the marking sanctions called for by the UCU. At NTU, over 50% of academic staff have received a pay rise of 4%, including an incremental increase of 3%, in addition to the 1% rise already given to all.
>
> If you would like to come in to chat about your petition I would be happy to speak to you. Please do let me know if you have any questions.
>
> All the best
> NTSU President

Figure 2.1 Email from SU official

and deprives them of agency at the same time as apparently giving them "voice" '. It is a skilful illusion. Not only must academic staff try to meet student expectations but also they may find marketing departments have heightened them further by 'selling' a fanciful vision of university by dint of association with lifestyle choices. Projecting sociability, availability of sports, retail facilities and a general portrayal of happiness, Haywood *et al* (2011) assert that students are being encouraged to 'dream'. Not only does this appeal to the imaginary undermine the seriousness of academic endeavour, it echoes the sort of marketing associated with luxury goods, but 'HEIs may find it easier to sell a lifestyle than students desire to study a complex subject in depth or to undertake the sort of intellectual exchange that we might hope a degree represents' (2011: 13).

Some recent examples have raised eyebrows in the sector. The University of Nottingham posts on its website a YouTube video entitled '7 Ways in Which the University of Nottingham Is Like Hogwarts'.[10] At the same time, the University of Gloucester tweeted on its open day, that the Cheltenham campus was 'the most Hogwarts of all our campuses'.[11]

In spite of the fake branding and shameless marketing strategies, not all students conceive of themselves as consumers. Cheeringly, there are many examples of students demonstrating that their powers of critique have not been blunted by the neoliberal discourse of entrepreneurship and economic rationalism which envelops them. Rogers and Furse wrote as two students at the University of Birmingham who were suspended from the university in 2014 after peaceful protest which did not result in criminal proceedings, but, instead, an internal disciplinary hearing ensued.

> Successful and famous courses such as archaeology, sociology and biological recording have been closed down when they don't fit with a narrow business logic [. . .] The changes to higher education that the government implemented in 2010 were supposed to usher in a new era of student choice and student control. Though we never asked for them and actively resisted the changes, their supposed intention was to empower the student consumer. Instead, marketisation has created universities that are increasingly intolerant of dissent.
>
> (Rogers and Furse 2014)

Similarly scapegoated by the University of London was Michael Chessum, for the 'crime' of defending the continuation of the university-wide SU. He wrote of the assault on student democracy: 'Students' Unions are characterized by the limited, bounded simulacrum of democracy furnished by voting and survey-filling mediated and interpreted by union managers and an all-powerful trustee board, comprising elected students and unelected externals selected for their expertise' (Chessum 2014). He adds, '[I]n the past decade, many unions have scrapped or sidelined a lot of the basic elements of student democracy, such as union councils and general meetings, replacing them with greater emphasis on surveys, market research and referendums'.

Chessum's clear rejection of the enclosure of student democracy is accompanied by the recognition that, although universities position students as consumer/customers, they are only too happy to behave very punitively towards them when the perceived interests of the institution are at issue. The contract between university management and students only obtains as long as students' desires fit within a strict neoliberal prescription. Far from being a construct of government policy and strategy, the student as consumer role coincides with a university managerial project to undermine the agency of the student body (Sabri 2011) by ensuring that decision making is exercised within sharply demarcated limits. Students are thus controlled and 'manufactured' to be consumers. In this way, students are arguably just as disempowered as academics.

The next section examines some of the ways in which SUs have changed their emphasis over the last two decades.

The role of SUs

If universities have been reconstructed in the neoliberal mould with a focus on marketisation and competition, then it is hardly surprising to find that SUs have mirrored this trajectory. Brooks (2014) and Brooks *et al* (2015) argue that SUs have been domesticated in recent years and co-opted by management to 'represent' the student voice. They have also been incorporated into debates over value for money and student satisfaction with the 'student experience' by dint of a question about the performance of SUs in the National Student Survey. It is also relatively easy to gain the acquiescence of a generation coerced by the prospect of debt.

At one time, SU officials would have exhibited solidarity with their fellow trade unionist lecturers in the event of industrial action. Happily, many chose to do so in the dispute over pension rights in the UK in Spring 2018. Even in the face of clear support, though, university managers found it convenient to manufacture a difference of interests between lecturers and their students. As a result, some SU officials have been seduced by the promise of career advancement and appear more concerned to make themselves acceptable to the businesspeople they encounter on boards of governors.

Failure to display obsequiousness to those in positions of power can result in the denial of the student democratic voice entirely. In a notorious episode in January 2018, the UK minister of state for higher education, Jo Johnson, made it clear that he would not endorse the recommended appointment of a student member to the board of the new HE regulator, the OfS, if that person had any affiliation with the National Union of Students, or even a local branch (The Commissioner for Public Appointments 2018). This was the ultimate irony; the body charged with upholding freedom of speech in universities, and implacably opposed to the no-platforming policies which had been a part of SUs since the 1970s, had themselves been found to be no-platforming students.

Students unions' function, inasmuch as they are accorded a role in governance at all, has narrowed to that of 'representation' with a corresponding decline in 'activism' and the student voice is assumed to equate to the student as consumer (Brooks *et al* 2015: 170–173). This is confirmed in Case Study 1 as we notice a large advertising function for SU websites. These days student elected officials are likely to see themselves as partners rather than adversaries of university managers, and with NSS scores and league tables in mind, their loyalty is courted by promises of career-enhancing opportunities and networks. Common cause centres around 'university reputation' with both management and students assuming a vested interest in its enhancement (Brooks *et al* 2015: 176). Once again, this ensures that individuals are empowered, whilst the interests of the majority of students are diminished. Other opportunities, such as political education and organising are subordinated to the careerism of a few.

If the suggestion is that SUs have become depoliticised, Raaper (2018) adds nuance to this issue. In a CDA of interviews with SU leaders, Raaper finds plenty of opposition to new legislation including dissatisfaction about the TEF and its proxy metrics, the instrumentalisation of higher education, marketisation and consumerisation. However, she finds that this opposition is also often 'fragmented by consumerist counter-arguments'.

As a case in point, Ridley (2017) details how change can be brought about when there is an effective alliance between academic and student union members. The context was a campaign over governance and accountability for high executive pay and privileges at the University of Bath in 2017. Despite this being a university with a high number of science and engineering students who are sometimes felt to be conservative in their political leanings, the students were active and vocal in pressing the campaign through to a successful conclusion.

> Bath UCU had been building links with students ever since the introduction of £9000 tuition fees in 2010. Carley said that it was at this point that students began to 'align themselves consciously' with staff, as there was a shared and growing resentment towards and political consciousness about the marketisation of higher education.
>
> (Ridley 2017)

In March of 2018, this was followed by a series of strikes over 15 days led by the University and College Union (UCU) in protest of management's attempts to make changes to pensions which would see lecturers receive hugely reduced income in retirement. Students refused management's narratives of selfish lecturers interrupting their studies, and instead joined their lecturers, librarians and IT staff on the picket lines in large numbers. Teach-outs were organised, which ranged from medieval poetry to a critique of the marketised, neoliberal university. By contrast, the media provided an unsympathetic portrayal of avaricious and wasteful vice-chancellors, and to the surprise of management which had become used to controlling the agenda, their viewpoint had little credibility. This seemed to offer optimism; it is still possible for students to exert power when they realise their voices amount to more than a consumer focus group. Having outlined recent critical discussions of SUs, we now turn to a language-focussed examination of the discourse of SU websites as the first case study in this chapter.

Case study 1: SU websites

The context outlined earlier inspired our examination of a sample of current SU websites. There was clearly a limit to how many websites could feasibly be subjected to a critical analysis. In this case study, two SU websites from each of the three UK university groupings were randomly selected for analysis. These were

Russell Group: University of Birmingham; University of Leeds
University Alliance: Coventry University; University of Lincoln
Guild HE: Newman University; Southampton Solent University

SU websites are multimodal texts and, as such, may be appropriately analysed using the tools of multimodal CDA, as described in the introduction.

SU websites contain a fairly standard set of sections which typically include a generic 'about us' introductory/overview section; a section focusing on student representation, advice and welfare; a section about student activities (some separate out student societies from 'employability'-focussed activities whilst other subsume the two together); an online store for purchasing university-branded products, tickets for events and other commodities; an events/what's on section; a section which contains legal and constitutional information about the union. Some have dedicated sections for 'campaigns' and 'awards' whilst others incorporate these into other sections. All websites contain various social media links and feeds, advertising tickers and some have 'live chat' systems in operation. There are, therefore, various strategies in place to engage students in the websites. Once there, they are coerced into performing an auditing function (e.g. Lincoln University website offers the chance to win £1,000 for evaluating modules – advertised on their SU home page).

Although all of the SU websites examined are remarkably similar in tone, style and content. The University Alliance and GuildHE websites generally contain more advertising space and their merchandise/shop sections are more prominent. The advertising platform function seems to be prioritised more than is the case for the websites of the two Russell Group universities, making the University Alliance and Guild HE unions seem more commercially focussed.

In the past, the central foci of SUs were student representation and voice, and the provision and organisation of student societies and activities. These continue to be integral components of SUs but, in more recent years, there has been a growing focus on the role of the SU in marketising students as 'products' of the university. This is manifested through highly visible 'jobs, skills and employability' sections of the SU websites examined and features which encourage students to advertise the university 'brand' (e.g. shop/merchandise sections of SU websites). This is illustrated in the typical examples in Figures 2.2–2.4.

This suggests an increasing corporatisation of SUs and a commodification of both the university itself and its students as a marketable 'product'. Although all of the websites contain information about student societies, these tend to be obscured within more general sections such as 'activities' and 'opportunities'.

SU websites now appear to function as advertising platforms for other companies and products outside the university. In the websites examined, all contained embedded advertisements for products such as takeaway pizzas, property agencies, alcoholic drinks, taxis, public transport companies and tickets for sports events with 'deals' on offer specifically for student consumers. Some examples are included in Figures 2.5 and 2.6.

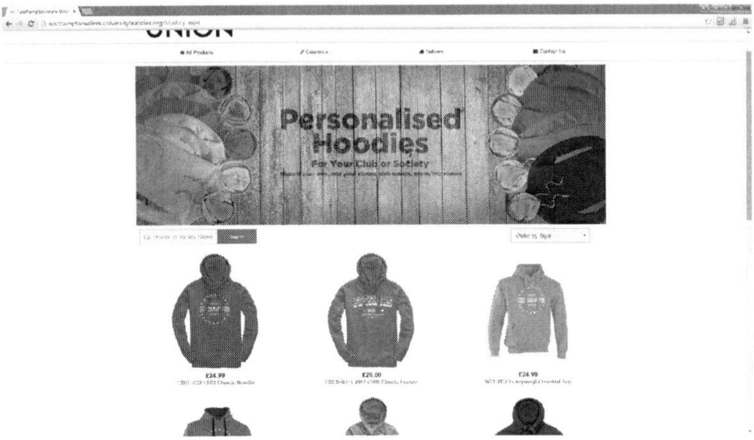

Figure 2.2 SU merchandise

Source: http://southamptonsolent.universityhoodies.org/Myshop.aspx

Figure 2.3 SU 'shop'

Source: www.cusu.org/shop/

SUs can clearly generate income from selling advertising space on their websites to external for-profit businesses. The SU websites are also used as advertising platforms for local entertainment venues and events with students being encouraged to 'purchase' and 'consume' badged club nights and venue promotions. Although local venues have always offered 'student nights', until recently, they have not been as rigorously marketed through the SU as we are now seeing.

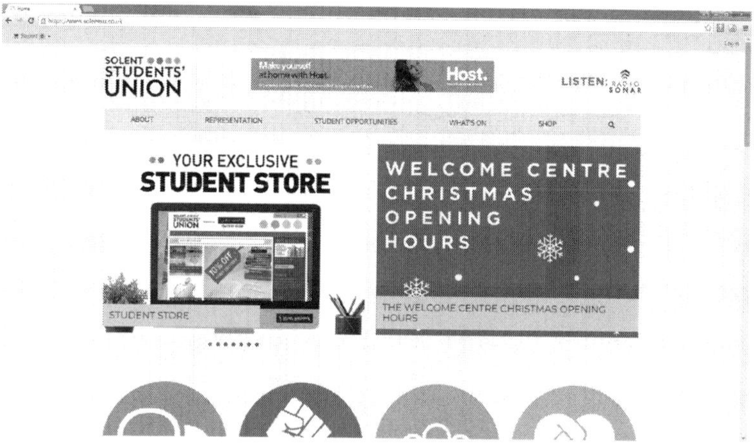

Figure 2.4 SU 'student store' website

Source: www.solentsu.co.uk/

Figure 2.5 Advertising on SU website 1

Source: www.guildofstudents.com/

A further notable feature of all of the SU websites examined is an emphasis on competition. All websites feature an 'awards' section which lists various awards and accolades such as teaching awards, 'school of the month', 'lecturer of the month' as well as awards for aspects of SU provision itself. Thus, SUs are constructed as being in competition with each other, just as universities as a whole are coerced into competitiveness through the neoliberal regime. Furthermore, SUs are complicit in the

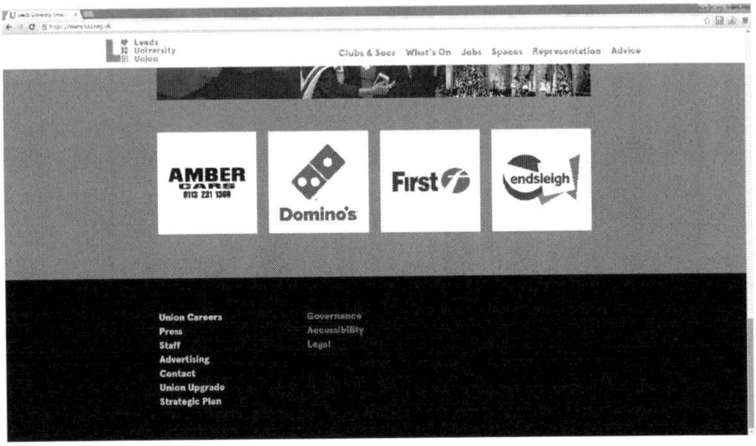

Figure 2.6 Advertising on SU website 2

Source: www.luu.org.uk/

colonisation of the corporate academic in their imposition of an award system for academic staff and schools. University management and administration are noticeably absent from such competitions – it appears to be only the 'student-facing' sectors of the university which are placed under scrutiny and colonised by these discourses of individualism and competitiveness. The culmination of these competitions is formal Oscar-style 'awards ceremonies' which typically take place towards the end of each academic year. Consider the examples in Figures 2.7–2.9 taken from the University of Lincoln and Newman University SU websites:

Thus, the overall ethos of the SU appears to have become more about encouraging competition across and between universities, rather than collaboration and unity. Newman University even has a regular 'You're great! Students think you're a legend!' competition in which particular staff members are nominated and awarded with a branded mug saying, 'You're great!' (Figure 2.10). Interestingly, words such as 'legend' are highly gendered with evidence showing that student evaluations will use 'legend' more in relation to male staff than female staff.[12] Thus, the words used in these SU competitions contain inherent gender bias against women.

The symbolic capital that attaches to such reward systems operates in stark contrast to that deployed by the metrics-dominated systems of REF and TEF. SU accolades are not considered to be esteem indicators in the external audit processes of REF and TEF and yet they are an integral part of the corporatisation process of academics.

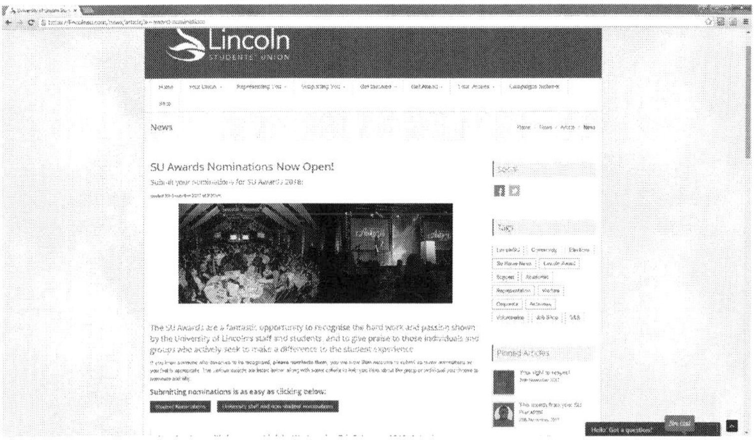

Figure 2.7 SU awards

Source: https://lincolnsu.com/news/article/su-award-nominations

- *Course of the Year*

  For this award, we ask you to take into account teaching quality, feedback and organisation of the course, and how this has developed over the last year. Does the course you are nominating stand out as dynamic and offer examples of work that others could take on board? Then you should nominate them.

- *Staff Member of the Year*

  This award is for an individual member of staff who has worked consistently to enhance the experience of students. You should nominate someone who has been helpful, supportive, approachable and patient, and who has ultimately positively affected the student experience.

- *Service Team of the Year*

  This will be awarded to a University professional services team who are constantly enhancing the student experience and offering a great standard of service. If you know a team who deserves to be recognised, get nominating!

- *The Inspirational Teacher of the Year*

  Nominees will be those whose teaching style or content and the support they offer has inspired students to reach their academic potential. Inspiring teachers are those who challenge and motivate their students, engaging them in meaningful academic activity. In short, they provide teaching that inspires students to learn and be successful.

Figure 2.8 SU award categories

Source: Adapted from https://lincolnsu.com/news/article/su-award-nominations

Figure 2.9 Advertisement for SU awards night

Source: www.newmansu.org/awards-nights.html

Figure 2.10 'You're Great!'

Source: www.newmansu.org/youre-great.html

The competitive neoliberal discourse appears incongruous in the context of the traditional collegiate ethos of SUs. Even the self-referential terms 'union' and 'guild' do not sit comfortably within neoliberal discourse and evoke a more overtly political trade unionist discourse with its associations of campaigning for students' rights. Although the older unionist discourse still clearly exists (it is embedded in the self-referential language of the SUs as well as website sections dedicated to campaigns and students societies), it now competes with discourses of commercialisation and accountability associated with neoliberalism.

All SUs now have 'strategic plans' which are closely aligned to the strategic plan of the university as a whole. Within these plans, equality and diversity is constructed as something which is 'marketable' – it becomes an advertising feature of the university rather than a genuine issue of well-being and social justice (Morrish and O'Mara 2011). Some SUs also have their own 'impact plans' bringing them even more in line with the dominant neoliberal discourse of the academy. SUs are constructed as accountable to their students who are, again, simultaneously positioned as both consumers (thus legitimising the accountability processes) and products.

SUs now have charitable status and we observe that attention is drawn to this on all of the websites, usually in the general information sections. All SUs consequently have a trustee board and information about the constitution of this is also provided on the website, along with the SU's own bye-laws and rules of membership. These 'legal/constitutional' components of SU websites are a relatively recent phenomenon and are perhaps indicative of the neoliberal turn in higher education more generally. The University of Birmingham contains a list of detailed regulations concerning membership of the Guild of Students. It is possible to purchase 'corporate membership' of the Guild, which imbues the Guild with the status of a business rather than a union-oriented organisation. Significantly, the trustee board of the Guild has to report to the University of Birmingham and university managers (e.g. director of finance, director of HR) are members of various Guild sub-committees.

The overall function of the contemporary SU, then, seems to be complex and multi-faceted but sits within the corporate ethos of the broader university which is largely constructed as a business selling products which need to be marketed. This includes its SU which consequently becomes accountable to the university, as evidenced through its ongoing production of strategic plans, impact plans and efforts to achieve various awards and accolades (which can then be advertised on the website – see Figure 2.11 for an example).

However, the SU is also a business (albeit a charitable one) in its own right. The SU attempts to sell its own products (events, catering outlets, societies, merchandise and so on) to student consumers. Furthermore, the SU plays a role in constructing students as university 'products', not just consumers, through its imposition of skills, employability and university branding.

Figure 2.11 SU accolades

Source: www.guildofstudents.com/

Perhaps the most sinister function of the SU, and one which aligns it closely with the neoliberalisation of the sector, is its increasing auditing role. Within the university, academic staff are constructed as neoliberal subjects who are products of the marketised university. As a result, academics are constantly being audited using increasingly complex and conflicting systems. The SU, with its system of awards, is one such auditing body.

At the same time as academic staff members are charged with managing student expectations, they may find marketing departments 'selling' the student experience by dint of association with lifestyle choices. Projecting sociability, availability of sports and retail facilities and a general portrayal of happiness, Haywood *et al* (2011) assert that students are being encouraged to 'dream'. It is within this context that we turn to the second case study in this chapter: analysing university prospectus and recruitment documents.

Case study 2: online prospectus and recruitment documents analysis

Until the mid-1990s, university prospectuses used to be brief documents descriptive of the courses offered and written in the stark language of a museum catalogue. They were not considered, until the post-2000 era, to be promotional documents requiring editing from the practised eye of the university's own marketing specialists. Fairclough (1995: 158) identified significant changes in the discourse of university prospectuses which he linked to 'enterprise discourse and the marketization of public discourse'. In other words, this was discourse that positioned universities as business entities, with competition as an essential element. Universities were beginning to see themselves as corporations in competition for students.

There are also regulatory constraints operating on universities. Bradley (2013: 76) points out that every university in the UK is required by HEFCE and equivalent organisations in Wales, Scotland and Northern Ireland, to post Key Information Sets (KIS) data on their websites. Prospectuses, though, do not receive the same scrutiny by the regulator and offer a platform for universities to display their own preferred statistics. The data, he finds, is often compromised by the omission of facts and selective reporting, misleading wording and inferences, carefully crafted comparisons and outright falsehood. These flaws centre on such aspects as employability, research and teaching quality.

Bradley (2013: 84–85) points to some reasons why universities should be held to high ethical standards in marketing. Higher education is an expensive commitment which cannot be tried out before 'purchase'. A large section of the target audience is young and may have limited experience of universities. They might reasonably place a great deal of trust in the honesty of the information provided in prospectuses. On the other hand, universities have a great deal to lose if their claims are found to be untrustworthy: 'Publications emanating from a university, including the prospectus, carry with them a public expectation that the claims they make are carefully presented, well evidenced and reputable' (Bradley 2013: 85).

In an era of, arguably, less regulation and government encouragement for 'new providers' to enter the market, the integrity of prospectuses becomes a more pressing issue. As we have mentioned earlier, the CMA and the OfS have pledged to ensure that universities are held to their promises.

In this case study, we continue to focus on the same sample of higher education institutions (HEIs) as in Case Study 1, but here we move to an analysis of their undergraduate prospectus and student recruitment website texts. Because these documents are lengthier and more 'text-heavy' than the SU websites, we were able to build a corpus and then analyse the keywords. This provided a useful starting point for identifying themes and semantic priorities in the texts. It also enables us to make comparisons across the three university groupings. We then conducted a critical analysis of SDS and metaphors used in the documents. These methods are described in more detail in the Introduction. Taken together, the corpus analysis of keywords and critical analysis of SDS and metaphors facilitated a detailed and systematic analysis of how the language of texts functions to embody and perpetuate neoliberal ideologies. All documents were taken from the same year (2016). In the remainder of this section, we firstly present and discuss the keyword analysis, and then move on to examining the critical SDS and metaphor analysis. For information, the sizes of the whole corpus and university group sub-corpora are as follows:

Russell Group sub-corpus – 78,489 words
University Alliance sub-corpus – 46,995 words
GuildHE sub-corpus – 124,341 words
Total corpus size – 249,825 words

Keyword analysis

Table 2.1 firstly shows the top 50 keywords from the whole data set. For comparison, Tables 2.2–2.4 then separately show the top 50 keywords for each of the three university groupings.

The keywords shown in Table 2.1 for the overall document set reveal a focus on work, employment and industry. Words whose meanings relate to subject knowledge are either absent or relatively low on the lists (*knowledge*, for example, is entirely absent and *academic* is the 24th keyword in the overall set). However, when the prospectus documents are analysed separately from the recruitment texts, the work/industry-focussed words appear to *not* be key in the recruitment documents. Several of the recruitment document keywords are focussed instead on what might be termed the practicalities of studying at university, such as *fees*, *accommodation*, *graduation* and *support*. This suggests that, whilst the prospectuses try to 'sell' the university by focusing on the future employment opportunities for potential applicants, the recruitment documents centre more on the day-to-day experiences offered by the university itself.

Although there are many similarities across the keywords of the three mission groups, *international* only features as a keyword in the Russell Group documents. *Academic* has a higher keyness in the Russell Group documents than it does in the UA and Guild HE texts. The particular subjects which appear as keywords in the Russell Group texts are science and mathematics, whereas a wider range of subjects appear as keywords in the UA and Guild HE documents.

This suggests more of a prioritising of the STEM academic subjects for the Russell Group institutions in their prospectus and recruitment texts.

When the mission groups are analysed separately, *industry* only appears as a keyword for the UA and Guild HE texts. The keywords

Table 2.1 Keywords – all prospectus and recruitment documents

1. skills	2. students	3. Solent	4. course	5. university
6. industry	7. year	8. study	9. experience	10. research
11. work	12. career	13. professional	14. degree	15. opportunities
16. develop	17. Hons	18. Lincoln	19. student	20. Newman
21. graduates	22. range	23. creative	24. academic	25. placement
26. management	27. learning	28. project	29. design	30. projects
31. Psychology	32. modules	33. including	34. BA	35. campus
36. key	37. graduate	38. placements	39. teaching	40. sport
41. courses	42. studies	43. programme	44. Birmingham	45. practical
46. opportunity	47. presentations	48. business	49. media	50. website

Table 2.2 Keywords – Russell Group prospectus and recruitment documents

1. students	2. university	3. Birmingham	4. study	5. year
6. student	7. campus	8. programmes	9. skills	10. programme
11. courses	12. Leeds	13. academic	14. research	15. website
16. degree	17. modules	18. offer	19. graduates	20. learning
21. range	22. online	23. BA	24. UK	25. BSc
26. undergraduate	27. graduate	28. international	29. opportunities	30. teaching
31. studies	32. careers	33. entry	34. honours	35. sciences
36. support	37. choose	38. employability	39. tuition	40. including
41. language	42. mathematics	43. taught	44. UCAS	45. science
46. grades	47. develop	48. experience	49. MSCI	50. accommodation

Table 2.3 Keywords – University Alliance prospectus and recruitment documents

1. Lincoln	2. university	3. students	4. graduates	5. Hons
6. research	7. opportunities	8. study	9. year	10. design
11. skills	12. career	13. placement	14. industry	15. student
16. course	17. graduate	18. work	19. campus	20. including
21. science	22. degree	23. BA	24. develop	25. modules
26. range	27. media	28. outline	29. business	30. Coventry
31. placements	32. journalism	33. academic	34. marketing	35. facilities
36. experience	37. management	38. social	39. professional	40. courses
41. careers	42. academics	43. creative	44. welcome	45. forensic
46. BSc	47. engineering	48. criminology	49. topics	50. UK

Table 2.4 Keywords – Guild HE prospectus and recruitment documents

1. skills	2. Solent	3. course	4. industry	5. experience
6. work	7. Newman	8. professional	9. career	10. develop
11. creative	12. key	13. management	14. Hons	15. project
16. projects	17. year	18. degree	19. study	20. students
21. opportunities	22. psychology	23. research	24. fashion	25. sport
26. presentations	27. creatives	28. placement	29. focus	30. practical
31. learning	32. design	33. range	34. overview	35. digital
36. teaching	37. education	38. production	39. placements	40. options
41. assessment	42. media	43. dissertation	44. academic	45. university
46. business	47. knowledge	48. marketing	49. including	50. understanding

social and *creative* are also absent from the Russell Group keyword list which, again, suggests a greater concern with academic STEM subjects in the Russell Group documents. The keywords generally suggest greater specialisation in particular subject areas for the UA and Guild HE documents and many of these might be described as more vocational than academic (e.g. *journalism*, *media*, *marketing*, *business*, *fashion*, *design*, *criminology*, *forensic*).

Whilst the keywords may provide a starting point for examining the general ideological concerns of the texts, a more detailed critical analysis can be conducted through analysing the SDS and metaphorical uses of language in the document sets.

SDS analysis

The prospectus and recruitment documents analysed are full of SDS which particularly take the form of adjectives describing various characteristics claimed for the university. These include *challenge/d*, *inspire/d*, *global experts*, *state-of-the-art*, *world-class*, *vibrant*, *outstanding*, *pioneering*, *cutting-edge*, *prestigious*, *unparalleled*, *innovative*, *distinctive*, *unique*, *excellent*, *commitment/committed to*, *leading-edge*, *quality*, *successful*, *award-winning*, *exceptional*, *high-quality*, *groundbreaking* and *international/ly*. Clearly, these words have an advertising function in the positive attributes they ascribe to the university 'products' that the prospectuses and recruitment texts are aiming to sell to potential applicants. Their meanings are vacuous, as they cannot be either proven or falsified. Also, because they are used prevalently by all of the institutions examined, it becomes impossible to tell which of the universities really are *groundbreaking*, *excellent*, *unparalleled* and so on when they all describe themselves using the same formulaic language. It is interesting to note that, sometimes, *revolutionary* and *revolutionised* are used as alternatives to *innovation* but this is relatively rare. Whilst the discourse of the 'corporate boast' is evident through the pervasive use of these SDS throughout most of the documents, elements of the Newman University documents stand out as being markedly differently. Within the Newman texts, we see the occurrence of words and phrases such as *values*, *ethos*, *community*, *care*, *ethics*, *diverse*, *love*, *welcoming*, *safe*, *relaxing*, *common good* and *social justice*. These SDS seem to move away from the individualistic, competition-focussed neoliberal discourse that is so strongly characteristic of the Russell Group and University Alliance prospectuses. Cited next is the 'Our Philosophy' page of the Newman University 2016 prospectus:

> Our Patron Blessed John Henry Newman provides the foundations of our educational philosophy. Born in 1801, he was a cardinal of the Catholic Church and an extraordinary thinker who argued that the role of the university is to train the mind rather than to stuff it with information. His ideal was a community where students and tutors discuss ideas and develop new knowledge; he was a fine tutor who made time for students. That, in essence, is the foundation of our approach to teaching and learning. We celebrate his belief that heart speaks to heart, as well as mind to mind, and that our real understanding of the world and of ourselves is shaped through shared times and insights. He saw the need for wisdom as much as knowledge and we feel this is as important today as it was when he first proposed it. His ability to touch, enlighten and enrich the hearts of so many people from so many different walks of life makes him such a fitting patron for us – and for our mission to provide inclusive higher education in contemporary British society.

We might suggest that the universities with a religious foundation might be more likely to emphasise values, ethics and ideals. Indeed, the 'Cathedrals Group' of UK universities (of which Newman is a member) describes itself as being different from other universities in that it is:

> based on ethical principles informed by faith-based values. Members share a common faith heritage and a strong commitment to values such as social justice, respect for the individual and promoting the public good through our work with communities and charities.[13]

In stark contrast to Newman, the Russell Group prospectuses appear to be characterised by a 'bigger is better' discourse. For example,

- At Birmingham we offer one of the broadest programme ranges of any UK university.

The underlying assumption is that a 'wide range' of courses is better than offering a smaller, more specialised selection. However, the claim lacks any reference point for comparison – a category of misleading advertising claims identified in Bradley (2013: 84).

Another selling technique used in all documents is that of the 'student voice' as evidence of quality. This takes the form of positive quotes and testimonials from students and external examiners. The documents also make use of survey results and statistics which are offered up as proof of the quality of courses. Some examples include the following:

- 90% of our final-year students rated their course as intellectually stimulating
- In the 2014 National Student Survey Birmingham achieved an impressive 89% overall student satisfaction rating, which is higher than the national average. Satisfaction with teaching is at its highest, with an overall score of 90%

Such examples contain underlying assumptions that the statistics being presented are good. But how do we know, for example, that 90% is good? The fact that the documents make use of a wide range of different measures and surveys across different years makes it difficult for readers to actually make sense of any of the statistics. There is no way of knowing which are more highly valued or reliable than others. And it is clear that selective use is made of the statistics (Bradley 2013: 79) due to the wide range of survey publication dates used across the texts. Some of the specific surveys mentioned in the text include the following:

NSS, 2013; 2014
REF 2014
The Graduate Market in 2015, High Fliers Research
High Fliers report, 2012
HESA report, 2013
DLHE, 2011/12; 2013
The Times and Sunday Times Good University Guide, 2014, 2015
Which University Guide, 2014
Complete University Guide, 2014, 2015
OFSTED Inspection Report, 2010
New York Times 45 Places To Go list
The Telegraph top ten most beautiful universities in Britain
Rough Guide Top 10 cities in the world to visit
Ukash
The Guardian University Guide/League Table 2015
Times Higher Education
QS World University Rankings

Throughout all of the documents, there is an implicit underlying assumption that all of the above are completely reliable and objective. In fact, such a numerous and varied selection of esteem indicating statistics offer each university the opportunity to 'cherry-pick' in order to present themselves in the most advantageous way.

Within the surveys, *satisfaction* (in relation to student satisfaction) is itself an SDS. *Satisfaction* is taken to be an indicator of quality when used in relation to student satisfaction. However, when the same word is used elsewhere, its meaning shifts to that of a 'pass/fail' measure. For example:

- A satisfactory DBS check is required before registration on the Applied Golf Management Studies, Sport, Physical Education and Coaching Science and Physiotherapy programmes. Those applying for BSc Physiotherapy will also be required to complete a satisfactory health declaration (University of Birmingham)

In instances such as the previous one, 'satisfactory' means that the applicant has to pass certain pre-requisites for entry such as the DBS and health declarations in order to be admitted to the courses. What emerges is a dual system whereby academic staff and the courses they teach are being judged as 'satisfactory' or not by students, and, at the same time, students are being assessed as to whether they 'satisfactorily' meet the requirements for being admitted to and passing courses. Satisfaction becomes meaningless in such a system of mutual scrutiny. In fact, much of the content of the course pages of the prospectuses is dedicated to 'entry requirements' which necessarily limits choice for students. This is another instance of the discursive construction of the illusion of choice, a recurring theme throughout the whole book. In Chapter 5, for example, we examine how the TEF white paper constantly refers to unfettered student choice and, in doing so, discursively constructs choice as unquestionably positive and unambiguously available to everyone. Choice is a key plank of neoliberal ideology. The fiction of its integrity, even while severely materially compromised, must be maintained.

Another sales technique used in the documents is the use of reports on awards and accolades won by universities. What is notable is that none of these are socially oriented. For example, there are no reports of awards for programmes such a teacher-training, nursing, social work and so on. The accolades considered worth reporting are those attributed to STEM subjects and university facilities. Despite the social contributions of universities featuring in their mission statements, these are not marketed in the prospectus and recruitment documents. This implies they are seen as having little or no market value.

The neoliberal focus on monetary and economic values is also reflected in the way that the documents include information about how much graduates are likely to earn. The inclusion of this information presupposes that the main reasons for potential students wanting to attend university are materialistic and financial, rather than social. Its inclusion also reflects the obligation on universities in the UK (and US) to publish this data in the form of KPIs. The focus on graduate earnings is used as a justification for tuition fees in that the university becomes conceptualised as an 'investment' – a personal one. In fact, all of the prospectuses contain a lot of financial information. Examples of the benefit of university being constructed as providing a return on economic investment include the following:

- We know that securing a graduate level position is the return you want from your investment in time and money
- Postgraduate study at Leeds is a major investment in your future
- When it is time to move on, you can be confident of the value of your degree. Birmingham graduates are highly regarded by employers here and abroad

The neoliberal emphasis on constructing an enterprising and monetary-oriented individual is further reinforced through the habitually positive values associated with 'entrepreneurialism' and 'industry'. This is particularly marked in the University of Birmingham prospectus from which the following example is taken:

- Acquiring practical experience and an entrepreneurial mindset is essential while at university.

From a critical perspective, we would question why 'practical experience' and an 'entrepreneurial mindset' are to be unquestioningly ascribed such positive value (through the use of the word *essential*). This actually produces a highly restricted view of the purpose of higher education. It is important to reflect on the alternative values which could have been presented as essential; we found no evidence in any of the prospectus documents of language which ascribed positive value to students' development of socially responsibility and moral mindsets as a result of participation in higher education. Such qualities clearly do not fit the neoliberal agenda of individual advancement and are, therefore, considered to be unmarketable.

In all of the documents, much attention is paid to location and locale. This suggests an underlying assumption that location is important with the result of large sections of the prospectuses sounding rather like holiday brochures. At times, the prospectuses, in particular, seem to be more about selling the place rather than the actual university or its courses. The typical example, which follows, is taken from the Southampton Solent University 2016 undergraduate prospectus:

A global village

Southampton is a lively and cosmopolitan hub of culture, entertainment, nightlife and shopping. just over an hour from London and a short distance from Bournemouth, Portsmouth and Winchester, it's *easy* to travel to Europe and beyond, either by ferry or from the city's airport.

Culture and entertainment

Just minutes from the main campus, the city has state-of-the-art auditoriums, studios, art galleries, restaurants, two major theatres and three cinemas. There's plenty going on all year round in this lively area, including numerous concerts, festivals, workshops, shows and events.

Nightlife and restaurants

The city has a great choice of restaurants. The Bedford Place area, popular with students, is *a* buzz of activity and offers a wide selection of boutiques, pubs, bars and restaurants.

Fantastic shops

Southampton has a great choice of shops. With the popular WestQuay and Marlands centres and other city outlets, it's one of the top 20 best retail destinations in the UK.

An interesting tension between the neoliberal emphasis on marketising the university, its products and its locale comes from the observation that SUs also feature heavily in prospectuses. The very notion of a 'union' (and a 'guild' in the case of the University of Birmingham), as we state earlier, implies older discourses of trade unionism and mutual cooperation, and is at odds with neoliberal discourses of competition and individualism. In the prospectus and recruitment documents, SUs are not presented as being business-focussed but as serving the needs of the student population and as offering communal spaces and activities which are socially, rather than economically oriented. The representation of SUs in the prospectus and recruitment documents is, in some ways, rather different from the way they are represented in their own websites – as we have already detailed previously in Case Study 1. SU websites do contain elements of neoliberal discourse which sit in tension with alternative discourses focussed on friendship, community and socially oriented collaborative endeavour.

In a similar way, we observe that there is a tension between references to a competitive job market and a friendly, non-competitive university environment throughout the prospectus and recruitment documents. There are many occurrences in which the 'market' is 'global' and competitive, but 'partnerships' are 'local' and collaborative. This creates a tension between the competitive global and the collaborative local and is further evidenced through the collocations of *global* and *local*, some of which are included in Table 2.5.

Collocates of *global* suggest more of a focus on the economy and job markets. The most frequent lexical collocates of *global*, shown in Table 2.6, include *business*, *industry*, *perspectives*, *marketing*, *economy* and *international*. There are also more occurrences of *global* being used in its nominalised form – *globalisation* – whereas this does not occur at all with *local*. This shows that globalisation is conceptualised as a process and a product in the documents whereas *localisation* is not, thus diminishing the significance to universities of the latter.

Collocates of *local* include *schools*, *NHS*, *community* and *government*. These collocate patterns are *not* about international competition. Whilst university prospectuses are used as an advertising platform for the locale,

Table 2.5 Sample concordance of *local*

1	country as well as serving the	local and regional areas within
2	full-time employment working for a	local Digital Marketing firm.
3	which places might become your	local haunts. CUSU has a strong
4	variety of genres and encourage	local artists to get involved
5	projects raising vital funds for	local charities. Ahead of the
6	scheme A2B helps students in	local partner schools from
7	each year, many of these in the	local community, Selly Oak. 93%
8	as a Higher Education Mentor in	local schools. Ellie also took
9	from industry and the	local community, whose guidance
10	internship for four weeks with a	local social enterprise. Work
11	variety of schemes, from being a	local conservation volunteer
12	the paid scheme works alongside	local authorities, including
13	internship opportunities in	local government and voluntary
14	have formed a partnership with	local NHS trusts to ensure that
15	statistics, computer analysis,	local government, defence research
16	variety of clients, including	local organisations such as the
17	through our partnerships with	local schools and hospitals.
18	work closely with employers or	local companies on projects within
19	course team has close ties to the	local music scene, enabling you
20	Many Solent students coach	local sports groups, help with
21	than £350 million a year to the	local economy. Following on from
22	having strong partnerships with	local employers. You may wish

Table 2.6 Sample concordance of *global*

1	including the prestigious	Global Challenge. Career prospects
2	situating these debates in their	global context. In both your
3	and become part of a powerful	global network of Birmingham
4	lecturers at Birmingham will be	global experts in their field
5	your home country as well as the	global job market. We keep up
6	due to a changing and uncertain	global economic climate. Acquiring
7	alumni in conjunction with larger,	global organisations. Their strong
8	funded as interns in top	global companies. There are
9	degrees will open your eyes to a	global business environment,
10	impacts, energy security,	global economic systems, changing
11	teaching at Birmingham and are	global leaders in corpus
12	that can compete successfully in	global markets, or to develop
13	and entry to a dynamic	global industry. Meets the
14	of situations. Working in a	global economy, you will approach
15	of major employers across the	global economy. All the awards
16	companies to be competitive in a	global marketplace. Course Outline
17	in your final year, such as	global marketing, entrepreneurship
18	excel at managerial roles in the	global business sector. Recent
19	entrepreneurial marketing and	global communications. Work

the university sees *international*, not *local* to be a signifier of prestige. Whilst *locale* may be a marketing advantage; to remain *local* is demeaning of reputation.

Nevertheless, a collocation analysis (see Table 2.7) of *partnership* reveals an overriding focus on the local rather than the global, with *local organisations*, *local employers*, *local schools*, *local authorities* and the *local community* featuring most noticeably. What partnerships are *not* is international, nor are they *between* universities.

A final discursive feature observed in all of the prospectus documents is that there is a clear register shift away from advertising discourse towards a legal register in the sections of the documents that deal with the regulations and laws governing university practice and procedures (which are, of course, required in the prospectuses in the same way that 'terms and

Table 2.7 Sample concordance of *partnership*

1	scale. We have formed a	partnership with local NHS trusts
2	within the community through our	partnerships with local schools
3	and practical learning. Strong	partnerships with local employers.
4	benefit from Newman's excellent	partnerships with schools in
5	students and having strong	partnerships with local employers.
6	of the whole child Effective	Partnerships that ensure all
7	freelance copywriting. Industry	Partnerships The University of
8	links with the wider community and	partnerships that will reach

conditions' are required for any other sort of legal transaction concerning goods or services). The legal register helps to create a more punitive discourse in which the power of the university as an institution is more heavily foregrounded. These sections contain legal information about the punitive consequences for students of non-payment of fees, course failure and so on. They do not, however, set out the punitive consequences for the university if it is seen to breach any of its own regulatory policies and procedures. Even in the face of interventions from the CMA, the underlying assumption here is that it is students who are more likely to need regulating than the university itself. Despite the other sections of the documents constructing potential students as consumers of university products, the legal sections make it clear who really has power in higher education. In fact, the only place in the legal section where we find the university being placed in a position of responsibility for breaking its own terms is in reference to the discontinuation of courses, as in the following example:

- If the University discontinues a programme, it will make reasonable endeavours to provide a suitable alternative.

In the realm of marketing regulation, discontinuing a programme may be considered akin to withdrawing a product after a sale. There is an attendant underlying assumption here that this is a practice that *does* occur in higher education. Furthermore, the university is not obliged to provide its student consumers of the discontinued programme with compensation or an alternative product – the condition it sets itself is only to 'provide reasonable endeavours' to provide suitable alternatives. *Reasonable* is an SDS and therefore impossible to challenge legally. This is one area in which universities have been required to concede territory to government constraint as they face increased expectations and tighter scrutiny with the introduction of the *Higher Education and Research Act* discussed in Chapter 5.

Critical metaphor analysis

The most notable metaphorical domains which are drawn on repeatedly throughout the prospectus and recruitment documents are those of sport and war. These domains tend to merge conceptually so that sport is often construed as warlike and war is presented as a competitive game. And we will see that these metaphors prevail throughout all of the HE documents examined throughout this book. Within these domains, the UNIVERSITY AS AN ATHLETE/SPORTS TEAM and UNIVERSITY AS A MILITARY UNIT metaphors map as follows:

UNIVERSITY IS AN ATHLETE/SPORTS TEAM:

Source	*Target*
Track record	Past achievements of the university
Baseline	Minimum requirements of a university
Tackling	University competes with other universities
Goals	What the university needs to do to be better other universities
Set a high bar	University aspires to be better than other universities
Champion	What the university becomes when it is better than other universities
Gaming 'metrics'	Universities try to cheat and manipulate
Level the playing field	Universities have to act fairly

UNIVERSITY AS A MILITARY UNIT:

Source	*Target*
Build an intelligence base	University spies on what other universities are doing.
Trigger (reviews)	University can engage in threatening and hostile action when people and teams aren't doing what the university wants them to.
Early warning mechanism	The university is under constant threat from the enemy (i.e. other universities). University is vulnerable.
Under attack	University and individuals/teams within it are vulnerable/can be damaged.

There has been much written about the cultural prevalence of sport/war metaphors in contemporary society both in the academy and in mainstream media. It has been widely recognised, for example, that the metaphor has been used extensively in relation to the UK's Brexit negotiations. In a 2017 article in the *Independent*, British Prime Minister Theresa May was reported as being criticised by EU Chief Negotiator Michel Barnier. May was reported as saying:

> And as we look forward to the next stage, the ball is in their court. But I am optimistic we will receive a positive response.[14]

This cultural prevalence of sport metaphors has, likewise, made its way extensively into university prospectus and recruitment documents. In the documents examined in this chapter, the sport metaphors are realised through words such as *goal/s*, *tackle* and *springboard* and metaphorical phrases such as *level* the playing field* and *track record*. Some examples are included below:

- one that is shaped around your individual goals, interests and career ambitions
- will give you the best possible chance of achieving your career goals
- This Foundation degree has been designed to ensure that graduates are equipped to tackle this challenge
- skills required to tackle the challenges of modern computing
- It can provide a springboard to professional training
- offers a high quality springboard into coaching sport from community to the elite level
- Rapid technological developments are levelling the playing field with regard to marketing
- and outstanding track record in collaborative research and process training
- The programme has a track record of international employment opportunities
- we have a strong track record in securing internship opportunities

Within the war domain, there are frequent references to pursuit, strategy, ranks and targets. For example,

- now have the chance to pursue our exciting Summer School programmes
- Newman University has pursued a strategy which places a stronger emphasis on research
- You will learn how to apply marketing techniques at both strategic and operational levels
- Joining the ranks of these professionals demands creativity
- which will track your progress and allow you to monitor your individual targets
- employers actively target our students for their drive, diversity, communication and problem-solving skills
- Some of these are targeted to help you build skills and experience

The discursive effect of the repeated use of these metaphors is to construct higher education, as adversarial, competitive, tough and aggressive and structured to reproduce the neoliberal subject who embodies these qualities.

The higher education experience is metaphorically conceptualised in two predominant ways in the documents: as a *journey* and as a *building*. A journey implies movement and mobility, with an implication of ending up in a different and better place than at the start of the journey. In the documents, journeys (and associated terms such as *launch*, *route*, *step*, *destination* and *pathway*) often refer specifically to careers and entrepreneurship as in the following examples:

- It is also a positive way to make valuable contacts in your chosen profession and to launch your career
- support to help you through your entrepreneurial journey
- the first step towards starting your own business
- especially relevant to a variety of employment pathways within the criminal justice and community safety sphere
- Other career destinations could include youth work
- offers a variety of services to students and graduates launching their own business
- Many successfully launch their own businesses
- Possible career destinations include community sport educator
- You may wish to embark on a new career path
- as well as following the teaching route
- could provide the next step towards a more rewarding and fulfilling career

The process of learning is also sometimes described in metaphorical terms as a journey, as in these examples:

- Students who follow a particular pathway through this degree programme
- your support becomes more personalised and tailored to your needs as your focus narrows to a particular pathway
- allowing you to create a pathway through the degree that best corresponds to your interests and strengths
- the course content will entail fixed pathways to ensure academic coherence and clarity
- an opportunity for you to embark on a creative journey
- A different kind of learning journey

However, learning is more predominantly conceptualised using the building metaphor discussed next. There are occasional journey metaphors referring to knowledge in terms of frontiers (overlapping with the war metaphorical domain).

- Biologists are pushing back the frontiers of knowledge

And we found only one example where a journey metaphor was used in more of a non-neoliberal sense to refer to a *faith journey* (in the Newman University prospectus).

- organised to fit in with the rhythm of your academic year while supporting you in your faith journey

The cumulative effect of the use of journey metaphors is that they construct their referents (learning, knowledge, careers) as linear and controlled processes. This is, of course, illusory in a way which helps to uphold neoliberal discourses of unremitting 'progress' as highly valued.

Even more prevalent than the journey metaphors are the building metaphors throughout all of the prospectus and recruitment documents. *Build** itself is used frequently to refer to knowledge, skills and experience.

- Engaging with research builds skills such as critical thinking and analysis
- The first year builds a foundation in core areas [. . .] In your second year, you build on this knowledge
- in addition to allowing you to put theory into practice and build real-world expertise and knowledge
- In your first year, you study a range of relevant topics while building theoretical and technical knowledge.
- You build a knowledge base through tourism-specific and business-related modules
- You will build on the mathematics that you have already studied
- so that you can build a degree that suits your interests
- This will be built on in your second and third year
- The first year is built around an interdisciplinary module
- building the depth of knowledge you need to be a successful engineer
- will help you to build a sound and up-to-date knowledge base in your subject
- you will build on your knowledge of psychological and sociological concepts

Beyond this, the most prevalent building terms used metaphorically are those associated with the initial construction stages in building – these include references to *grounding* and *foundations*, and they are used repeatedly to refer to subject knowledge and conceptual understanding.

- As well as a thorough grounding in the academic elements of drama
- offers students the opportunity to acquire a solid grounding in and critical understanding of social science
- and prepare the ground for career progression
- Provides a solid grounding in the underlying physical and mathematical principles

- giving you a firm grounding in scientific skills
- and gain a strong foundation in research methods
- The first year of the BEng and MEng programmes provide a solid foundation in mechanical engineering theory and practice
- The first year equips you with a foundation of social science
- while providing you with a solid foundation in the key aspects of the discipline.
- In your first year you will be given a foundation in the analysis and practice of theatre,
- Our foundational first year gives you an excellent grounding in the major historical periods
- which will provide a firm foundation for future continuous professional development leading to a masters degree
- A broad curriculum in the first and second years provides strong foundations for specialisation in the third year
- The first year introduces you to the cornerstones of literature

We note in the previous examples how many occurrences of *foundation/s* and *grounding* are pre-modified by adjectives whose meanings are those associated with strength, security and power (e.g. *solid*, *firm*, *strong*). Strength is highly valued in these metaphorical constructs of knowledge as a building. Alternative metaphors such as 'roots' may be strong but could also be associated with other positive attributes such as adaptability and effectiveness – these qualities are important to knowledge and understanding but are not captured particularly well by the *grounding/foundations* building metaphors.

The notion of *underpinning* also occurs frequently in the documents. This is an interesting use of the building metaphor as underpinning is usually a remedial process in construction (it is used to hold up failing buildings and prevent them from collapsing). *Underpinning* is used in two main senses in the documents. In the first, it is used to refer to teaching being underpinned by research and/or the student experience being underpinned by research and teaching. Therefore, students are the beneficiaries of a foundational process of shoring up in these metaphorical constructions, either directly through teaching or indirectly through research.

- We are proud of our reputation for providing a high-quality student experience underpinned by inspirational teaching
- Research underpins the student experience at the University of Lincoln
- It is underpinned by high-quality scientific research and field investigations

- All of this is underpinned by our commitment to academic excellence in teaching, research and professional expertise
- cutting-edge research underpins the teaching you receive on this programme

The discursive effect of these metaphors is to construct a notion that teaching and the 'student experience' will fail without research. *Underpinning* in its second sense refers to elements of knowledge underpinning other elements in specific subject areas.

- you consider the history, theories and research techniques that underpin investigative journalism
- the elements of sports science which underpin the principles of good quality coaching
- whose work is underpinned by a depth of knowledge and breadth of experience
- The field of study underpins the hi-tech world we live in
- which underpins the formulation and synthesis of drugs

Through these metaphors, as in the journey metaphors, knowledge and learning are constructed as uni-directional, linear, insular and planned, rather than organic, responsive, unpredictable, adaptable, or even transformative. Thus, certain conceptualisations of knowledge are prioritised over others through this discursive effect. In some places, there are even references to *capstones* (usually to refer to a dissertation or final assignment on a degree programme) – in building, the final stone that completes the building.

- and there will be a capstone dissertation project

Other building-related terms include *forge* and *tools/toolkit* which are used to describe skills and careers. *Forge* includes a meaning of bringing into being, so it is significant that it is applied to the career after higher education, and not to the process of producing knowledge during it.

- Some graduates have used their skills to forge a career outside the discipline
- These skills will give you the tools to success in your future career
- where students develop a comprehensive toolkit of skills

In sum, the KNOWLEDGE IS A BUILDING metaphor embodies the following cognitive mappings:

KNOWLEDGE IS A BUILDING:

Source	*Target*
Underpinning	Course content based on research
Preparing the ground and laying foundations	First year of an undergraduate course
Building (process of)	Studying more modules
Capstone	Final dissertation/thesis
Tools used for building	Academic skills

Building metaphors have been identified as operating frequently in other discursive contexts such as political discourse (Charteris-Black 2004). The cumulative effect of the building and journey metaphors are to construct learning and the overall experience of higher education as linear, controlled and contained. Buildings are bounded and inorganic – they are designed and strategic rather than naturally evolving from their environment. It is easy to see how such metaphors function to reinforce the ideology of the self-serving individualistic neoliberal subject (in the form of the student consumer of higher education) who can be designed and controlled to fit the purpose of the controlling institution.

As in other documents examined throughout this book, there are other metaphors which seem to offer alternatives to the inorganic building metaphors. We find some instances of nature metaphors being used to refer to creativity and research, as in these examples:

- this course also offers a holistic approach that <u>nurtures</u> individual creativity
- Newman University has a <u>growing research culture</u>
- It has <u>blossomed</u> into a discipline that has changed the world beyond recognition

Here, it seems that research can be organic and can be 'nurtured' rather than aggressively designed and executed. Interestingly, and perhaps surprisingly, nature metaphors are also used to refer to entrepreneurship and business:

- Effective management in business is essential for companies to <u>thrive and grow</u>
- The University of Lincoln is proud of its approach to <u>nurturing</u> entrepreneurialism in its students
- our dedicated business <u>incubation</u> centre, which can provide offices, mentoring and business planning support
- it all started with an idea <u>hatched</u> at Birmingham

In these examples, businesses and business ideas are conceptualised as living organisms through the nature metaphors. We may speculate that the neoliberal concern with creating entrepreneurial individuals is discursively constructed as 'natural' to hide its ideological purpose.

One interesting use of organic metaphors applies to descriptions of the physical campus of the university. *Heart* is used routinely to metaphorically construct, or particular aspects of it, as a living organism. *Heart* is used as an organic alternative to 'middle' or 'centre' to describe universities in terms of their physical location in relation to the surrounding city or region:

- We're located in the very heart of the cultural and commercial capital of the South
- The University of Leeds is a single campus in the heart of Leeds
- Located in the heart of England with a proud heritage and excellent academic credentials
- Coventry University is situated in the heart of the city and occupies a compact campus.
- Situated at the heart of the UK rail and motorway network
- there's always something to discover in the city at the heart of the UK
- Birmingham is at the heart of the UK's road and rail network
- Our student accommodation in the heart of Coventry

In other instances, *heart* is used to locate particular university buildings or facilities within the broader campus:

- The Union building is located right at the heart of campus
- the School of Mathematics at the heart of its Brayford Pool Campus
- accommodates students in a variety of residences with a popular social centre at its heart
- situated on campus in the heart of the Student Village

Heart is also used to situate university values in relation to each other. In the following examples, research and teaching style are valued as the heart of learning, the library is valued as the heart of learning experience, and creative practice is valued as the heart of the specific course. The entities to which the heart metaphor is attributed in these examples are, therefore, construed as enabling the learning process to happen – they are presented as feeding life-blood to them in a way that connects them organically.

- Whichever subject you choose to study, research will be at the heart of your learning
- Our interactive teaching style puts you right at the heart of your learning

- We place students at the heart of everything we do
- our library will be at the heart of your learning experience
- The development and refinement of your own creative practice is placed at the heart of the course

Discussion

The linguistic evidence presented and discussed in the two previous case studies is compelling in its determination to construct students as consumers. It is ironic that a university which should allow young people to search and inhabit multiple and evolving identities should seek to homogenise their outlook so thoroughly. This is obscured by the mythology of the 'personalisation' agenda. It is designed to echo the legislative title, 'putting students at the heart of the system', but instead is selling some misleading fallacies. With the imposition of dashboards, targets, learning outcomes and indicators, there is a concern that this leads not to a personal intellectual trajectory, but rather the opposite course of control and containment of learning.

The origin of the consumerist discourse lies in the uniquely high tuition fees paid by students in England. This is, we maintain, a deliberate strategy by the UK government in order to, firstly, construct neoliberal subjects who accept responsibility for their own education and, secondly, to shift the narrative of higher education, from public good and a necessity for a democratic society, to higher education as personal benefit in a stratified, marketised system.

The analysis of SUs exemplifies the shift towards a consumer outlook and away from activism and provision of a platform for the student voice. This endorses the findings of Brooks *et al* (2015) that the activist function of SUs has been subdued in recent years. New findings in our data based on systematic linguistic analysis have included the new focus on marketisation and the commodification of both the university and the positioning of students as products via a new prominence for employability. Whilst this may be seen as a benign innovation, when it sits alongside advertisements for pizza and financial services, this context offers a different interpretation which coincides with other changes in the neoliberal university. Students, like university buildings and academic staff, become another asset to be exploited for financial gain when they are coerced into acting as 'brand ambassadors' for the SUs and, by extension, the universities.

Another aspect of neoliberalisation apparent in the SU websites is the foregrounding of competition, but this time taking the form of an invitation to students to participate in an audit and ranking of academic staff and departments. SUs appear to mirror the discourses of the university management tiers to which they are coupled; themes of strategic plans, impact and accountability are paraded. At the same time, these discourses find themselves in competition with traditional discourses of trade unionism. SU websites do contain elements of neoliberal discourse which sit in tension with alternative discourses focussed on friendship, community and socially oriented collaborative endeavour. It cannot be surprising that this is a cohort of students which has been socialised to find audits such as TEF, NSS and discourses such as 'value for money' palatable.

Consumerist and neoliberal ideology is found extensively in the universities' own marketing literature to the extent that Bradley (2013) questions their integrity. It is possible that there is no intent to deceive, but that the competitive nature of the quasi-market in higher education requires universities to present the best possible news about themselves, sometimes at the expense of currency and accuracy. We may speculate whether the university prospectuses merely reflect or help construct the role of student as consumer. Perhaps it is both.

But the most powerful effect emerging from the prospectuses is the discourse which constructs the university's own identity which manifests as self-promotion packaged in a repeated set of SDS adjectives: *world-class*, *outstanding*, *pioneering*, *cutting-edge*, *prestigious*, *unparalleled*, *innovative*, *distinctive*, *unique*, *excellent award-winning*, *exceptional*, *high-quality*, *groundbreaking*. Bradley's (2013) study which we have drawn on extensively in the discussion of university marketing materials has nevertheless overlooked the extent to which reliance on such a small sub-set of promotional adjectives is central to the advertising strategy. In our sample, though, Newman University stood out as eschewing this discourse, preferring to signal its commitment to values of community, ethics and social justice. Given the hyper-promotion of university websites, perhaps it is inevitable that the CMA should tighten its scrutiny of universities. However, this has opened up the limits of its scope in regulating the behaviour and the consequences of university education to debate, as the Siddiqui case mentioned earlier makes clear.

Despite universities celebrating their social contribution in mission statements (Morrish and Sauntson 2013), these are not specifically marketed to students, with the exception of Newman University. Instead, prominence is given to those features which have purchase on individual aspiration or function as clear status signifiers: employment, graduate earnings, the league table position of the university. Additionally, universities which are able to do so, for reasons of attractiveness to students, like to sell the location of a university.

For the majority of universities, their academic, pastoral and social provision is endorsed with the language of competition, and sustained by metaphors of war and sports. Newman University favours a counter-discourse which is anchored in metaphors of individual *blossoming*, and the *nurturing* of students. This metaphor of organic growth is occasionally used elsewhere, but with a rather different perspective;

entrepreneurialism is *nurtured* at the University of Lincoln, whilst ideas are *hatched* at the University of Birmingham.

We wish to suggest that the possibility of counter-narratives are not restricted to the religious foundation universities – indeed, the idea of student as consumer has received widespread criticism in politics and society generally over the last few years since tuition fees in England reached £9,000 per year. We are cheered to find alternative conceptualisations of students and their relationship to learning and the academy. For example, Sabri (2013) points to the US NSSE (National Survey of Student Engagement) which moves the focus from consumption to an obligation to engage in a more active way.

Neary and Hagyard (2011) develop an alternative pedagogy of student as producer of knowledge, whilst Nordensvard (2011: 166) offers instead the student as citizen: 'A student is positioned with values for the common good of society [. . .] a student could be seen as someone abiding to democracy and its struggle, abide to a common good beyond the individual pursuit for profit'. For Nordensvard, the graduate should be willing to offer their knowledge and minds in the service of others. This ethos is prominent in new work in alternative pedagogy by Hall and Winn (2018) which seeks a role for 'mass intellectuality' in opposition to the agenda of skills, technology and the knowledge valued only for its role in the service of the economy.

For students who are realising the limits of the consumerist promises, the notion of mass intellectuality exposes the paradox that the market has shaped them into less democratic and neoliberal subjects, whilst still believing themselves to be free (Davies and Bansel 2007: 254). We contend that it is only at moments of crisis and resistance that subjects enter the forcing ground of critical engagement and are allowed intellectual transformation. Ironically, the marketised, consumerist university with its structured learning environments, learning outcomes, aims, objectives and assessment criteria does not ordinarily grant this.

There have been hopeful signs for a change of, if not ideological shift, then ideological clarity. These have emerged in the context of student support for two significant academic union campaigns at the University of Bath, and a more general strike by workers facing drastic contraction of their pension scheme in the UK. Students have taken to the picket line and attended teach-outs which have seen alternative pedagogy merge organically as lecturer and students have sat and learned together. This may reveal to students that they have been sold a false prospectus of personalisation which has entailed the abandonment of collective learning, peer education, or even Robbins' ideal that higher education should 'transmit a common culture and common standards of citizenship' (Robbins 1963). We wait to see whether this has indeed been a pivotal moment and a challenge to the neoliberal academy, but it is increasingly evident that students are not entirely comfortable with being treated as consumers (Anonymous Academic 2018).[15]

Notes

1. www.gov.uk/government/news/putting-students-at-the-heart-of-higher-education
2. www.theguardian.com/education/2016/dec/04/graduate-sues-oxford-university-1m-failure-first-faiz-siddiqui
3. www.universitiesuk.ac.uk/policy-and-analysis/reports/Documents/2016/consumer-rights-universities.pdf
4. www.hepi.ac.uk/2017/11/09/much-much-cross-subsidies-teaching-research-british-universities/
5. See, for example, www.insidehighered.com/news/2015/06/15/are-lazy-rivers-and-climbing-walls-driving-cost-college
6. www.theguardian.com/education/2015/may/28/exam-stress-students-cuddle-piglets-relieve-revision-anxiety
   www.bbc.co.uk/news/uk-england-bristol-32707572
   www.bbc.co.uk/news/uk-england-somerset-27434656
7. www.timeshighereducation.com/news/buzzwords-helped-universities-get-gold-tef
8. https://analytics.jiscinvolve.org/wp/files/2016/04/CASE-STUDY-I-Nottingham-Trent-University.pdf
9. www.longviewoneducation.org/propaganda-behind-personalised-learning/)
10. www.youtube.com/watch?v=4hhFAZU8Mbk
11. www.glos.ac.uk/discover/campuses/pages/our-campuses.aspx
12. www.nytimes.com/2015/02/07/upshot/is-the-professor-bossy-or-brilliant-much-depends-on-gender.html?_r=0
13. www.cathedralsgroup.ac.uk/
14. www.independent.co.uk/news/uk/politics/brexit-michel-barnier-talks-not-a-game-david-davis-brussels-a7992691.html
15. www.theguardian.com/higher-education-network/2018/mar/02/my-students-support-our-strike-they-dont-want-to-be-passive-consumers

References

Barnett, R. 2013. *Imagining the University*. London: Routledge.

Bousquet, M. 2008. *How the University Works*. New York: New York University Press.

Bradley, J. 2013. Integrity in higher education marketing? A typology of misleading data-based claims in the university prospectus. *International Journal for Educational Integrity* 9 (2): 74–88.

Brooks, R. 2014. What role do students' unions play in today's HE system? https://blogs.surrey.ac.uk/sociology/2014/08/20/what-role-do-students-unions-play-in-todays-he-system/ (Accessed 28 December 2017).

Brooks, R., Byford, K. and Sela, K. 2015. The changing role of students' unions within contemporary higher education. *Journal of Education Policy* 30 (2): 165–181.

Cable, V. and Willetts, D. 2012. *Higher Education: Students at the Heart of the System*. London: Department for Business, Innovation and Skills.

Charteris-Black, J. 2004. *Corpus Approaches to Critical Metaphor Analysis*. Basingstoke: Palgrave.

Chessum, M. 2014. Students' unions are being co-opted and depoliticised. *Times Higher Education*. www.timeshighereducation.co.uk/comment/opinion/stu

dents-unions-are-being-co-opted-and-depoliticised/2014384.article (Accessed 28 December 2017).
Collini, S. 2012. *What are Universities For?* London: Penguin.
Davies, B. and Bansel, P. 2007. Neoliberalism and education. *International Journal of Qualitative Studies in Education* 20 (3): 247–259.
The Dearing Report. 1997. The national committee of enquiry into higher education. https://archive.is/20121224091502/https://bei.leeds.ac.uk/Partners/NCIHE/
Department for Business, Innovation and Skills. 2010. *The Browne Report: Securing a Sustainable Future for Higher Education: An Independent Review of Higher Education Funding and Student Finance.*www.gov.uk/government/publications/the-browne-report-higher-education-funding-and-student-finance (Accessed 1 September 2017).
Department for Business, Innovation and Skills. 2016. *Success as a Knowledge Economy: Teaching Excellence, Social Mobility and Student Choice.* London: Department for Business, Innovation and Skills.
Doxdator, B. 2017. The propaganda behind personalised learning. www.longviewoneducation.org/propaganda-behind-personalised-learning/ (Accessed 16 December).
Fairclough, N. 1995 [2010]. *Critical Discourse Analysis.* Harlow: Longman.
France, P. 2018. Personalized learning is a problem of privilege. www.edsurge.com/amp/news/2018-01-21-personalized-learning-is-a-problem-of-privilege?__twitter_impression=true (Accessed 23 January 2018).
Geesin, B. 2016. Raising the surveillance subject: Children with toys that are intelligent and interactive. *Surveillance and Security in the Age of Algorithmic Communication (IAMCR)* conference, University of Leicester, UK, July.
Hall, R. and Winn, J. eds. 2018. *Mass Intellectuality and Democratic Leadership in Higher Education.* London: Bloomsbury.
Haywood, H., Jenkins, R. and Molesworth, M. 2011. A degree will make all your dreams come true: Higher education as the management of consumer desires. In M. Molesworth, E. Nixon and R. Scullion, eds. *The Marketisation of UK Higher Education and the Student as Consumer.* London: Routledge. 183–195.
Maringe, F. 2011. The students as consumer: Affordances and constraints in a transforming higher education environment. In M. Molesworth, E. Nixon and R. Scullion, eds. *The Marketisation of UK Higher Education and the Student as Consumer.* London: Routledge. 142–154.
Molesworth, M., Nixon, E. and Scullion, R. 2009. Having, being and higher education: The marketisation of the university and the transformation of the student into consumer. *Teaching in Higher Education* 14 (3): 277–287.
Molesworth, M., Nixon, E. and Scullion, R. eds. 2011. *The Marketisation of UK Higher Education and the Student as Consumer.* London: Routledge.
Morrish, L. and. O'Mara, K. 2011. Queering the discourse of diversity. *Journal of Homosexuality* 58 (6–7): 974–990.
Morrish, L. and Sauntson, H. 2013. 'Business-facing motors for economic development': An appraisal analysis of visions and values in the marketized UK university. *Critical Discourse Studies* 10 (1): 61–80.
Neary, M. and Hagyard, A. 2011. Pedagogy of excess: An alternative political economy of student life. In M. Molesworth, E. Nixon and R. Scullion, eds. *The Marketisation of UK Higher Education and the Student as Consumer.* London: Routledge. 209–223.

Nixon, E., Scullion, R. and Hearn, R. 2016. Her majesty the student: Marketised higher education and the narcissistic (dis)satisfactions of the student consumer. *Studies in Higher Education*: 1–21.

Nordensvard, J. 2011. The consumer metaphor versus the citizen metaphor: Different sets of roles for students. In M. Molesworth, E. Nixon and R. Scullion, eds. *The Marketisation of UK Higher Education and the Student as Consumer*. London: Routledge. 157–169.

Prinsloo, P. 2017. What I heard, what I did not hear and what I wish I had heard . . . Reflections on the world conference on online learning, Toronto. *Open Distance Teaching and Learning* blog. https://opendistanceteachingandlearning.wordpress.com/2017/11/21/what-i-heard-what-i-did-not-hear-and-what-i-wish-i-had-heard-reflections-on-the-world-conference-on-online-learning-toronto-2017/

Raaper, R. 2018. Students' unions and consumerist policy discourses in English higher education. *Critical Studies in Education*. (online) https://doi.org/10.1080/17508487.2017.1417877

Ridley, D. 2017. Governance as trade union strategy: Interview with bath UCU's Michael Carley. https://hemarketisation.wordpress.com/2017/12/27/governance-as-trade-union-strategy-interview-with-bath-ucus-michael-carley/ (Accessed 1 September 2018).

Robbins Report. (1963). *Higher Education: Report of the Committee Appointed by the Prime Minister Under the Chairmanship of Lord Robbins*. London: Her Majesty's Stationery Office. www.educationengland.org.uk/documents/robbins/robbins1963.html (Accessed 18 May 2015).

Rogers, K. and Furse, S. 2014. We have paid a heavy price for our peaceful student protest. *The Guardian*. www.theguardian.com/commentisfree/2014/jul/24/heavy-price-peaceful-student-protest-birmingham-university) (Accessed 1 September 2018).

Sabri, D. 2011. What's wrong with 'the student experience'? *Discourse: Studies in the Cultural Politics of Education* 32 (5): 657–667.

Sabri, D. 2013. Student evaluations of teaching as 'fact-totems': The case of the UK National Student Survey. *Sociological Research Online* 18 (4): 15.

Sclater, N., Peasgood, A. and Mullan, J. 2016. Learning analytics in higher education. *JISC*. www.jisc.ac.uk/sites/default/files/learning-analytics-in-he-v2_0.pdf (Accessed 1 September 2018).

Turnbull, S. 2018. A guide to UK league tables in higher education. *HEPI Report*. www.hepi.ac.uk/2018/01/04/guide-uk-league-tables-higher-education/ (Accessed 1 September 2018).

Williams, J. 2011. Constructing consumption: What media representations reveal about today's students. In M. Molesworth, E. Nixon and R. Scullion, eds. *The Marketisation of UK Higher Education and the Student as Consumer*. London: Routledge. 170–182.

Williams, J. 2013. *Consuming Higher Education: Why Learning Can't Be Bought*. London: Bloomsbury.

3 Marketing the goods

Context

A market revolution has swept into higher education in the UK, and this has become a new priority for British universities, accompanied by a 33% increase in marketing spend since 2010–11 (Sandler Clarke 2014). Universities have relied on corporate funding for many decades (Thompson 1970; Washburn 2005), and in this sense, marketisation and relations with business and the economy is nothing new. It is perhaps the balance of this activity, which is changing, and with it, argues Washburn, the danger that commercial forces will transform every aspect of academic life.

Whatever the arguments, there is no doubt that universities now see themselves in marketised and commodified terms. The competition for students has made universities re-order their priorities from promoting knowledge to the promotion of self and 'brand'. Sanigar (2013), using corpus linguistic methods, examines the language of university websites and what she analyses as a dialectical relationship between language and a marketised society. She finds a more covert kind of market-oriented discourse, using the strategic placement of positive, but semantically malleable, evaluative adjectives (e.g. *quality, world-class*) collocating with lexical items like *research*. Sauntson and Morrish (2010) conducted an analysis of university mission statements in order to determine what universities consider their products to be. Unsurprisingly, it was revealed that universities consider these to be *research, students* and *knowledge. Knowledge* was treated as a 'product' which the university owns as a commodity, rather than a process, and so can be 'sold' and marketed to potential students and perhaps other stakeholders (2010: 78).

Not only must they compete for students, but universities have also felt obliged to justify themselves in economic terms. The neoliberal traits of marketisation and competition are readily apparent in all public communications (including those analysed in the previous chapter). However, the market in higher education defies the transactional analogy. Burrows (2012) argues that the nature of markets in higher education is a form of simulation. League tables and constant audit of metrics, designed to further regimes of accountability, have mimicked the market by transforming universities into sites of competition. Of more concern, Burrows notes, are the 'structures of feeling' that are sedimented by these regimes. Universities, despite displaying very little actual distinctiveness in the UK, are nevertheless concerned with marketing a brand image. Wæraas and Solbakk discuss the nature of branding: 'While a physical product may be very similar to other products, a brand is identified as something unique. It is something that exists more in the minds of consumers than in the product or the organization itself' (2008: 451). Despite their finding that 'a university may be too complex to be encapsulated by one brand or identity definition' (2008: 1), universities, nevertheless, seem to imagine that branding commodifies some indefinable quality of a university which, nevertheless, constitutes a 'unique selling point', and may secure 'uptake' of the product. To this end, universities have continued to engage in self-promotion and marketing more intensively than in the past, and university mission statements are one strategy used to market and 'brand' the university and its 'products' in what might be seen as a challenge of promoting intangible products to 'consumers' and in a relatively undifferentiated market.

The statements of missions and visions that now routinely appear on university websites reflect their reorientation from an academic-facing value set towards a corporate one which embodies the following dimensions: marketisation (the imposition of markets on public sector organisations), financialisation (the view that all transactions have a financial basis) and commodification (the refiguring of goods and services into a purchasable commodity) (Apple 1995; Morrish 2000; Morrish and Sauntson (2013); Pratt 1995).

Case Study 3 in this chapter analyses an updated corpus of mission statements from a wider range of UK HEIs than was examined in the 2010 study. The corpus is analysed using the selective elements of corpus linguistics outlined in the Introduction (keywords and some of their collocation patterns). Sample mission statements (one from each 'mission group') are also analysed in greater detail using APPRAISAL analysis in order to provide a more nuanced examination of how evaluative language is used in the statements in order to construct the university as a commodified entity.

Case Study 4 examines another marketable commodity in the 21st-century university – that of the 'KPIs' of diversity. This case study also incorporates an analysis of US as well as UK data for comparison. We will argue that, in the deeply corporatised university of the 21st century, diversity accompanies *excellence*, *transferable skills*, and *accountability* as markers communicating 'we are competitive players'. However, it is apparent that some categories of diversity are more front stage than others in this naïve marketing strategy. We will argue that universities prefer their diverse minorities to embody their difference in a visible way.

People of colour, people with disabilities are all brought within the purview of diversity and considered to be an asset to the institution. Instead, what appears in statements are broadly based 'strands' of diversity which correlate with bodily intelligible differentiation by race, ethnicity, gender, and so on. In this way difference is discursively invoked, but simultaneously erased. As we will contend, the 'invisibility' of LGBT+-identified people is preferred, lest they bring universities and colleges into disrepute. In the second case study of university marketisation, we analyse a collection of diversity statements from UK and US universities, for comparison of approach. As with the first case study of university mission statements, the diversity statement study uses the same analytical tools of corpus linguistics and APPRAISAL analysis in order to explore how university values are embedded in (and reiterated through) diversity statements.

Case study 3: UK university mission statements

In our previous study of UK university mission statements (Sauntson and Morrish 2010), we presented as evidence the analysis of a detailed corpus linguistic analysis of all of the available mission statements at the time for UK universities in the Russell Group, 1994 Group and Million + group. We found that marketisation, commodification and globalisation play key roles in the university's construction of its own identity and 'brand'. The analysis also revealed that students are positioned, simultaneously, as consumers, units of profit, and as 'products' of the university. Furthermore, we observed that the frequent claims of uniqueness included with the mission statements were tempered by a kind of discursive uniformity and standardisation. However, there was also evidence that counter-hegemonic/non-neoliberal discourses have not been entirely erased suggesting that neoliberal rhetoric does not sit entirely comfortably or without challenge within the HE context.

In the current study, we followed the same procedure as the 2010 study. We collated a corpus of university mission statements, accessed between July and September 2015. The whole corpus amounted to 13,913 words. Within this corpus, we identified three sub-corpora, representing the three main 'mission groups', detailed below. The sizes of each sub-corpora were: the Russell Group – 4,816 words; University Alliance – 3,941 words; Guild HE – 5,156 words. According to the universities' UK website: 'The Universities in the UK are diverse in their missions and location. A number of these have formed groups with common interests. These include the various regional university associations and also the so called "mission groups" '. Since the 2010 study, the 1994 Group has been disbanded. This study compares mission statements from the Russell Group, the University Alliance and the Guild HE Group. We have sought, as far as possible, to choose groups who might make a claim for distinctiveness of mission. In particular, the Guild HE has emerged in the last few years as a significant champion of smaller, teaching-focussed universities with a local or regional remit. There have also been some changes to the specific universities belonging to each of these major mission groups. However, the characterisation of the groups remains very similar to that of the 2010 study:

- Russell Group of the 24 major research-intensive universities of the UK (www.russellgroup.ac.uk/). (24 universities sampled). 'The Russell Group represents 24 leading UK universities which are committed to maintaining the very best research, an outstanding teaching and learning experience and unrivalled links with business and the public sector' (tag line from website)
- University Alliance Group: 20 smaller, internationally renowned, research-intensive universities. (www.unialliance.ac.uk/). (20 universities sampled) 'Britain's universities for cities and regions' (tag line from website)
- Guild HE Group mainly comprises post-1992 universities. There are 30 full members and 8 associate members. For this study, we have just included full members (www.guildhe.ac.uk/) (30 universities sampled). 'Distinction and diversity in higher education' (tag line from website)

Corpus analysis

The first stage in the corpus analysis was to compile keyword lists for each mission group sub-corpus (see Tables 3.1 to 3.3). As explained in previous chapters, keyword lists are a common starting point in corpus analysis as they can provide information about the most salient themes and concerns in the texts comprising the corpus. As in other chapters, the reference corpus used for the keyword analysis is the British National Corpus.

They keyword analysis is revealing in terms of how thematic and ideological priorities are embedded into the mission statements for each group. High on the keyword list for the Russell Group are *world* and *global* (positions 7 and 8, respectively). *Global* does appear in the UA list (at number 19) but neither *world* nor *global* appear in the Guild HE keyword list. *World* is only a keyword in the Russell Group list (and *globally* is also a keyword at number 38).

Interestingly, *research* is a higher keyword in the UA list (2) than it is in the Russell Group (3) and is lower in the Guild HE list (10). The highest keyword for the Guild HE group is *learning*. *Learning* does appear in the other keyword lists but in lower positions (4 in UA and 15 in the Russell Group). *Excellence* is high in all three lists suggesting it is almost formulaic in its use within these kinds of texts.

Table 3.1 Keywords – Russell Group mission statements

1. university	2. students	3. research	4. excellence	5. teaching
6. academic	7. world	8. global	9. staff	10. knowledge
11. LSE	12. scholarship	13. innovation	14. diversity	15. learning
16. vision	17. education	18. community	19. committed	20. alumni
21. highest	22. quality	23. universities	24. sustainability	25. outstanding
26. collegiality	27. international	28. student	29. environment	30. partnerships
31. society	32. campuses	33. graduates	34. Warwick	35. mission
36. leading	37. distinctive	38. globally	39. challenges	40. well-being
41. university's	42. providing	43. values	44. sustainable	45. internationally
46. transparency	47. social	48. creativity	49. freedom	50. understanding

Table 3.2 Keywords – University Alliance mission statements

1. university	2. research	3. students	4. learning	5. excellence
6. knowledge	7. communities	8. enterprise	9. develop	10. enterprising
11. graduates	12. teaching	13. internationally	14. innovation	15. education
16. professional	17. sustainability	18. creating	19. global	20. student
21. staff	22. environment	23. academic	24. inspiring	25. quality
26. working	27. creativity	28. opportunities	29. community	30. partnership
31. individuals	32. promote	33. employability	34. engagement	35. partners
36. vision	37. ambitious	38. strategic	39. professions	40. achieve
41. creative	42. diversity	43. organisations	44. outstanding	45. create
46. partnerships	47. international	48. society	49. business	50. lives

Table 3.3 Keywords – Guild HE mission statements

1. learning	2. students	3. university	4. excellence	5. creative
6. staff	7. professional	8. education	9. community	10. research
11. academic	12. environment	13. committed	14. arts	15. internationally
16. AUCB	17. student	18. teaching	19. quality	20. mission
21. inclusive	22. practice	23. distinctive	24. social	25. ethos
26. institution	27. develop	28. knowledge	29. graduates	30. values
31. engagement	32. employability	33. sustainable	34. support	35. scholarship
36. vision	37. development	38. cultural	39. value	40. catholic
41. employable	42. nationally	43. provide	44. inclusivity	45. sustainability
46. higher	47. respect	48. maintain	49. commitment	50. diverse

Keywords which are common to all three lists, and which therefore characterise the formulaic genre of the university mission statement the most clearly, are *university*, *student/s*, *research*, *excellence*, *teaching*, *knowledge*, *academic*, *environment*, *learning*, *staff*, *education*, *community/ies*, *quality*, *diverse/ity*, *vision*, *sustainable/sustainability*, *international/ly*, *graduates* and *creative/creativity*. These are arguably the main 'buzzwords' for UK universities at the time of writing. What is perhaps more interesting to examine are the keywords which feature in one list but not in the other two – in other words, the keywords which are unique to one particular mission group. Whilst the common keywords can help to reveal the discursive priorities of all universities, isolating keywords unique to each mission group can point to the discursive priorities and ideological alignments of universities according to their mission group.

The keywords which only appear in the Russell Group list are *world*, *alumni*, *highest*, *campuses*, *challenges*, *understanding*, *freedom*, *well-being*, *leading*, *collegiality*, *transparency* and the names of specific universities. Whilst it is not surprising to see *world*, *highest* and *leading* appearing as unique keywords in the Russell Group statements, words such as *freedom*, *well-being*, *collegiality* and *transparency* are perhaps less expected. We note that corpus techniques such as keyword analysis can reveal findings which are counter-intuitive.

In the Russell Group sub-corpora, *freedom* collocates with *academic* and *thought*, as in these examples:

- The University's core values are as follows: freedom of thought and expression (Russell)
- we will build on the University's long traditions of independent scholarship and academic freedom (Russell)
- Academic freedom and curiosity: All academic staff and students should be able to follow their academic interests in order to engage in research, teaching and learning of the highest quality (Russell)

Well-being is usually used to refer to the well-being of students in the Russell Group mission statements:

- a champion for our students, dedicated to their development and well-being (Russell)
- provide the highest quality learning and teaching environment for the greater well-being of our students (Russell)

When *transparency* is used, it refers to the actions of 'the university' as a fairly abstract entity. Emphasis is placed on the positive value of openness and accountability:

- transparency – we want to be accountable for our decisions and actions (Russell)
- Integrity: openness, transparency and honesty (Russell)
- Transparency: We strive to be clear and open about what we do and why (Russell)

We may deduce from examining the frequent collocations of these unexpected keywords that the Russell Group has felt obliged to incorporate these values into its mission statements and is using appeals to academic freedom, commitment to the well-being of students, a sense of collegiality rather than competition, and declarations of openness and transparency as USPs within the group. Interestingly, these are some of the key issues over which Russell Group universities have been criticised in recent years. For example, there is the well-documented case of Professor Thomas Docherty who was suspended in 2014 by the University of Warwick on charges of insubordination, which it was later forced to drop. There is evidence of a new 'weaponised' form of disciplinary regime in the form of performance management unfolding in universities (Morrish 2015). Morrish and Sauntson (2016) find that academics are encountering many structures which compromise academic freedom. It may be that Russell Group universities are aware of the negative perceptions that surround them and are attempting to challenge these directly by including them in their mission statements.

The keywords which are unique to the UA mission statements are *lives*, *enterprise/enterprising*, *working*, *inspiring*, *opportunities*, *individuals*, *promote*, *ambitious*, *strategic*, *achieve*, *organisations* and *business*. Several of these words reflect the 'aspirational' nature of the UA institutions as ranked immediately following those in the Russell Group (e.g. *ambitious*, *inspiring*, *strategic*, *achieve*). There is also the emergence of a discourse of corporate 'enterprise' which does not appear in the other two groups at all. Keywords such as *enterprise*, *enterprising*, *working*, *organisations* and *business* fall into a semantic field of work and business and perhaps, therefore, reflect a key marketing strategy of the UA which is to emphasise their economic value outside the university itself. This is further supported through words such as *partners*, *partnership* and *innovation* which are keywords in both the UA and Russell Group statements, but not in the Guild HE set. The keywords *professional*, *employable* and *employability* also appear in the UA and Guild HE statements. Some examples of this economic discourse emerging through these keywords and their collocations are:

- Encourages innovation and enterprise, in particular through partnerships with industry, business and the community (Russell)
- Developing future generations of leaders in scholarship, research, the learned professions, the public sector, business and innovation (Russell)
- opportunities for innovative partnerships with business, charitable foundations, and healthcare (Russell)
- we will be known for the quality and range of our partnerships with the professions, business, industry and government (UA)
- We seek to foster excellence, innovation, creativity and enterprise among our students, staff and partner organisations (UA)

- Our enterprise culture will deliver sustained innovation and international impact (UA)
- providing programmes with an emphasis on employability; the application of enterprise and research to defined needs (UA)
- is a research-rich, business-focused, professional university with a global reputation for academic excellence (UA)
- A learning environment and promotion of a student culture that enhance personal development and employability (GuildHE)
- Improve student employability through career guidance and by showcasing their work to industry professionals (GuildHE)

The keywords which only appear in the GuildHE statements are *catholic*, *ethos*, *nationally*, *respect*, *AUCB*, *practice*, *arts*, *higher*, *inclusive/inclusivity*, *institution*, *support*, *cultural* and *maintain*. This suggests a rather different discourse than either the Russell Group or UA. Keywords such as *inclusive*, *inclusivity*, *respect*, *support*, *maintain* and *ethos* signify more of a 'social responsibility' discourse than can be found in the Russell Group UA statements. *Nationally* appears in place of *international/ly*, *world* and *global* which reflects the different aspirational level of the GuildHE group. The inclusion of *arts* in the GuildHE statements is the only reference in the entire corpus to a subject area which could potentially give readers an indication of the content of learning that they can expect from such universities. The inclusion of *Catholic* reflects the fact that some of the Guild HE institutions have religious affiliations. However, it is interesting to note that Catholic is the only religious denomination which appears as a keyword, suggesting that the Catholic foundation universities reference their religious ethos more explicitly than any of the other faith groups.

Examining the frequent collocations of some high-ranking keywords is also revealing in terms of how discourses are manifested in the language of the documents. For example, in the Russell Group statements, *student** collocates with words which indicate something to do with 'quality' and which often have a superlative meaning, for example, *high-quality*, *greatest* and *talented*. Just as *research* is frequently described in terms of its high quality in the Russell Group statements, *students* seem to be constructed as another 'high-quality' product which is being used to market the university.

- Recruits and retains the <u>highest possible calibre of staff and students</u> and provides an environment in which they can flourish (Russell)
- By attracting <u>ambitious and talented students</u>, staff, and business partners, we will firmly establish ourselves among the top ten UK universities by 2015 (Russell)

- We will recruit extraordinary students. LSE will recruit students with the greatest ability, motivation, and potential to benefit from LSE teaching (Russell)

Conversely, this type of collocation is rarely found in the UA and GuildHE statements.

Knowledge is a word which has fairly high keyness in the Russell Group sub-corpora. Closer examination of how the word *knowledge* is used in the statements reveals that *knowledge* does not collocate with *student**. This suggests that the way knowledge is being presented in this mission group has little to do with students creating or developing knowledge. Instead, knowledge is treated as a 'product' which the university owns as a commodity, and which can, therefore, be 'sold' and marketed to potential students and perhaps other stakeholders. So the frequency of collocations such as *dissemination* with *knowledge* and *knowledge transfer* suggest that knowledge is being constructed as a fully formed product which can be passed on by the university – knowledge is a product rather than a process in which students are invited to become engaged as co-producers. Some examples are included below:

- the contribution which the University can make to society through the pursuit, dissemination, and application of knowledge (Russell)
- We seek the highest distinction in research and scholarship and are committed to excellence in all aspects of education and transmission of knowledge (Russell)
- to transfer the knowledge it generates to business and the community, regionally, nationally and internationally (Russell)
- Committed to leadership in the advancement, dissemination and application of knowledge within and across disciplines (Russell)

In the mission statements of the UA and GuildHE universities, *knowledge* (with lower keyness than in the Russell Group statements) collocates with other commodities and products which the university is offering in its mission statements such as *skills* (especially in GuildHE group statements), *learning* and *research*, as in the following examples:

- Exploited the synergy between higher learning and research to nurture new knowledge and types of practice (GuildHE)
- create and sustain a vibrant community for learning and knowledge (UA)
- to achieve their potential through high-quality learning, research and knowledge transfer (UA)

The high value of knowledge as a commodity is often emphasised through frequent collocating modifiers such as *cutting-edge*, *exemplary*, and *highest quality* – these modifying adjectives collocate particularly frequently with *knowledge* in the Russell Group statements. In the University Alliance group statements, there appears to be more emphasis upon what can be done with knowledge, so we see it collocating more frequently with verbs such as *increase* and *exploit* and nominalisations such as *exploitation*, *transfer* and *exchange*, as in the following examples:

- Knowledge transfer/knowledge exploitation excellence (UA)
- to enrich our students, partners and the wider society through education, training, research, scholarship and knowledge transfer (UA)
- transforming futures – through our research, learning and teaching and knowledge exchange (UA)

From these findings, it seems that nouns appearing in the semantic field of what we might term 'pedagogy' are the main 'products' which are being marketed in the Guild HE statements whilst research and prestige and rank markers are the main products being marketed by the Russell Group universities. The UA group statements seem to draw on a combination of both. These findings are consistent with those of our previous 2010 study.

Indicators of prestige and rank are evident when we examine the relative keyness of *world* across the three groups. A key concern of Russell Group universities is proving that they are world-leading (as will be shown later, *leading* collocates frequently with *world*, particularly in the Russell Group statements) and these universities are increasingly positioning themselves towards an international market. Globalisation is a feature of neoliberal discourse so the use of *world* and *global* in Russell Group statements contributes to this theme. *Global* (but not *world*) does also appear in the other two lists but lower down suggesting that prioritising globalisation and internationalisation in mission statements is not so important for these universities as it is for the Russell Group ones. *World* (especially when collocating with *leading*) appears to be used as a marketing strategy, as a means of signalling the high quality of the work of the university:

- We produce <u>world-leading</u> and internationally excellent research that drives excellence across the University (UA)
- further develop our reputation as a <u>world-leading</u> university (UA)
- As a <u>world-leading</u> centre of academic excellence we aim to (Russell)
- inspiring our students, producing <u>world-leading</u> research (Russell)

Other key nouns also appear to serve a similar function, for example, *excellence* and *quality*. *Leading* appears as a key adjective for the Russell Group but does not appear in the Guild HE or UA keyword lists. What is clear from examining collocations is that *leading* is being used in the Russell Group to advance a claim about quality. As exemplified earlier, a common left collocate in the Russell Group statements is *world* which further emphasises the Russell Group's preoccupation with globalisation and with using its international status as a marketing tool. *Leading role* is also a notable right-hand collocation in the Russell Group:

- committed to making a positive, distinctive and measurable impact on society, and playing a <u>leading role</u> (Russell)
- play a <u>leading role</u> in the economic, social and cultural development of the North East of England (Russell)

In terms of the self-promotion function of branding, this rests for most universities on some rather abstract claims for uniqueness, which takes place through a recycling of essentially the same few nouns and adjectives, though their relative order of keyness may vary for each mission group. The teams of managers who write these documents are charged with propounding a particular institutional narrative recounted through the lexicon of business and industry. It is interesting to note that these key nouns are abstract and semantically vague. It could be argued that, because nouns such as *excellence* and *quality* are used so frequently in the statements, that their meanings start to become questionable. In particular, there is such frequent reference to *excellence* that Moriarty (2014) has characterised this as 'the vacuity of excellence'. As explained in the Introduction, Urciuoli (2000) refers to such words as SDS. In our corpora, we can see that branding cements itself through these unarguable, but non-distinctive virtues.

The semantic patternings described earlier indicate a high usage of evaluative language (especially in the form of adjectives). In order to explore this further, we now turn to APPRAISAL analysis of the data set.

Appraisal analysis

JUDGEMENT and APPRECIATION are the attitudinal markers that predominate throughout all of the mission statements. The attitudinal sub-category of AFFECT is low across the mission statements of all of the groups. However, on the occasions when AFFECT does occur, it usually takes the form of positive markers of HAPPINESS or SECURITY. The HAPPINESS occurrences are mostly to do with the university being engaged in the act of celebrating things such as its success (happiness occurs as a result of success) as illustrated in these examples:

- Engaged with our graduates and rejoicing in their success [Russell: HAPPINESS]
- Celebrating our position as a people led organisation [UA: HAPPINESS]
- we delight in creating, sharing and applying knowledge [UA: HAPPINESS]
- we celebrate social and cultural diversity [GuildHE: HAPPINESS]
- valuing and celebrating all achievement [GuildHE: HAPPINESS]
- the University celebrates its Christian foundation [GuildHE: HAPPINESS]
- proud of and celebrates its history, heritage, environment and accomplishments [GuildHE: HAPPINESS; SECURITY]

The SECURITY occurrences in all groups of mission statements are usually to do with the university feeling confident and proud (of itself), as in the following examples:

- Confident in its place as a leading international research university [Russell: SECURITY]
- Tackling global challenges with confidence [Russell: SECURITY]
- Our strategy for 2020 sets out a confident and ambitious future [UA: SECURITY]
- We are justly proud of our record in preparing students for professional lives [GuildHE: SECURITY]
- We proudly stand in the tradition of Catholic education [GuildHE: SECURITY]

In the JUDGEMENT category, positive CAPACITY is the highest sub-category in all of the groups' mission statements. TENACITY and PROPRIETY occurrences are also high in all groups indicating that, through their mission statements, the universities are presenting themselves as capable, tenacious and moral institutions. The focus is on the universities claiming that they are good, able and moral in their behaviour.

- The University of [. . .] is an international powerhouse of learning, discovery and enterprise. [Russell: CAPACITY]
- Provision of effective and efficient customer-focused services in all aspects of our work [Russell: CAPACITY]
- Through our education and research we transform people's lives and change the world for the better. [Russell: CAPACITY]
- We believe in the equitable treatment of all [Russell: PROPRIETY]

- Respect and tolerance will characterise the conduct of our relationships [Russell: PROPRIETY]
- Committed to excellence in all aspects of education [Russell: TENACITY]
- Our vision builds on [. . .]'s current success [UA: CAPACITY]
- Being a vibrant and effective learning community [UA: CAPACITY]
- We're already an ambitious, world-class university. [UA: CAPACITY]
- We value diversity, fairness and equality of opportunity [UA: PROPRIETY]
- We will act ethically to minimise our impact on the environment [UA: PROPRIETY]
- Our mission includes a commitment to engage fully with the community [UA: TENACITY]
- We deliver these through constant innovation, enhancement and attention to excellence [GuildHE: CAPACITY]
- Celebrates its history, heritage, environment and accomplishments [GuildHE: CAPACITY]
- An ethical approach to all activities in which the University and its staff are engaged [GuildHE: PROPRIETY]
- Accessible academic and professional education based on respect for others, social justice and equity [GuildHE: PROPRIETY]
- [. . .] University is committed to being a leader in learning [GuildHE: TENACITY]
- [. . .] University strives to be a Market Led, Student Centred University of International Significance [GuildHE: TENACITY]

However, a closer inspection of the high occurrences of TENACITY reveal that they are often refer to the university 'trying to' and 'striving to' achieve certain things, as in the following examples:

- We aim to demonstrate our commitment to the communities of Cardiff and Wales [Russell: TENACITY]
- We are committed to developing sustainability [Russell: TENACITY]
- Always striving to be better than our previous best [Russell: TENACITY]
- Infused with a commitment to student learning [Russell: TENACITY]
- We are committed to understanding others' opinions, beliefs and cultures [Russell: TENACITY]
- We are committed to the principle of academic freedom [UA: TENACITY]
- We are an ambitious and forward-thinking institution [UA: TENACITY]
- We will maintain our commitment to driving social inclusion [UA: TENACITY]
- Being committed to sustainability [UA: TENACITY]

- We are committed to the continuing education and development of all staff [GuildHE: TENACITY]
- We will strive to be an inclusive community [GuildHE: TENACITY]

These typical examples suggest that a kind of irrealis (Sauntson 2018) CAPACITY and PROPRIETY operates across all of the mission statements. The texts are not making statements about what universities actually are, but what they are *aiming* or *aspiring to be*. This is a subtle rhetorical device which presents an image of the university in very positive terms without making false claims about its actual real-life practices.

In all of the groups, the NORMALITY occurrences usually refer to innovation and claims about the university being progressive.

- We have been pioneering in a range of other fields [Russell: NORMALITY]
- Fostering a culture in which innovation plays an important role [Russell: NORMALITY]
- Unconventional, risk-taking, experimental, radical, responsive [GuildHE: NORMALITY]
- We see our College as a crucible, or laboratory, for artistic experiment, exchange, entrepreneurship and innovation for *new* thinking [GuildHE: NORMALITY]

VERACITY occurrences within the JUDGEMENT category are relatively low, suggesting that veracity as a behavioural characteristic is not something which is valued highly by the universities – they rarely make statements about aspiring to be truthful and honest.

In all of the UK and US mission statements, the APPRECIATION category is mainly realised as markers of positive VALUATION. Unsurprisingly, there are many occurrences of positive VALUATION in all of the statements and this is one of the key discursive features that make the mission statements in all groups sound like a 'corporate boast'. Positive VALUATION markers often co-occur with positive CAPACITY and PROPRIETY statements, as in the following examples:

- A world-class research-intensive university [Russell: CAPACITY; VALUATION]
- Recruits and retains the highest possible calibre of staff and students [Russell: CAPACITY; VALUATION]
- To recruit and develop the world's most promising students and most outstanding staff [Russell: CAPACITY; VALUATION]
- A people led organisation that recruits, values and invests in high quality staff [UA: CAPACITY; VALUATION]

Within the positive VALUATION (and positive reaction) occurrences, the APPRECIATION is attributed in most cases to 'the university' itself as a kind of abstract entity, as the previous examples show. In the Guild HE statements, some of the positive VALUATION markers refer to more specific descriptors such as *specialist institution* and *conservatoire*.

- Maintain the College's reputation as a world-class, practice-based, professional *conservatoire* [GuildHE: VALUATION]
- To be a world-leading *institution of the theatrical and performing arts* [GuildHE: VALUATION]
- In the running to become a world-class *creative institution* [GuildHE: VALUATION]
- To be the best *specialist university for arts, design and media study* in Europe [GuildHE: VALUATION]
- *High quality* education for life in *contemporary arts practice* [GuildHE: VALUATION]
- To provide the highest quality undergraduate and postgraduate degree-level and continuing professional education and training in all aspects of *theatre and performance* [GuildHE: VALUATION]

This has the effect of making the GuildHE statements sound slightly less formulaic in terms of their evaluative assertions.

In several cases, *students*, *graduates* and *staff* are attributed positive VALUATION. In doing so, the discursive effect is that they appear to be attributed value as objects rather than people.

- Reward of the University's staff as its greatest asset [Russell: VALUATION]
- To recruit and develop the world's most promising students and most outstanding staff [Russell: VALUATION]
- A people led organisation that recruits, values and invests in high quality staff [UA: VALUATION]
- Attracting and developing outstanding people [UA: VALUATION]

Students are attributed positive VALUATION more frequently in the Guild HE statements than they are in any of the other groups. Other things/entities that are valued positively across the whole data set are *research and scholarship* and *learning and teaching*.

- Deliver teaching and facilitate learning of the highest quality [Russell: VALUATION]
- We combine inspirational teaching, world-class research [UA: VALUATION]

- World-class research, scholarship and education will have secured us a place among the top 50 universities in the world [Russell: VALUATION]
- Top quality teaching, research and professional management that provide rounded support to all our students and staff [Russell: VALUATION]
- We will encourage and support high quality teaching and research [UA: VALUATION]
- We produce world-leading and internationally excellent research that drives excellence across the University [UA: VALUATION]
- The delivery of a high quality student experience [GuildHE: VALUATION]
- Offers excellent programmes of study sustained by teaching and research of the highest quality [GuildHE: VALUATION]

Campus and *environment* are also attributed positive VALUATION in many of the statements but particularly in the Guild HE Group. *Ethos* and *community* are valued positively in the GuildHE and UA groups only.

- Provide a high quality teaching environment [GuildHE: VALUATION]
- Foster an ethos in which individuals are valued and diversity is celebrated [GuildHE: VALUATION]
- The provision of facilities that are fit for purpose [GuildHE: VALUATION]
- Maintaining a safe environment in which to learn and relax [GuildHE: VALUATION]
- A vibrant learning community for staff and scholars [GuildHE: VALUATION]
- A strong ethos of research and entrepreneurship [UA: VALUATION]

In sum, what this case study reveals, is an overwhelming pre-occupation with corporate branding which is, ironically, highly formulaic. We see the language of neoliberalism repeated throughout the statements in ways which reinforce corporate, rather than, academic values. We now turn to an analysis of diversity statements from samples of UK and US universities.

Case study 4: UK and US university diversity statements

In this case study we elected to use data from both UK and US universities. An earlier study by Morrish and O'Mara (2011) had already identified the differing legal contexts which have conditioned approaches to diversity in UK and US universities. We did not use data from the US in Case Study 3 on mission statements. This was for two reasons: US mission statements tend to be short statements of a college ethos or its actual purpose, e.g. to educate women, or scientists and engineers – they are descriptive of educational purpose rather than attempts to position the universities within a corporate sphere. Secondly, diversity of mission is an actuality in US higher education and is taken for granted. It is precisely the fear of diversity of purpose that haunts UK universities. What is interesting is how these institutions stake their claim for parity of international esteem, and of course excellence, whilst still asserting distinctiveness.

In the US, diversity has predominantly been framed by civil rights struggles, women's equality, Title IX and in the last five decades, affirmative action. Whereas in the UK, diversity agendas in universities and other public institutions haves been informed by a series of legislative acts designed to challenge discrimination based on a range of characteristics (e.g. Sex Discrimination Act, 1975; Race Relations Act, 1976; Disability Discrimination Act, 2000). More recently, the 2010 Equality Act has replaced all former legislation regarding equality and diversity in the UK by bringing together all 'protected characteristics' into a single piece of legislation. In the UK in particular, audit culture has impelled diversity agendas in universities. Morrish and O'Mara (2011: 978) note that a key reason that universities have appropriated the language of equality and diversity is because compliance with the legislation is auditable:

> In other words, *diversity* is a marketable signifier – its invocation masquerades as the cultural capital of the university, to be bestowed on all who tread within its walls and resonating with the promise of corporate success. It has become another brick in the edifice of 'academic capitalism'.
>
> (Slaughter and Leslie 1997)

In both the UK and the US, diversity statements, like mission statements, perform the primary function of marketing the university as an institution committed to the equality and diversity agenda as it is defined by the law. This makes them a rich source of data for analysing in terms of how their language embeds (and perhaps, in some cases, challenges) neoliberal ideologies.

In order to build our corpora for this study, we selected UK and US universities which were similar in status. We chose 17 universities (3,227-word sub-corpus) from the UK Russell Group, and a 14 (4,747-word sub-corpus) from the analogous grouping in the US Research Universities. Two more corpora were constructed from the diversity statements of 22 universities from the UK Million+ think tank which reflects the interests of largely post 1992 teaching intensive universities (6,797-word sub-corpus). The clearest US group of similar universities is the group characterised by the *Chronicle of Higher Education* as US Four Year comprehensive institutions (awarding bachelor's and master's degrees) (19 universities; 4,040-word sub-corpus).

Corpus analysis

The same procedure was used for analysing the corpus of diversity statements as was used for analysing the mission statements in Case Study 3 – an analysis of keywords followed by an examination of the collocations of some of these words. Table 3.4 shows the 20 highest keywords in the whole corpus.

This list gives an initial indication of the thematic priorities of all of the diversity statements taken together as a whole set. Like the mission statements, there is a lot of uniformity across the diversity statements from the different kinds of universities ('research-intensive' and 'non-research-intensive') and from institutions in the UK and the US. Tables 3.5 to 3.8 give a breakdown of keyword lists according to each mission group sub-corpus.

What we see in these tables first of all is a remarkable uniformity in the keywords. However, in the UK university statements, there are some differences in the order of each of the various aspects of diversity (referred to as 'protected characteristics' in the UK Equality Act) appearing the keyword lists. The Million+ set contains a wider range of words indicating aspects of diversity (*disability*, *gender*, *orientation*, *ethnic*, *race*, *sexual*, *religion*, *belief*, *marital*) than the Russell Group set (*gender*, *disability*, *race*, *sexual*, *age*, *belief*). Whilst the Russell Group list contains *age*, this is absent from the Million+ set. The Million+ list contains *ethnic* (suggesting a more explicit acknowledgement of ethnic identity as well as race), religion and marital status whereas these are all absent from the Russell Group list.

The Russell Group keyword list also contains words which have a generally negative meaning in relation to equality and diversity – *discrimination*, *harassment*, *victimisation*, and *bullying*. Out of these, only *discrimination* and *harassment* appear (lower down) in the Million+ keyword list suggesting the Russell Group statements place more emphasis on what happens as a result of a *lack* of inclusion – a more 'punitive' discourse seems to emerge as a result of this.

It seems significant that *discrimination* does not appear as a high keyword in either of the US diversity corpora. By contrast, it features in both the Million+ and Russell Group UK corpora. This difference in emphasis reveals the greater focus on issues of legality in the UK, and perhaps a procedural 'box-ticking' approach to diversity. The evidence of the US diversity statements shows a greater will to achieve diversity for the public good (e.g. through keywords such as *community, campus, committed)*.

Table 3.4 Keywords – diversity statements (whole corpus)

1. diversity	2. equality	3. university	4. students
5. staff	6. diverse	7. community	8. discrimination
9. faculty	10. gender	11. committed	12. disability
13. orientation	14. inclusive	15. campus	16. excellence
17. student	18. backgrounds	19. sexual	20. race
21. respect	22. environment	23. policy	24. promote
25. opportunity	26. mission	27. vision	28. academic
29. ethnicity	30. statement	31. religion	32. values
33. college	34. harassment	35. dignity	36. commitment
37. promoting	38. ethnic	39. perspectives	40. ensure

Table 3.5 Keywords – UK Million + diversity statements

1. equality	2. diversity	3. university	4. staff
5. students	6. discrimination	7. policy	8. disability
9. gender	10. committed	11. orientation	12. opportunity
13. ethnic	14. community	15. race	16. procedures
17. action	18. sexual	19. diverse	20. inclusive
21. ensure	22. dignity	23. policies	24. backgrounds
25. student	26. promoting	27. religion	28. environment
29. respect	30. belief	31. marital	32. responsibilities
33. valued	34. opportunities	35. socio	36. harassment
37. origin	38. commitment	39. aims	40. values

Table 3.6 Keywords – UK Russell Group diversity statements

1. equality	2. diversity	3. university	4. discrimination
5. staff	6. students	7. committed	8. gender
9. diverse	10. inclusive	11. disability	12. orientation
13. promoting	14. environment	15. respect	16. opportunity
17. policy	18. harassment	19. victimisation	20. excellence
21. ensure	22. race	23. university's	24. achieve
25. sexual	26. promote	27. bullying	28. community
29. aim	30. legislation	31. equalities	32. dignity
33. potential	34. members	35. vision	36. values
37. age	38. belief	39. commitment	40. action

The US lists both contain the word *campus* whereas this does not appear in either of the UK university lists. *Campus* tends to be used in relation to statements about ensuring student and staff safety on campus, suggesting there is greater emphasis placed on physical safety by the US universities. Finally, *vision* and *mission* appear in the lists for the US Four Year and US Research lists but do not appear at all in the UK Million+ group and appear low down in the Russell Group list. The relative keyness of these words in the US statements suggests that they are more

Table 3.7 Keywords – US Four Year diversity statements

1. diversity	2. diverse	3. faculty	4. community
5. college	6. students	7. campus	8. inclusive
9. university	10. statement	11. vision	12. geneseo
13. earlham	14. excellence	15. ethnicity	16. differences
17. staff	18. gender	19. perspectives	20. student
21. programmes	22. orientation	23. goals	24. sexual
25. backgrounds	26. committed	27. mission	28. understanding
29. environment	30. values	31. educational	32. CWU
33. cultural	34. learning	35. academic	36. aspirations
37. global	38. race	39. Wartburg	40. trustees

Table 3.8 Keywords – US Research diversity statements

1. diversity	2. faculty	3. campus	4. diverse
5. community	6. university	7. excellence	8. academic
9. students	10. staff	11. mission	12. inclusion
13. student	14. equity	15. backgrounds	16. gender
17. ethnicity	18. affirmative	19. MIT	20. programmes
21. perspectives	22. MIT's	23. disability	24. orientation
25. respect	26. promote	27. OED	28. UWS
29. committed	30. office	31. institutional	32. discrimination
33. California	34. Caltech	35. Dartmouth's	36. UCLA
37. sexual	38. OID	39. AA	40. Illinois

directly linked to the universities' mission statements. Their absence/low occurrence in the UK university sub-corpora indicates that the mission statements and diversity statements are not cross-referenced and are treated largely as separate entities. In other words, whilst it is common practice for UK universities to have diversity statements, 'diversity' and 'inclusion' are not necessarily part of the university's mission in the way that they are for US universities.

The keyword analysis of the corpora suggests that these diversity statements are also largely made up of semantically imprecise SDS including *diversity, respect* and even *equality*. This supports previous findings by Morrish and O'Mara (2011). In the current keyword findings, these terms occur in high positions in all of the lists.

Equality, for example, emerges as a keyword for the Million + group when compared against whole diversity statement corpus (with 27.79% keyness). This suggests that the Million+ diversity statements explicitly refer to 'equality' much more frequently than the statements in the other groups. 'Equality' (more than 'diversity' and 'inclusion') therefore strongly emerges as a thematic and discursive priority for the Million + group. Secondly, *college* was a keyword for the US Four Year sub-corpora (with 27.68% keyness). This is perhaps less meaningful but reinforces the importance of physical 'place' in the US Four Year statements.

In the US university keyword lists, the aspects of diversity and inclusion which appear in both are *gender*, *sexual orientation* and *ethnicity*. These appear in a relatively similar position across the two lists suggesting greater uniformity across the different types of US universities than was found in the UK ones. The US Four Year set also includes *race* and the Research set includes *disability*.

The names of the universities appear in the keyword lists of the US university statements whereas they do not appear at all in the UK lists. This is particularly the case for the US Research university statements (11 out of 40 keywords are the names of universities compared to 3 out of 40 for the Four Year group). This suggests the individual identities of the universities are more explicitly embedded into the diversity statements than they are in the UK statements. The US universities, especially the Research group, may be using the diversity statements more explicitly for marketing purposes than the other groups.

The word *campus* appears in the keyword lists for the US universities but not for the UK ones. *Faculty* also appears in the US university keyword lists but not in the UK ones, perhaps because *faculty* is the more usual term for what would be called 'academic staff' in the UK. An examination of the co-texts of these keywords reveals that they are used in relation to keeping students and staff physically safe on campus and in their faculties – again, this is a consideration which is not acknowledged at all in the UK university diversity statements. This might be an acknowledgement of the increased risk of violence experienced by people of colour on US campuses, not least by the campus police. Such incidents have been well documented in the *Chronicle of Higher Education* in recent years.

A final observation is that the word *excellence* appears in all sub-corpora keyword lists except for the UK Million+ group. On closer examination, it appears that *excellence* only appears as a keyword for the US Four Year group because it is used with a very high frequency in the diversity statement of one particular university, to the point where it skews the analysis. We have, therefore, disregarded the appearance of *excellence* as a keyword in the US Four Year corpus.

- We're committed to working with staff to achieve excellence through equality and diversity (Russell)
- The University of Cambridge is committed in its pursuit of academic excellence to equality of opportunity (Russell)
- The University values diversity and recognises that a diverse staff and student group contributes to its continued achievement of excellence (Russell)

- Johns Hopkins is a community committed to sharing values of diversity and inclusion in order to achieve and sustain excellence (US Research)
- Diversity should also be integral to the University's achievement of excellence (US Research)

What is interesting about the previous examples is that excellence is not used as an attribute of diversity itself; rather, *excellence* is achieved through *diversity*. Diversity, therefore, is discursively constructed as a tool for achieving excellence in domains other than equality, diversity and inclusion.

These universities are claiming *excellence* (or at least claim to be 'striving for excellence') in a domain which has few measurable parameters. *Excellence*, then is being used to sustain corporate image-making, rather than indicating a genuine commitment to equality, diversity and inclusion. In the deeply corporatised university of the 21st century, *diversity* accompanies *excellence* as a marker indicating 'we are competitive players'.

As in Case Study 3, we now turn to the APPRAISAL analysis of the diversity statement data set.

Appraisal analysis

The occurrences of AFFECT in the diversity statements are very similar to its use as an evaluative sub-category across the mission statements. Occurrences of HAPPINESS are higher than they are in the mission statements and this is mainly a result of the inclusion of assertions about the universities celebrating (i.e. being happy about) diversity.

- We <u>celebrate</u> our diversity [Russell: HAPPINESS]
- It encourages staff and students to <u>enjoy and celebrate</u> its diverse culture [Russell: HAPPINESS]
- We <u>actively celebrate</u> diversity [Million+: HAPPINESS]
- The University of [. . .] <u>celebrates</u> and values the diversity of all students and staff. [Million+: HAPPINESS]
- <u>We are most pleased</u> to welcome you to this vital informational site. [US Research: HAPPINESS]
- Please join me and our campus in <u>celebrating</u> our diversity [US Research: HAPPINESS]
- A mutually respectful environment that recognizes and <u>celebrates</u> diversity among all students, faculty, and staff. [US Four Year: HAPPINESS]
- We <u>celebrate</u> diversity in all of our educational and employment endeavors [US Four Year: HAPPINESS]

Within the attitudinal sub-category of JUDGEMENT, PROPRIETY occurs with the highest frequency for both of the UK groups. It is interesting to note the much larger gap between PROPRIETY and second highest judgement sub-category of CAPACITY for the Million+ group. This gap is much smaller for the Russell Group statements, suggesting that the Million+ group statements place more positive emphasis on the moral dimensions of diversity rather than making claims about their capabilities around dealing with diversity issues. But in both of the UK and the US groups, the JUDGEMENT sub-category of TENACITY operates in the same way as it does in the mission statements in that it indicates that the claims made are not what the universities *actually do* in terms of equality and diversity, but what they *aspire/aim to do*. The TENACITY markers in all of the groups make the statements aspirational and irrealis rather than being a true and accurate report of what the universities actually do in terms of equality and diversity.

- The University of [. . .] is intent on advancing equality and diversity [Russell: TENACITY]
- [. . .] University is committed to supporting, developing and promoting equality and diversity [Russell: TENACITY]
- Here at [. . .] University, we are committed to valuing diversity and promoting equality [Million+: TENACITY]
- The University of [. . .] is committed to promoting equality of opportunity in all of its activities. [Million+: TENACITY]
- [. . .] is committed to creating and supporting a community diverse in every way [US Research: TENACITY]
- [. . .] has made great progress in developing an ongoing culture of diversity, yet we constantly strive to do even better [US Research: TENACITY]
- [. . .] is committed to providing a diverse and inclusive community [US Four Year: TENACITY]
- We will strive to recruit and retain a diverse administration, staff, faculty, and student body [US Four Year: TENACITY]

The result is that the diversity statements do not actually commit to very much at all. This similarity in the use of TENACITY markers means that the diversity statements end up sounding very much like mission statements. The aspirational register is perhaps to be expected in mission statements but arguably less so in diversity statements which are supposed to serve a different purpose.

In the US diversity statements, CAPACITY is much higher in the Research group than all of the other sub-categories of JUDGEMENT. In the Four Year group, CAPACITY and PROPRIETY occur with similar frequency. This suggests that the Research group statements focus more on claims about capability than morality.

Within the attitudinal sub-category of APPRECIATION, *environment* and *community* are the things which are attributed the most positive VALUATION after 'the university' itself as an abstract entity. This occurs across all of the UK and US groups.

- We want to create a supportive and inclusive *environment* [Russell: VALUATION]
- We provide a safe, supportive and welcoming *environment* [Russell: VALUATION]
- In order to accommodate a more diverse University *community* [Russell: VALUATION]
- The University of [. . .] seeks to establish an inclusive *community* [Mission+: VALUATION]
- We seek to create a *community* in which diversity is valued [Million+: VALUATION]
- The rick mix of backgrounds, heritages, ages, experiences and skills that spark innovation and create a fruitful and vibrant *community* [Million+: VALUATION]
- The structural supports needed to manage our lively, provocative and stimulating *community* [US Research: VALUATION]
- Creating a rich and inclusive *community* of learners [US Four Year: VALUATION]
- Leading to a supportive, affirming and positive *environment* for all students, faculty and staff [US Four Year: VALUATION]

However, in the US groups, there is generally a wider and more diverse range of things and entities that are positively valued than there are in the UK groups. The patterns of VALUATION in the UK statements are fairly uniform and formulaic. There seems to be more room for individuality in the statements from the US universities.

Discussion

This chapter has revealed a university sector increasingly preoccupied with self-promotion and corporate branding. The paradox, however, is that the formulaic nature of university mission statements betrays a rather undifferentiated approach to the mission of higher education institutions. British universities have felt compelled by government incentives to brand themselves in pursuit of excellence in teaching, research, graduate education, local outreach, international impact and economic relevance to the extent that all believe they must fulfil each mission. What can be detected by corpus analysis, though, are shifts in focus and emphasis: research is the priority for the Russell Group; students take precedence in the Guild HE universities.

We have demonstrated that the mission statement reflects the current obligation for universities to reflect corporate rather than academic values. This is consonant with the way universities have been compelled to recast themselves in the mould of neoliberal ideology. We see the following themes in the statements:

Marketisation: students and research are commodified by universities and treated as their products. Not even knowledge escapes, as it too, is treated as a product, rather than a process. Diversity, too, is deployed as a signifier of competitiveness and virtue. In the UK, diversity statements emphasise compliance with legal requirements, in a context where such compliance is auditable. As we have seen elsewhere, those factors which are observable and measurable are more likely to receive institutional attention. By contrast, in the US, diversity is held to be a public good (though also marketable). In contrast to wider public debates about diversity threatening to compromise academic standards, it is presented as an essential component of excellence. However, use of TENACITY markers such as *committed to* and *intent on* mean that institutions commit themselves to very little other than aspiration towards greater diversity and inclusion.

Corporatisation: The mission statement fulfils the task of corporate image-making. This is evident in the way they publicise their signifiers of prestige and rank. These claims are established via a small recurring set of adjectives and nouns such as *world-leading, quality* and *excellence* – APPRAISAL markers of APPRECIATION. These are particularly prevalent in the mission statements of the high-status Russell Group universities, but all universities feel able to make these declarations of reputational distinction.

These same themes also emerged from the analysis presented in Case Studies 1 and 2. In terms of APPRAISAL markers, mission statements feature markers of CAPACITY as universities wish to portray themselves as capable institutions. Once again, their aims and aspirations are framed by a number of irrealis markers such as *committed to* and *strive to be.*

We may be seeing a sector in which differentiation of mission is widening. The University Alliance presents its members as an aspirational group of universities which mould their identity around being oriented towards business. The Russell Group maintain excellence in research. The GuildHE universities have a clear focus on students and teaching.

In US diversity statements, we see indicators of an ethos which still holds the university as a public good and to that end diversity and inclusion are signalled as commitments. It is interesting that inclusion does not feature in the UK diversity statements, but in the US, diversity is just the precursor to inclusion. It is not enough to bring about a campus diverse in its representation of gender, ethnicity, sexuality and disability – there must be representation amongst these groups at every level of the institution to realise the goal of inclusion. Paradoxically, the TEF, which we address in Chapter 5, may offer the incentives (in the form of metrics of 'outcomes') that will compel universities to confront lack of inclusion and differential outcomes for all categories of students.

The best that we can say of UK HE mission and diversity statements is that they offer a platform for universities to present themselves as capable, moral and worthwhile institutions. On the other hand, we see the mission and diversity statements used to accomplish a rather mundane exercise in visibly performing compliance. We can, though, understand the reasons why universities are so anxious to satisfy government edicts and demonstrate obedience before audit. In 2016, Jo Johnson, minister of state for universities and science, said:

> We want compliance to be a strong feature of our system. It is important that the sector should do all it can to be compliant with Home Office regulations [. . .] [home secretary] mentioned compliance and quality. High-quality institutions are compliant institutions; they are one and the same.[1]

This stated equivalence of quality with compliance was something which had been assumed by universities, but it had not been stated so baldly by their government masters before. The move towards an increasing regulatory burden on universities, and its capture via 'metrics' will be explored in the next two chapters.

Note

1. http://wonkhe.com/blogs/quality-compliance-and-international-students-doublespeak/

References

Apple, M. 1995. Cultural capital and official knowledge. In M. Berubé and C. Nelson, eds. *Higher Education Under Fire*. New York: Routledge. 91–107.

Burrows, R. 2012. Living with the h-Index? Metric assemblages in the contemporary academy. *The Sociological Review* 60 (2): 355–372.

Moriarty, P. 2014. The vacuity of excellence. http://physicsfocus.org/philip-moriarty-vacuity-excellence/ (Accessed 18 May 2015).

Morrish, L. 2000. A feminist's response to the technologization of discourse. *The European Journal of Women's Studies* 7: 229–238.

Morrish, L. 2015. https://academicirregularities.wordpress.com/2015/07/10/the-paradox-of-the-underperforming-professor/; https://academicirregularities.wordpress.com/2015/08/17/the-disciplinary-dashboard-from-reception-class-to-retirement/ (Accessed 18 May 2017).

Morrish, L. and. O'Mara, K. 2011. Queering the discourse of diversity. *Journal of Homosexuality* 58 (6–7): 974–990.

Morrish, L. and Sauntson, H. 2013. 'Business-facing motors for economic development': An appraisal analysis of visions and values in the marketised UK university. *Critical Discourse Studies* 10 (1): 1–20.

Morrish, L. and Sauntson, H. 2016. Performance management and the stifling of academic freedom and knowledge production. *Journal of Historical Sociology* 29 (1): 42–64.

Pratt, L. 1995. Going public: Political discourse and the faculty voice. In M. Berubé and C. Nelson, eds. *Higher Education Under Fire*. New York: Routledge. 35–51.

Sandler, C.J. 2014. Marketing spend up, but applications fail to follow suit. *Times Higher Education*. www.timeshighereducation.co.uk/news/marketing-spend-up-but-applications-fail-to-follow-suit/2012107.article 20 March 2014 (Accessed 18 May 2015).

Sanigar, M. 2013. Selling an education. Universities as commercial entities: A corpus-based study of university websites as self-promotion. *Leeds Working Papers in Linguistics and Phonetics* 18: 85–114.

Sauntson, H. 2018. *Language, Sexuality and Education*. Cambridge: Cambridge University Press.

Sauntson, H. and Morrish, L. 2010. Vision, values and international excellence: The 'products' that university mission statements sell to students. In M. Molesworth, E. Nixon and R. Scullion, eds. *The Marketisation of UK Higher Education and the Student as Consumer*. London: Routledge. 73–85.

Slaughter, S. and Leslie, L. 1997. *Academic Capitalism: Politics, Policies and the Entrepreneurial University*. Baltimore: Johns Hopkins University Press.

Thompson, E.P. 1970. *Warwick University Ltd: Industry, Management and the Universities*. London: Penguin.

Urciuoli, B. 2000. Strategically deployable shifters in college marketing, or just what do they mean by 'skills; and 'leadership' and 'multiculturalism'? *Language and Culture Symposium 6*, Binghampton University. http://language-culture.binghamton.edu/symposia/6/index.html (Accessed 20 June 2018).

Waeraas, A. and Solbaak, M. 2008. Defining the essence of a university: Lessons from higher education branding. *Higher Education* 57: 449–462.

Washburn, J. 2005. University Inc.: The Corporate Corruption of Higher Education. New York: Basic Books.

4 Language and audit culture 1

Research and performance management

Context

Audit culture

Every academic recognises that the demands of audit, 'performance management' and accountability have infiltrated their workplace to the extent they have become its central organising principle. Some can remember the beginnings of a culture of accountability, starting with research and encompassing teaching, impact and now knowledge exchange in the UK. Even over the course of writing of this book, we have seen an escalation in the use of metrics by university managers, compilers of league tables and not least, amongst academics themselves. All have internalised these as accurate reflections of the worth of research outputs and indeed, the worth of individual researchers themselves. Since 2016, teaching, too, has been nationally evaluated, primarily in English universities (see Chapter 5). In addition, the scale of work intensification has escalated as academics find their every lecture, seminar and research output is logged on a dashboard and scrutinised by layers of managers and human resource officers.

This new emphasis on quantification of work has arisen alongside a repositioning of the university as site of capital accumulation rather than as a site for the development of humanistic values (Thorpe 2008). Hall and Bowles (2016) invoke the Marxist notion of subsumption: 'The process through which inherent constraints on labour capacity of a particular sector of the economy are overruled and subordinated to the demands of capital'. As we will see, precise calculations and maximisation of workloads via metric scrutiny and performance management heighten the subordination of academic labour to the profit motive.

Audit culture evolved from Taylorist techniques aimed at improving efficiency and capacity of workers (Shore 2008: 279). The escalation of audit has been associated closely with a requirement to account for and justify public expenditure, and more recently for private expenditure in the form of student fees. Davies (2014) explains this through the paradigm of neoliberalism where:

> What it means is that processes traditionally left in the realm of politics must now be reconfigured in calculative, economically rational terms. Yes, you can carry on expressing demands publicly; but you must now do so in ways that makes the costs and benefits of your demand explicit.

With the growth of NPM (Deem *et al* 2007), audit has been liberated from the world of finance and become fully sedimented into all aspects of university administration. It has taken on what Strathern (2000: 2) describes as 'the contours of a distinct cultural artefact'. Peck and Tickell (2002) argue it is the function of neoliberalism to instil these behaviours in order to reorganise patterns of life. But the aim lies beyond shaping of behaviour; there is a clear desire to produce self-governing subjects who have learned to behave as economic units (Davies 2006; Morrissey 2013).

NPM has moulded individual behaviour, but has also realigned the ethos of the whole public sphere. Holmwood (2014) argues that, through NPM, audit has become a tool of government in order to 'shape universities, opening them up to market processes and reinforcing management control' and that recent reforms have been framed within a discourse which emphasises the economic value of universities and their role in developing human capital, rather than any public value.

Audit is now an inescapable feature of life as a university academic to the extent that many feel their primary purpose is to provide measures and validation of their work over and above the performance of the work itself. As Peseta *et al* (2017: 454–454) contend:

> The demand to count, measure, rank, quantify, evaluate and judge the work of universities (along with those who labour and study in them) haunts virtually all aspects of our work: from the quality of research, to targets for income generation, counts of patents, citations of articles and public testimonies of policy impact made visible and likeable online; from the quality of curriculum, to teaching with technology, responding to student feedback, watching the employment destinations and salaries of graduates as a comment on the value of their education; to whether a university is healthy, sustainable, sufficiently globalised or doing enough to position itself as the world leader in this or that discipline. Every day, our conduct is being shaped to procure a commitment to institutional indicators, targets, standards and benchmarks that help us to diagnose ourselves (and others) as worthy and successful academics.

The growth of metrics

Whatever its original purpose, audit has been absorbed into the institutional culture of universities. The new patterns of life which the neoliberal subject must assimilate to are bounded by data points of audit whose number expands over time and are dictated by the ability of technology to produce them (Morrish 2019a). Currently, many annual performance reviews will wish to see an assemblage of outputs, journal rankings, journal impact factors, citation counts, and download numbers from academic platforms such as ResearchGate. They are demanded precisely because they are the metrics which technology and audit have made available.

A recent review (Wilsdon 2015) offered recommendations for the responsible use of metrics, including their continued use in conjunction with peer review, and for universities not to base promotions and appraisal procedures on them. To this end, there is now a Metrics Toolkit which aims to expand the range of available metrics and tailor their responsible use according to discipline and type of output. Nevertheless, even this requires the academic to believe that metrics define their worth. There is another derivative metric, the 'h-index' – an index which allows comparison between the citations of each piece of published work (Burrows 2012) and this has become the primary vehicle for establishing ascendancy amongst academics, particularly in science. The impact of metrics on the academic psyche does not seem set to recede.

As time has gone on, tools for monitoring research have accumulated: e.g. REF, internal peer review of published research, internal 'dry runs' of the REF and seminars on how to target submissions at high-ranking journals. Many of the reporting measures are sustained by proxy metrics outside the control of academics. For example, the value of research is often now imputed from the level of grant funding secured or the published report may be evaluated according to the journal impact factor; an academic's work may be excluded from the REF audit if its subject matter diverges too far from the wider research group focus. This constitutes a disincentive to pursue curiosity-driven research. Many academics have presented reservations about the integrity of the metrics which dominate academic careers (Bishop 2013a; Colquhoun 2016; Morrish 2014; Sayer 2015), nevertheless they have been allowed to skew institutional priorities, reputation and funding levels.

The only predictable course of audit is that its demands will increase. Late in the cycle of the 2014 REF, the organising body, HEFCE, introduced a requirement for research units to justify a certain proportion of its research in terms of its social and economic 'impact'. Additionally, for the next research audit in the UK, (REF 2021), all publications must be freely available via open access routes within three months of publication in order to be eligible. As a measure of how quickly the criteria for research performance change, some academics are finding that scholarly monographs contracted just two or three years ago are being devalued because the metrics are not as easy to ascertain for this particular form of publishing. This marginalisation of books has also turned on the fact that they have hitherto not been 'open access' or available for free electronic download. Increasingly, both technology and the needs of audit now determine the platform for dissemination of research.

The overarching purpose of the veneration of metrics is to prove 'excellence' in institutional terms (see Chapter 3 for a discussion of *excellence* as an SDS). Of course, not all universities can be excellent, despite their claims to possess it. The compulsion to be excellent has led to a great deal of parody and Moriarty's (2014) comments on 'the vacuity of 'excellence' captured the feelings of many critics. Knights (2013) portrays the experience as follows:

> rooms full of intelligent people spending hours then days working on re-iterations of strategic plans bespeaks a form of essentialism where policy words and phrases – *vision*, *excellence*, *quality*, *transparency*, *mission, added value, embracing change* and the like – are treated as though they contain stable meanings.
>
> (2013: 183)

Moore *et al* (2017) argue compellingly that excellence is not a discoverable quality; it is a fiction. At best it is a discursive strategy to normalise the achievements of the most talented and ambitious academics and make everyone else seem deficient by comparison.

The managerial appeal of metrics

Metrics have been embraced by managers who felt they had too long lacked a rational way to evaluate academics. However, the imposition of what Morozov (2014) calls 'a future of algorithmic regulation' can be shown to be counter-productive. Holmwood (2011) comprehensively exposes the misunderstandings of the way scholars in the humanities and social sciences work. The TRAC mechanism of audit was developed to assign FEC of research, including indirect costs such as usage of the estate. He also casts doubt on whether it is possible to discern a distinct boundary between teaching and research in the humanities, and whether large grants and equipment are necessary at all in these disciplines. Nevertheless, grant capture is rapidly becoming mandatory for all scholars seeking promotion.

Managers have not been alone in their fetishisation of grant 'capture'. Those who stand to benefit the most (mainly bioscience and engineering) have welcomed grant-mandatory culture. However, there are plenty of critics, even within the experimental sciences (Bishop 2013b, 2014; Colquhoun 2012; Edwards and Roy 2017; Lilienfeld 2018) who argue that this practice is distorting scientific research and may incentivise questionable research practices and lead to a stifling of academic freedom (Morrish and Sauntson 2016). And the allocation of research funds is, of course, politically motivated. Bishop points to a devaluation of science which may be cheaper to run, and also to an effect whereby there is a backlog of research which never gets written up when the imperative is always to secure the next tranche of grant funding. Colquhoun documents a shameful episode when several professors were fired at Queen Mary University, London for lack of grant accumulation relative to an arbitrary departmental norm, the justification of which was to enable the university to rise in league tables. If further substantiation of a distorting effect of metric targets should be needed, Colquhoun reveals that if they had been imposed on Peter Higgs, he would not have remained employed long enough to make his great discovery:

> Peter Higgs had no papers at all from the time he moved to Edinburgh in 1960, until 1964 when his two papers on what's now called the Higgs' Boson were published in *Physics Letters*. That journal now has an impact factor less than 7 so Queen Mary would not have counted them as 'high quality' papers, and he would not have been returnable for the REF. He too would have been fired.
>
> (Colquhoun 2012)

There is evidence that perverse incentives are becoming more prevalent in science, and that competition for funds has led to some fraudulent research claims and retraction of journal articles. Some recent cases are discussed by Morrish (2016), Michalek *et al* (2010) and Edwards and Roy (2017), whilst Bishop (2013c, 2016) points to a reproducibility crisis in psychology, to some extent because high-impact journals favour publishing articles with surprising, newsworthy results.

The urge to appear outstanding has also had an effect on the discourse of scientific writing. In a world where academics are obliged to offer up each piece of work to be evaluated as internationally significant, world leading and so on, they will seek to signal such a rating discursively. A study by Vinkers *et al* (2015) uncovered a new tendency towards hyperbole in scientific reports. They found the absolute frequency of positive words increased from 2.0% (1974–80) to 17.5% (2014), which amounts to a relative increase of 880% over four decades. 25 individual positive words contributed to the increase, particularly the words *robust*, *novel*, *innovative*, and *unprecedented*, which increased in relative frequency up to 15 000%).

What we can surmise from these cases is that metrics are failing to accurately measure performance and, more worryingly, they also act to distort and corrupt science to the extent that there is a risk of losing public confidence. Shore (2008) documents one particularly notorious case of audit distortion that resulted in the dispersal of one of the most innovative research units in the social sciences in the UK. The Department of Sociology and Cultural Studies at University of Birmingham was closed in 2002 when just one of the imposed 'KPIs' – performance in the 2001 Research Assessment Exercise – dropped below target. This internationally renowned department was closed, and its staff made redundant. He writes:

> These new systems of audit are not, as they claim, just neutral or politically innocent practices designed to promote 'transparency' or efficiency; rather, they are disciplinary technologies – or 'techniques of the self' – aimed at instilling new norms of conduct into the workforce.
>
> (Shore 2008: 283–285)

Shore and Wright (2015: 430) write that seemingly mundane practices shape the way in which people are governed 'producing accountable and transparent subjects that are simultaneously docile yet self-managed'.

Accountability has transformed performance monitoring into an exercise in corporate coercion and hyper-surveillance. In a 2016 lecture, Docherty quoted former archbishop of Canterbury, Dr Rowan Williams, who offers an analysis of how complicity is constructed in a society. Drawing on the example of the Third Reich which he calls 'a masterclass in executive tyranny', Williams blames an 'erosion of a sense of the ridiculous' when excess and wrongdoing become normalised and tolerated. Accountability atomises the world into a series of processes wherein we hide our subjectivity behind bookkeeping. Whilst Docherty was keen to emphasise that in HE, the stakes are obviously far less grave than in the prison camps, nevertheless, when finance invades politics, it installs corruption and false accounting.

Audit culture is both product and vehicle for marketisation (Thorpe 2008: 105). League tables cast us all as competitors. KPIs bring us all within the realm of the calculable and ensure our focus on just a few main issues. Thorpe (2008: 425) further argues 'there is a coercive dimension to that accountability; organisations must present themselves in terms of that narrow, predetermined script of expert assessors'. This has instilled permanent mistrust between employers and employees (Lorenz 2012) and has become what Strathern (2000) calls the 'tyranny of transparency'.

Case study 5: research 'quality' and REF

Mechanisms for monitoring and auditing university research have now spread to many places in the world. They are particularly prevalent in the Northern European HE systems: Denmark, Sweden, Iceland and Netherlands (Berg *et al* 2016). However, the system on which they are all modelled, the REF (formerly the Research Assessment Exercise) was inaugurated in the UK. A short history of its genesis can be found in Berg *et al* (2016). According to website, the key purposes of the REF are:

- to inform the selective allocation of funding for research,
- to provide accountability for public investment in research and produce evidence of the benefits of this investment, and
- to provide benchmarking information and establish reputational yardsticks, for use in the higher education sector and for public information.

(www.hefce.ac.uk/rsrch/ref2021/)

The requirements of the REF as they were set out in the 2014 exercise are well-known to UK academic readers but may not be widely appreciated further afield. The assessment cycle takes place every five to seven years, and yet priorities, expectations and reporting mechanisms have changed with each iteration. The 2014 REF required all HEFCE-funded research units to submit for evaluation four 'best' pieces of research for each research-active academic in post on 31 October 2013. These could be monographs, refereed journal articles, book chapters, etc. Pieces were given a ranking by what was claimed to be a process of 'expert peer review'. Each of these research 'outputs' was graded 1–4 according to a judgement of nationally recognised, internationally recognised, internationally excellent, or world-leading quality. Two other measures contributed to the unit/department's overall score. The research 'environment' was evaluated according to whether it was conducive to producing quality research of in terms of its vitality and sustainability. The other measure was 'impact', and for each ten scholars entered, there had to be at least one case study which detailed how their work had impact – either economic or social. Paradoxically, the sort of scholarly influence desired by most academics carried no weight.

Chief amongst the critics of the REF were Derek Sayer whose 2015 book marshalled evidence that the REF has failed in its claim to offer international benchmarking of UK research, since so few of the judging panellists are from overseas. He claimed that the reduction in the number of panels in 2014 meant that members of broad subject-themed panels were attempting to make judgements of significance, originality and rigour on research which did not even lie within their primary field of expertise. The lack of sufficient breadth and depth on panels meant that the exercise amounted to nothing more than skim reading masquerading as rigorous judgement, and the resulting subjectivity certainly did not match the rigour of the peer review demanded for publication.

It should be borne in mind that, particularly in medicine and bioscience, there is support for a research quality audit based on metrics (e.g. citations, journal impact factors, h-index). Nevertheless, the question of research assessment and disbursement of funding is a contested subject in the UK. For this reason, we decided to analyse the discourse within which those discussions are carried out. The following corpus analysis will examine these features in the discourse of documents relating to REF 2021 and institutional documents submitted to the 2014 REF audit.

The data for this case study comprises texts taken from the REF website at the time of writing – these include the Stern Review report (2016), general REF 2021 framework document, HEFCE consultation on the second REF, REF consultation webinar, REF staff and outputs webinar, and the initial decision on the REF 2021 document. Also included are the REF2014 submission documents for two UK HEIs (X University and Y University) comprising, for each institution, impact statements, environment statements, general outputs information, and the institutional research strategy. Taken together, the whole corpus is 91,752 words.

Corpus analysis

Firstly, the keyword analysis for the corpus is presented in Table 4.1. Throughout all of the documents, the keywords suggest that there is again a tension between competition and collaboration. Universities are encouraged to collaborate with each other (e.g. in terms of producing co-authored REF outputs) but the whole process is one of competition – reflected in the high keyness of words such as *assessment*, *panel/s* and *criteria*. The terms *research* and *REF* appear to be synonymous within the documents, suggesting that research as an academic activity is increasingly being defined in terms restricted to eligibility for REF audit.

Table 4.1 Keywords – REF documents

1. research	2. REF	3. outputs	4. impact	5. panels
6. assessment	7. submissions	8. panel	9. submission	10. staff
11. HEIs	12. submitted	13. UOA	14. funding	15. unit
16. HEI	17. institutions	18. submitting	19. studies	20. UOAs
21. interdisciplinary	22. criteria	23. output	24. template	25. data
26. impacts	27. equality	28. institutional	29. environment	30. quality
31. guidance	32. bodies	33. UK	34. HESA	35. excellence
36. academic	37. review	38. case	39. PGRs	40. RAE
41. institution	42. consultation	43. FTE	44. [university name]	45. researchers
46. annex	47. strategy	48. metrics	49. paragraph	50. include

SDS analysis

All of the documents contain numerous SDS, many of which also occur as keywords (such as *excellence* and *impact*). Many of the SDS are adjectives which refer to the 'quality' of research. Despite the REF focus on metrics, these adjectives refer to qualities which are not measurable or definable. They include *exceptional*, *innovative*, *cutting-edge*, *world-leading*, *distinctive*, *inclusive*, *substantial*, *substantive*, *important*, *outstanding*, *creative*, *significant*, and *sustained*. Although the REF documentation attempts to define features such as *world-leading* and *significant*, they remain strategically deployable and therefore open to contestation and variability. However, the actual 'content' sections of each institution's individual REF documents do *not* contain SDS or metaphors (or very few compared to the other sections). It is predominantly the REF procedural documents themselves that are characterised by their frequent use of SDS and metaphorical language.

Throughout the documents, there are frequent references to a 'research culture'. It is perhaps interesting to note that there are no corresponding references to 'teaching culture' in the teaching audit documents. In the REF, individuals are not actually audited – the audit focuses on teams/units. However, the REF has become increasingly individualised in its operationalisation with individual staff members' published outputs being graded using the system, rather than a collective body of research. In TEF, it is institutions which are ostensibly audited. At first sight, this looks like conflicting systems of evaluation between REF and TEF, with REF focusing on individual research contributions and the TEF evaluating institutions. However, we can see the beginnings of the TEF becoming an individualised audit procedure in the way that the REF is, for example, through scrutiny of individual module evaluations for staff members.

Another notable feature of the documents is their use of a legal register. Examples include the following:

- sources to corroborate the impact
- As this is in the earliest stages, corroboration comes through testimony in a series of emails
- Submissions may legitimately include areas of research which fall within the descriptors of other UoAs
- where the output itself is in itself deemed to constitute sufficient evidence of the research.
- The material must be sufficiently substantial to constitute evidence
- The sub-panels will take all these factors into account as appropriate when weighing the evidence provided
- The integrity, coherence and clarity of the narrative accompanying each case study will be essential to the panels when forming their

judgements, and key claims made in the narrative should be capable of corroboration
- User feedback or testimony

The final sections of main REF document, in particular, are characterised by legal discourse and there are numerous references to *evidence* and *testimony*. This creates the effect of HEIs and individual units of assessment as being 'on trial' and discursively places them in a defensive position. Despite the frequent use of legal register terms such as *evidence*, there are no clear definitions of what the terms mean. As stated earlier, this lack of clear definition and the prevalence of SDS is a key characteristic of the discourse of the whole document set (and of all of the documents examined throughout this book). We note that the only definition of research 'impact' appears in the main REF document:

- For the purposes of the REF, impact is defined as an effect on, change or benefit to the economy, society, culture, public policy or services, health, the environment or quality of life, beyond academic

But this definition does not specify if *effect*, *change* and so on are positive or negative, and *benefit* is a largely subjective and unmeasurable term. In some cases, the meanings of SDS can be taken from their collocational patterns in the documents. *Growth*, for example, is only ever economic and financial – its collocations never indicate any meanings relating to social, moral or cultural growth as a result of research conducted in HEIs. For example:

- increasing economic growth, greatly important through these
- generally show faster rates of growth in output
- with the estimated costs growing from £66m for the 2008
- such investment is a major factor in growth. It is also a critical part

The main REF document contains a section on equality and diversity in relation to selection of staff for inclusion in the REF. There is an underlying assumption here that universities do (or at least have the potential to) routinely discriminate against certain staff and break equality and diversity legislation. (Performance Management documents, for example, are clear examples of harassment and discrimination whereby professorial staff are cross-examined and made to meet standards and undertake duties not previously defined by university management – this is discussed further in Case Study 6.) The very principle of 'selection' implies competition, hierarchy and is open to exploitation and abuse. The document contains lots of references to Equality and Diversity legislation and acts as a clear warning to universities. However, there is no indication anywhere in the document of what staff in HEIs should do if they believe their HEI to be disregarding this legislation and the Equality and Diversity framework put into place by the REF. This recalls the argument made by Morrish and O'Mara (2011) that the focus on Equalities legislation together with vague language leads to questions about whether claims and promises are genuine (2011: 981). Reference to the need for an 'appeals procedure' for individual staff acknowledges a need for safeguarding and indicates a mistrust of HEI managers. At the time of writing, it remains to be seen if the new REF Equality and Diversity regulations will be tested by any submitting institutions and, if so, how such issues will be handled by REF.

Critical metaphor analysis

The main metaphorical domains used throughout the documents are those of sport/war; building; and nature/growth. Metaphors relating to engineering and acting/performing also occur fairly frequently. Each of these domains will be discussed in turn.

As in other documents examined throughout this volume, metaphors relating to sport and war are prolific throughout the REF documents examined. This is a key feature of the neoliberal discourse which proliferates the current UK HE context and is reflective of the increasing competitiveness of HE. We, again, see the frequent use of *strategy* in relation to research, implying that research is a competitive domain.

- Our strategy will invest in research leaders and teams
- competing effectively for strategic managed programmes
- Strategically targeted applications for Doctoral Training initiatives
- Many core features of the current research strategy demonstrate continuity
- CSICAD provides a key focus for strategizing how the unit's research findings can be mobilized to produce impacts on practice and policy
- Some team members hold strategic positions in international networks
- This section should provide evidence of the achievement of strategic aims for research during the assessment period, and details of future strategic aims and goals for research
- to engage with strategic initiatives and more targeted grant-making bodies
- For strategies to increase registration and completion of PhD projects
- we adopted an increasingly strategic approach and implemented policies to embed the impact agenda more systematically within the research culture

Another frequent manifestation of the war/sport metaphorical domain is the reference to *goals* and *targets* throughout the documents:

- This additional work on target definition and setting
- at conferences and through targeted events
- a series of mutually reinforcing goals which encourage research excellence
- This section should highlight the University targets in relation to this particular strategy
- facilitating the discussion of research plans and goals at annual Performance Development Reviews
- attracting high quality academic and research staff and research students with a target to increase inward mobility
- Its central goal has been to expand its research output
- recent staff appointments in the Department have also targeted areas of existing research strength

The discursive effect of war and competition is further enhanced through references to *winning*:

- adopting a managed approach to winning responsive mode funding
- Maximising QR and winning funds for all types of research
- expanding and winning funding for knowledge exchange initiatives

Even more sinister are the references to *capture* – a word which arguably evokes the domain of war rather than sport – *capture* implies a degree of aggression, power and tactical planning as well as implying that the 'target' is difficult, elusive and adversarial.

- fully exploit the realistic opportunities for research grant capture
- Research teams which outperform benchmarked grant capture
- this has been captured in the form of publishers' sales figures
- The team will work with the University's Research and Enterprise Support Office to ensure that impact is captured and accurately recorded
- External grant capture presents particular challenges in a climate of economic contraction
- with workshops on submitting work for peer review, external grant capture etc.
- The capture of external grants from funding councils and other bodies is a priority for a mature research team
- To conduct horizon scanning and intelligence gathering to contribute to the University-wide approach for efficient grant capture
- processes which support horizon scanning, proposal development, research grant capture

In the final two examples, *capture* occurs close to *horizon scanning* and *intelligence gathering* which are also terms which evoke war and combat.

The effect is to construct obtaining external grants as warlike and aggressive military strategies. The collocates of capture are often *metrics*, *impact* and *grants*, suggesting that these aspects of academic research are particularly elusive (but still available for *capture*). Importantly, these collocation patterns create a meaning which suggests there may be valuable work being conducted in universities which is not 'captured' or represented through the REF procedures:

- it is also recommended that the aspects captured by the impact template
- emphasis on a) expanding grant capture capacity to strengthen the
- for a wider variety of impacts than were captured in the case studies

A closely related term to *capture* is *pursuit* and this also appears a number of times throughout the document to refer to external research grants, for example:

- the successful *pursuit* of further research grants based on a track record of research excellence.

Other terms in the sport semantic field include *baseline*, *scorecard*, *penalty* and *training*:

- The REF results will provide the baseline measure for research quality
- The targets will be developed for each campus and compiled into an institutional scorecard
- with no penalty for research which is plainly within a distinct tradition
- the University's first class environment for career development and training

Another common metaphorical domain emerging from the analysis presented throughout this book is that of construction, and the REF documents are no exception. As well as explicit references to *building* and *building on*, there are frequent metaphorical uses of construction terms such as *underpinning* and *foundations*, as in the following examples:

- the University's Knowledge Exchange and International strategies and underpins Strategy 2020
- The Research Strategy 2015–2020 builds on the success of the previous strategy
- provide an intellectual foundation for our research strategy
- While these revised aims will continue to underpin our strategy
- we aim to build on our existing expertise

- they also produce or underpin impacts of the kind exemplified below
- These strategies build on foundations already established during this census period
- As well as underpinning these theoretical papers
- The research underpinning this case study
- Each project builds on previous creative work and recommendations
- prioritising the completion of PhDs and building capacity for 2019
- Evidence for the relationship between the underpinning research and the impact claimed
- An underpinning principle of the REF is that all forms of research output will be assessed on a fair and equal basis

*Underpin** collocates particularly notably with *research* and *impact*, suggesting that the metaphor creates a semantic link between *research* and *impact* by which *impact* is dependent upon research (i.e. research underpins impact). We have already noted that, in building, underpinning is a remedial process. The semantic effect of the metaphor, then, is to create the idea that impact is fragile and will fail without research. This cementing of the dependence of impact on academic research obscures the fact that real-world impact and change often comes about as a result of non-research processes such as activism and political lobbying. For academics involved in such activities, as well as in academic research, there is no way of assessing or valuing such activities in REF terms as impact must be based on publications. It is only narrowly REF-defined research which can result in impact.

Other building references include *structures* and *infrastructures*, as well as *forging* and features of construction such as *central plank* and *bridge*:

- shapes investment decisions in the University's research infrastructure and research base
- arising out of discipline bridging and international collaboration
- we have taken the opportunity to revise and refocus the intellectual infrastructure.
- Such collaborative activity is a central plank of our strategy to develop future research funding.
- Researchers in the Unit have forged meaningful relationships and durable interactions
- The wider University vision underpins these activities and, at Departmental and UoA levels, this commitment is supported through structures

The *nature* metaphors in the documents mainly refer to natural growth as an organic process.

- including the continued growth of research at the University's campuses

- The growth and development of a wide range of high quality long-term research collaborations
- The growth of the University's market share of national and international research funding
- the growth of postgraduate student provision.
- by growing the community of PGR students

The metaphorical use of growing (a natural process) contrasts with the metaphorical use of construction seen earlier. External research funding is often metaphorically constructed as a landscape or environment as in the following examples:

- The funding landscape
- the challenges of recruiting doctoral students in the current funding environment.

Examples such as these create the impression that research funding allocation is a natural feature and process, thus disguising the fact that it is really a social and political process. Interestingly, disciplines and units of assessments within REF are sometimes referred to in terms of *health*, which is arguably another metaphor relating to nature (or, specifically, to the natural human body):

- excellent research can be undertaken in a wide variety of research structures and environments, and that the health of the disciplines within Main Panel D is well served by that variety
- The extent to which the research environment ensures the future health and well-being of the unit

The idea of particular subject areas being 'healthy' or 'unhealthy' is a way of classifying research quality in a different way from that which is used in the REF documents (world leading, etc.). Health and well-being are, of course, usually used to refer to people in a non-metaphorical way. There is an implicit assumption in the documents examined here that health and well-being are not being used to refer to the physical health of the actual people who comprise 'the unit' or 'the discipline' (which would bring with it a duty of care) but to the quality of work produced by those individuals.

The engineering metaphors are most frequently used to refer to how the university manages, or is expected to manage, research as in the following examples:

- The systems-based approach to research management
- To introduce a wider range of instruments to recognise and reward individuals

- employing mechanisms for the wider dissemination of research findings.
- Mechanisms and systems in place for research leave are reviewed by the Faculty Research Committee
- Impact takes place through a wide variety of mechanisms.

Equity in terms of the REF reviewing process is metaphorically described as *calibration* in the main REF document:

- *Calibration procedures* will be described in more detail in the panel criteria and working methods document.

Accelerate and *pump* are motion-related engineering terms used to describe collaborative research and impact in the documents:

- To increase and accelerate impact from the research base
- to pump prime collaborative research

One discursive effect of this metaphorical domain is the presentation of research performance in the REF as something that can be engineered or manipulated. The university as an engineered machine which produces research de-personalises and de-humanises those working within institutions to produce the research.

Finally, the use of a number of acting and performing metaphors draws attention to the ephemeral nature of the REF exercise (and this same finding emerges in the performance management documents examined in Case Study 6). *Playing a role* implies falsity and temporality and suggests research is performative rather than having any inherent value. Examples of such metaphors include the following:

- This delivers 410 studentships for the Consortium for arts and humanities, which will play a major role in the future sustainability of postgraduate research in our UoA
- Other researchers act as consultants and use their research to shape and inform professional practice
- have played an active role in shaping the nature of the research
- some researchers have taken a proactive role in identifying potential beneficiaries
- Building on these partnerships plays a central role in our future impact strategy
- Cox also continues to play a major role in promoting the status
- where PhD students frequently share the platform with the guest speakers

In sum, the analysis reveals repeated SDS and metaphor usage which creates cumulative discursive effects of aggression, competitiveness and hostility.

Holmwood (2014) writes that the use of metrics and the technological gift of 'big data has rendered academics available for continuous micro-management. Thus, the turning of the audit screw is reducing the substance of academic life to "measurable moments" with academic freedom subordinated to market-based judgments of worth'. It is now prevalent in some business schools for professors to be known as 4*4s – people who have four outputs in four-star journals, and for this to be the benchmark for excellence (Butler and Spoelstra 2014: 541; Parker 2014: 5). Insofar as the discourse of metrics and competition has become normalised within institutions, it is common for senior management teams to agree to institutional targets for research evaluation such as the following (from Holmwood 2014):

> Target 2.1: To achieve and maintain a REF GPA above the current Russell Group average of 2.71 (new benchmarks to be set following REF2014);
> Target 2.2: To increase the quality of the University's research portfolio, as measured by three-year field weighted citation impact, by 20 per cent by 2020 (1.68 in 2013);
> Target 2.3: To double the proportion of publications in a three-year period in the top 10% of most cited outputs (21% in 2013).

As Shore (2008) details, the existence of a UK research unit depends entirely on its performance on the REF. It does not depend on other indicators of health – international reputation, PhD students, other forms of income – e.g. teaching or teaching quality assessments; instead, research ambitions have been entirely shaped with regard to feeding the audit and secondly convincing management that this has been achieved.

In effect, heads of department and deans are charged with ensuring individual academics are responsibilised for delivery of the institution's ambitions and targets. We might compare this to a kind of dressage training where the academic is schooled in going through the motions of audit (Bendix Petersen and Davies 2010). Case Study 6 shows how this expectation is codified in the management and evaluation of individual academics.

Case study 6: performance management and professorial review

Performance management has staked its claim in UK universities over the last decade and, increasingly, academics and other professional staff are surveyed and rendered auditable by outcomes-based performance management techniques. A useful definition of performance management comes from Franco-Santos *et al* (2014: 12):

> At work, individuals are said to perform when they are able to *achieve the objectives established by management*. Organisations are thought to perform (or to be successful) when they satisfy the requirements of their stakeholders and are more effective and efficient than their competitors.
>
> (Our italics)

Contemporary approaches to Human Resource Management appear to assume that employees are fundamentally lazy and so close scrutiny and accountability for outcomes are necessary to counter this (Franco-Santos and Doherty 2017: 20)

In fact, the reality amongst university academics is more complex in an environment where the requirement to be transparently competitive ensures that a set of KPIs constitute a hierarchy amongst academics. It may be that human resource officers suspect academics of backsliding, but at the same time '[apparatuses] to oversee performance management appear to rely centrally on liberal notions of freedom, individuality and competitiveness' (Morrissey 2013: 7) so that the individual's aspirations are linked to the institutional strategy by activating both their anxiety and their desire to be competitive. Morrissey draws on Foucault's concept of governmentality in which particular techniques of performance management bring into being and configure new, coerced academic subjectivities. He terms these 'conditioned agency' (2013: 15) which appear to draw on discourses of liberation and empowerment as well as more central notions of competitiveness.

We can recognise an intricate chain of coercion which institutions deploy over individuals, but we can trace the origin all the way to political attempts to extend their control of universities. As Thorpe contends, 'making universities 'entrepreneurial' has translated into making them governable by the central state' (Thorpe 2008: 104) and, as the work itself has been appropriated in the service of government targets, '[A]rticles in journals become merely displays to an agency of the state, an indicator to the powers that they are getting value for money' (Thorpe 2008: 110).

Performance management began in universities to evaluate the performance of departments or research teams; however, more recently, the use of metrics in individual performance management has become widespread, and consequently there has been disquiet amongst academics. Two of the most controversial metrics are the h-index and the journal impact factor. These are now commonly asked for in performance review documents, and we show an image of such a document submitted for professorial review in Figure 4.1.

Research

Publications:

4–6 articles in the last five years, of "internationally excellent" quality (e.g in the top 10%ile of the field)

- As first or last author; or a middle author with substantive and critical contribution.
- H-Index 25 and above

Grants:

- Sufficient grant income to maintain their own laboratory/desk-based research group with 4 or more regular research workers.
- Obtaining 25% or greater salary recovery on research grants (as PI and Cl)

Students:

- Primary supervision of three or more PhD students, with additional secondary supervision.

Esteem:

- Routinely invited to speak at international meetings, organizing symposia and invited speaker. Chair and oragniser of national meetings, Reviewing articles for high-impact journals;

Figure 4.1 Research expectations for professors at [university name]

The San Francisco Declaration on Research Assessment (DORA) has this to say about the journal impact factor:

> These limitations include: A) citation distributions within journals are highly skewed [1–3]; B) the properties of the Journal Impact Factor are field-specific: it is a composite of multiple, highly diverse article types, including primary research papers and reviews [1, 4]; C) Journal Impact Factors can be manipulated (or 'gamed') by editorial policy [5]; and D) data used to calculate the Journal Impact Factors are neither transparent nor openly available to the public [4, 6, 7]. http://am.ascb.org/dora/

In some disciplines, principally within the sciences, the h-index has become the management signifier of choice. It is almost mandatory in review documents or in applications for internal research funding, and at one Russell Group university, there is strong encouragement to collaborate only with those with a higher h-index.

The underlying supposition of this approach to performance management is that all measures must improve, year on year, and that all categories (impact, esteem, grant capture, research quality) must be optimised. It is also apparent that teaching is not expected to be a priority for professors, nor is it incentivised. This leads to a situation where the race for metrics distorts the very research which is done 'because they promote instrumental and opportunistic behaviour rather than genuine academic inquiry' (Butler and Spoelstra 2014: 539). The process of constant assessment and accountability can actually impede research as documentation for performance management, or any other reporting task, escalates. Knights (2013: 185) writes:

> To perform the rituals for setting about a task (the massive documentation of a 'project initiation document' or PID, the reporting in detail at every stage on outcomes) easily turns into a symbolic substitute for actual work in the field.

There are now commercial platforms which specialise in recording metrics and so faculty find themselves 'dashboarded'. Rutgers academics objected to a four-year deal with Academic Analytics costing $492,500 (Flaherty 2015). Their objection was that such archives of data often contain errors and offer only a limited view of an academic's contribution to the institution. It is a coincidence of particular categories and sources of data which determines the criteria for judgement in the first place (Morrish 2019a). This accident of availability cannot be allowed to drive evaluations if they wish to secure public confidence.

As we see in Figure 4.1, the initial objects of surveillance have been those who might have been thought to have proved their worth incontrovertibly – professors. At some institutions, they must often undergo six-month performance reviews (as frequently as newly appointed probationers); if long-term projects which develop slowly, or lengthy grant applications, mean there is little to report, this can lead to a misplaced sense of under-achievement. Newly conceived 'reward' structures have been installed along with multiple professorial 'bands'. Progression to the next level must be achieved, in some universities, within five years, and this depends on meeting certain 'drivers' illustrated in the earlier example, which include securing a research grant as PI every two years, producing REF 3* and 4* 'outputs', supervising graduate students, producing a significant impact case study, leading high-prestige international collaborations and, of course, continuing to teach. Failure to reach these exacting expectations can result in professors being placed under performance management procedures – the academic equivalent of a headteacher's report. This is the institution exercising extreme coercion to ensure that its needs are met in terms of league table advancement and capital accumulation. It should be pointed out that the potential repercussions of performance management are extremely serious; an employee who is found not to have 'improved' according to the criteria may be dismissed. Others, of course, refuse this process and resign or leave the profession.

The data set for Case Study 6 is taken from documents relating to a professor at a post-1992 UK university who was undergoing 'performance improvement procedures'. The documents comprise: two transcripts of 'improving performance' meetings held between the professor, a manager and a HR representative; two of the institution's documents which set out role expectations for professors. This corpus is 8,439 words in size. All of the documents are used with the permission of the employee who, for context, was quickly able to secure another professorial appointment at a highly ranked university outside the UK.

Corpus analysis

The keywords in Table 4.2 give an indication of the kind of work that is valued by the institution from those who are employed as professors. In particular, keywords such as *international*, *income* and *outputs* provide an indication of the kinds of activities valued by the institution.

Perhaps rather surprisingly given its increasingly central role in guiding research in universities, *REF* is not a high keyword. Paradoxically, the person being 'performance managed' in these documents has an exceptionally strong research profile in REF terms; nevertheless, the achievements are downplayed in the discussions, with more emphasis being placed on the managers' assumptions about what is 'lacking' in terms of their work output. Indeed, the discursive manipulation of constructing the reviewee's work in negative terms, and thus in need of defending, is compounded through the use of legal register throughout the documents. This is signalled through the use of words such as *case* and *evidence*, as in the following example:

- You have made a strong case regarding external esteem

The deployment of a legal register has the discursive effect of evoking a criminal trial, with the reviewee positioned as a defendant and the managers and HR staff as the prosecution. This contributes to a discourse of criminalisation in relation to academic staff who are discursively positioned through the legal register as lazy and being bad at their jobs. This contributes to the erosion of public confidence in academics. The discourse has the effect of aligning managers as serving public interests and positioning academics as doing the opposite.

Table 4.2 Keywords – performance management documents

1. research	2. teaching	3. discipline	4. academic	5. external
6. international	7. learning	8. contribution	9. esteem	10. band
11. professors	12. professorial	13. income	14. commensurate	15. sustained
16. university	17. outputs	18. student	19. pedagogic	20. relevant
21. strategy	22. evidenced	23. HR	24. development	25. assessment
26. activities	27. students	28. mentoring	29. level	30. quality
31. undertaking	32. oversight	33. excellence	34. school	35. conferences
36. undertake	37. equivalent	38. PhD	39. successful	40. prof
41. postgraduate	42. application	43. leadership	44. example	45. management
46. REF	47. supervisions	48. bodies	49. impact	50. role

SDS analysis

The 'defence' of the reviewee is rendered impossible through the systematic use of SDS such as *standards*, *quality*, *significant*, *high profile*, *sustained*, *excellence* (including *sustained excellence*), *successful* and *impact*. Throughout the documents, there is a tension between implying that there is competition between universities (and between individual professors), and the value placed on universities and professors collaborating with each other. As in other documents examined throughout this book, there is no clear indication of whether HEIs should be competing against or collaborating with each other with discursive meanings frequently shifting between these two seemingly polar positions.

The terms *professor* and *professorial* do, themselves, behave like SDS when examined in context. Table 4.3 shows that the terms frequently collocate with *extent of* and with '*band numbers*' (1–4), which indicate the relative seniority of professors in the particular institution under scrutiny in this case study.

The semantic environment of *professor/ial*, then, suggests it has no clearly defined meaning but rather operates on a continuum of non-delineated and semantically ambiguous 'extent' which may itself 'grow'. This potentially leaves professors open to a never-ending audit of their

Table 4.3 Sample concordance of *professor**

1	achieved when the role of a Band 1	Professor has grown sufficiently
2	taking into account the extent of	Professorial experience.
3	at a comparable level. Band 2	Professors perform at a
4	within five years. Band 1	Professors on the Teaching,
5	with appropriate level outputs.	Professors within Band 1 will
6	appointed directly to Band 3.	Professors focussed on teaching
7	their host School. At NTU Band 1	Professors will have an
8	within five years. Band 1	professors should focus on the
9	standard is that identified in	Professorial Band 1, for example

academic activities with constantly shifting priorities being set down capriciously and without warning by university managers.

Critical metaphor analysis

Although the competitive signalling of sport/war metaphors are a staple of neoliberal discursive formations, they are particularly dense in this particular document set, appearing every two or three utterances. Examples include the following:

- the aim is for you to no longer be under the procedure
- We are getting closer to appropriate targets
- The strategy for attracting PhD students is appropriate
- to understand the funding environment and the grant capture team
- What strategy can you have to improve upon success rates
- If we can capture the detail within the three-year plan then that might be fine
- I suggest a report which details forward application strategy over 3 years
- One target then will be to submit the ESRC application
- Perhaps it would be possible to produce a brief plan of forward income generation strategy going forward
- I can give evidence of pursuing this objective
- Secure at least one successful funding application as principal investigator every two years
- securing income commensurate with discipline norms
- providing mentoring and coaching to secure a high level of performance
- Sustained contribution to shaping and influencing academic strategy

Target, *pursue* and *capture* are particularly warlike and connote hostility and aggression. The terms mainly refer to money and research grants, as in the following examples:

- Would it be helpful to target some more achievable grants?
- at that number would be to say the target is £35,000 per year. The amount
- a three-year plan for grant capture. Could I apply for
- the funding environment, and the grant capture team. The possibility of smaller

Similar collocation patterns occur around *target* and *capture* in the REF documents which reinforces the idea that research grants are elusive and need to be taken through rapid, forceful, and adversarial processes rather than through protracted collaboration and mutual endeavour. Related to this, *secure* also collocates noticeably with *grants* and *funding* in the documents suggesting need of containment. It also invests the grants with a kind of animacy so that they are envisaged as evading capture by hostile and aggressive academics, rather than being earned and constructed by a facilitator of new research and knowledge.

- principal investigator every two years, securing income commensurate with
- Income Generation: Secure at least one successful funding
- Your band Income relates to securing research income
- not in our control whether we actually secure the external income
- strategy and exploration of how best to secure income. Perhaps we could put a

In this sense, the repeated metaphorical use of words signalling a source domain of military tactics, such as *capture*, *target* and *secure*, in relation to grant income constructs external funding as an 'enemy' of individual academics within the performance management documents.

Also prevalent are metaphors pertaining to the domain of acting – for example:

- Undertake relevant administrative and academic management duties as are expected of the role
- Band 2 Professors perform at a significantly higher level
- fulfil major international roles within their discipline
- Evidence of performance at this level
- Take a leading role in developing capacity and capability of staff
- on the basis of performance within five years
- Play a leading role in development and training activities
- in addition to a major institutional leadership role within the University
- A leading role in high-impact work which influences government

The prevalence of acting metaphors gives the impression that the individual under scrutiny is 'performing' rather than 'being' and that this 'performance' is temporary and susceptible to the whims and tastes of varying audiences. In fact, the metaphorical domain of acting as it is applied to academic work creates a sense of academic work only being valued on a temporary basis. Academic work is constructed not as a vocation or even a job, but just as a role. 'Performing a role' invokes a sense of inauthenticity for the academic staff member – what they do is purely 'for show' rather than having any inherent substantive value in itself.

A final metaphorical domain which appears throughout the documents is that of finance and business. In examples such as the one that follows, the managers explicitly refer to the university as a commercial enterprise:

- selling and delivering programmes to the external market; undertaking consultancy on behalf of the University, working for a commercial team

Thus, the professor becomes an entrepreneur, or, indeed, even a university 'product' which is promoted and sold on the global market; in effect, they are a commodity whose measures of value are always temporary and in flux. The analysis of this data set shows that, ultimately, the criteria for acceptable performance are shifting and that the university professor can always be discursively constructed as 'underperforming' at the whims of university management teams. Indeed, the criteria seem to be set so broadly and at such a high level, that any professor might be found wanting, depending on how capriciously management wished to apply the policy.

Discussion

The alienation of academics

The spread of performance management in public institutions has been global, and we have referenced studies which reflect this from Australia, UK, Netherlands, Iceland, Sweden, Denmark, Finland, US and Ireland. As Lorenz (2012) notes, NPM, which has given birth to outcomes-based performance management, has resulted in deprofessionalisation of employees and stripping of their professional autonomy. This is what Hall (2018) and Hall and Bowles (2016) in a Marxist analysis, refer to as proletarianisation, inducing overwork, insecurity, ill-health and exploitation. Shore (2008: 289) writes:

> [T]he new regimes of audit have also precipitated a shift in the management of universities, which are now defined in terms of their administrations and management teams. Academics are no longer treated as constitutive members of the university but as its employees, an individualized proletarian workforce that must be subordinated to the organisational hierarchy of managers, people of whom the 'University' must demand excellence.

It is self-evident that under these conditions, the ethos of being an academic has changed as a result of performance management (Kallio *et al* 2015: 3). Careers must now be refocussed on quantitative rather than qualitative judgements, market-oriented work, and researchers subjected to early competition and judgement against senior academics (2015: 19). In a study of Australian early career researchers, Petersen (2016) detailed how they all felt the need to follow what is 'hot' – i.e. popular or of the moment in research terms, and were encouraged to 'do a dirty' and produce rapid, rather than careful research resulting in journal articles where speed becomes valued over quality. This had a profoundly alienating effect on the relationship of the researchers to their work: 'The ECRs who struggled with the performance frameworks also in many cases struggled to articulate the value and worth of their work outside of the productivity discourse' (Petersen 2016: 114).

The analysis of the discourse of performance management presented in this chapter reveals that the professor has been instrumentalised and objectified (Morrish 2015; Nussbaum 1995) to the extent that they are valued primarily for research outputs and for their ability to 'capture' funding. Even the research outputs are monetised through their potential for earning REF quality-related money and otherwise, as signifiers of institutional reputation. Research is treated as a game of strategy. It is startling to encounter the language of war in the context of performance management which, ostensibly, is supposed to support the employee. Instead, it is more redolent of Žižek's (2009) concept of symbolic violence.

The distortion of academic careers

We have now reached the point where available data, audit and performance management and their impact now dominate the lives of academics who are, to quote the title of the well-known blog piece by Holmwood, 'tracked and fecked' (2011). As Morrissey (2013: 805) states:

> The fear for many is that the limits and possibilities of academic productiveness today (and, by extension, the broader values and functions of higher education) are being overly determined by primarily economic delineations of productivity, which miss out on broader civic, political and social educational values.

The discourse of productivity and 'REF-able' research locks the individual into a distinctively neoliberal subject formation – indeed, the ideal corporate subject.

The result has been what Carrigan (2015) calls 'the accelerated academy'. He writes, 'The imagined slowness of university life has given way to a frenetic pace, defined by a perpetual ratcheting up of demands and an entrepreneurial ethos seeking new and quantifiable opportunities'.

This has led to some undesirable behaviours becoming more prevalent in the contemporary academic environment. Morrish (2016) details instances of academics admitting lying and inflating the impact of their research to get grants, whilst Bishop (2016) points to a reproducibility crisis in psychology, a reluctance to report negative results, and an overriding concern with garnering social media attention.

We have argued that these behaviours are congruent with neoliberal values of competitiveness and entrepreneurialism in an academic context and that these values do *not* serve public interests. Prioritising this, rather than the integrity of the work, precipitates its own crisis of legitimation and anxiety. The effect of audit and surveillance is felt in both mind and body (Sparkes 2007). In a widely circulated piece, Gill (2009) brings the strategy of reflexivity to bear on her own experience of a neoliberal university as the context within which she is expected to do research. She describes the sense of overload, panic, stress, shame and guilt elicited by the incessant demands of the university, and the feelings of failure when one does not meet those demands.

In the UK, performance review and REF submission loom large as 'drivers' of academic stress. In the US, tenure and promotion take their toll, especially on women, who may face domestic as well as professional expectations coinciding with this life stage. This is a reflection written by a female US academic about her upcoming mid-tenure review:

> For some of us, it's not that we are afraid to lean in. It's that we have jumped in head first and are barely treading water even when we are considered 'successful.' It's not that my success has come at the expense of family or that my career advancement has been stifled by raising a family. It's that my success in academe is simply not the kind of success that I envisioned myself. Success should feel good, make you beam with pride, feel as if all your hard work was worthy of something bigger. I envisioned, and frankly deserve, a type of success in which the next panic attack isn't just around the corner and in which supportive spouses don't feel like they must resort to ultimatums to cultivate a meaningful family life.
>
> (Sangaramoorthy 2015)

As this example shows, it is important to recognise the differently gendered effects of the neoliberal preoccupations with competitiveness, efficiency and increasing productivity. Without wanting to appear essentialist about the particularities of the effects, we need to take into account the realities of many women's lives. Lynch (2010a, 2010b) and Evans (2010) both refer to the 'careless' university which rewards only 'careless' employees with no familial claims on their time. Lynch (2010a: 57) and a culture of 'carelessness' which has been exacerbated by new managerialism. Senior and even permanent positions are denied those who have caring responsibilities or who must cater to the emotional needs of others. The culture of performance assumes a life unfettered by other demands.

> There are now global opportunities for mobile transnational academics, but the expectations of performance that govern these posts, and set the gold standard for leadership at all levels in the academy, are those that only a care-less worker can fully satisfy.
>
> (Lynch 2010b: 57)

Women, writes Evans, must be prepared to perform according to the metrics of success that have been derived according to norms of masculine lives. There are often extra impositions faced by women of colour in the academy. As well as acting as role models and sources of counselling and affirmation for students of colour, institutions often burden such faculty members with promoting and building diversity. These assignments soak up time, and expectations of published outputs are rarely adjusted accordingly even in institutions that claim to care about diversity. For the most part, it is barely acknowledged except in the form of an equality and diversity department whose wording reflects legal compliance and whose adoption ensures little more than statistical monitoring. There is no intervention against the compulsory conformity, the inscriptions applied by racist structures on bodies seen as different – these all belie institutional claims and commitments to diversity.

For all of us there is a common theme. Our professional lives are dominated by the need to provide discursive evidence that we are compliant with the managerial regime in the form of performance management reviews, teaching evaluations, student satisfaction surveys, REFs and so on. Failure to echo the discourse results in illocutionary silencing (Sauntson 2013), since one has become literally unintelligible to the managerial mind. By locating critique outside the range of the sayable, our resistance is blunted (Davies and Bendix Petersen 2005: 85).

The shift in ethos and concomitant repercussions should now be evident from the linguistic data we have analysed in this section and the growing number of dissenting voices we have cited.

The dissent incorporates a number of critics of NPM and neoliberalism who work within the critical management studies paradigm (Butler and Spoelstra 2014; Franco-Santos *et al* 2014; Gabriel 2012; Parker 2014; Taberner 2018). This work suggests that NPM has failed because, despite a focus on 'efficiency', effectiveness has been undermined, even as scrutiny has intensified in the academy (Taberner 2018: 141–142). As many other critics agree, the reporting function has crowded out 'core functions' like teaching and research, whilst perceptions of surveillance and bullying have become prevalent.

Several scholars (Davies 2014; Thorpe 2008) see audit and performance management as a new governmentality (Foucault 2007). Thorpe describes a process of 'unsettling established practice, replacing established informal, tacit understandings of institutional goals with explicit (but often not well understood), centrally mandated targets, and by creating a climate of coercion and fear' (Thorpe 2008: 107). Davies (2014) explains how audit has become detached from any thought of accountability for the public good and instead has become a disciplinary regime by 'governing through unhappiness'.

> The function of competition, from a neoliberal perspective, is to save centralised politicians or experts the trouble of becoming embroiled in normative or democratic disputes. It also allows the politics of austerity to be somewhat concealed [. . .] The suffering that it causes people, through stress, guilt, self-blame, isolation from colleagues, is a way of reducing their desire to stick with it.

Shore sees resistance and challenge as futile, writing that once audit has colonised a workplace, it is irreversible, and with it, creativity and initiative (2008: 292). And so, the compliance of employees with management priorities is ensured by mandatory and continuous 'change management'.

It is also apparent that permanent anxiety is now institutionalised in universities (Berg *et al* 2016; Thorpe 2008). Hall and Bowles (2016) compare universities to an 'anxiety machine'. Citing Tokumitsu (2014), they remind us that few other professions stake their personal identity so intimately on their work output. The extent of mental illness experienced by academics in the UK has been extensively commented upon in the higher education press (Brady 2018; Grove 2018; Jones and Oakley 2018; Krause 2018; Oswald 2018). Its causes are largely agreed to be unattainable targets, a culture of surveillance, precarious employment and excessive workloads. Looking at the examples in Case Study 6, we see reference to expected targets and a suggestion that they are not being achieved. Management frames this as the employee being subjected to 'performance management' in order to 'empower' them to achieve the targets the institution has demanded of their rank. Let us remind ourselves that this rank is professor, and that the person will have been promoted under a process of internal scrutiny and external peer review. It is not hard to imagine the ways in which this kind of erosion of autonomy and esteem will have an adverse impact on mental health, magnified by the semi-public implementation of the process.

The fact that causes of declining mental health in universities are known, and yet remain unaddressed, deserves condemnation. Employers have a legal duty to identify significant and foreseeable risks to the health of an employee and to take action to prevent harm and caused by work (Landau Law n.d.). But when work overload, burnout, stress and mental health problems have become widespread and normalised, the institution feels justified in claiming that no individual employee's stress or workload is more than any other's. Additionally, the notion that academic work should be done out of love makes an analysis of exploitation hard for the individual to internalise. Anxiety is deliberately intensified, driven by the system designed to maximise performance and outputs. Hall and Bowles (2016) invoke the analogy of the peloton in a professional cycle race where the expected speed is matched to that of the leader. The result is a radically altered academic identity in which everyone else is made to feel as if they are not doing enough. This leads to chronic anxiety, itself a diagnosable category of mental illness (neurosis).

It is warranted, in this context, to invoke Cooper and Whyte's (2017) notion of institutional violence. They move beyond Galtung's (1969) idea of structural violence – the prevention of people from meeting their basic needs – because it encompasses no obvious actor and no perceivable intent. Cooper and Whyte argue that in many instances it is possible to trace actors, actions and intent: 'To talk about institutional violence means that we need to see violence not as "exceptional" or "unusual" events but "ordinary" and "mundane" processes that routinely the violence of austerity and over time deteriorate our mental and physical health' (Cooper and Whyte 2017: 23–24).

It is also relevant to note that in universities, the assumption is that all legal requirements are being complied with, including health and safety legislation. The institution will therefore act towards employees as if these obligations are embedded in policies, are functioning and there is no intent to curb their force. This was the case in institutional responses to the 2014 death by suicide of Professor Stefan Grimm at Imperial College, London (Carrigan 2015; Colquhoun 2016; Davies 2014; Grove 2015; Morrish 2015). In a similar sad case, Malcolm Anderson took his own life at work at Cardiff University in 2018. It was reported at the coroner's court that he had been given 418 essays to mark in just 20 days, and that he had raised the issue of excessive workload with his manager, as the procedure demanded (Pells 2018). His claim was not acted upon, however, and neither were the general complaints about the viability and sustainability of the workload model which the UCU branch had raised in the months previously.

When institutional policies and procedures are altered without consultation or flouted with impunity, the employee loses faith in their integrity and protective power. As Thorpe points out, once you have removed any sense of change or management led by principle, once you have established permanent and rapid change, you can literally impose anything as nothing seems to have legitimacy any more (Thorpe 2008: 107). But it is more serious than just a loss of confidence. There has been a huge rise in universities' referrals of staff to occupational health and counselling services (Morrish 2019b), and as we reported earlier, there have already been suicides which have resulted from workplace stress induced by excessive workload and practices of performance management. This goes further than an analysis of institutional violence; we might predict future allegations of corporate manslaughter (Health and Safety Executive) if the known stressors are not alleviated.

Alternatives

There is currently a shockingly toxic environment for academic staff in UK higher education. Academics, it seems, are easy dupes for enforced competitiveness, especially when it delivers privileges to groups who are socialised to affirm exceptional intellectual success. Although we have demonstrated that there are aspects of this system which are excessive, distorting and damaging, debates about the merits of the REF are very polarised in the UK. There are some who feel it has led to improved research strength in universities, and that it has offered support for research to new and previously excluded areas – gender and queer studies would be beneficiaries in those terms.

Those who have had lengthy careers know that a situation of endemic stress and anxiety is not inevitable or unalterable. Despite the witness of institutional memory, resistance to audit culture has been rare across the world. However, in September 2012, German academics boycotted the Centre for Higher Education (CHE) ranking system which ranked universities on a green, yellow and blue traffic light system. They were particularly angered by a new rating of individual academics on the basis of number of publications. An open letter of protest was signed by 300 economics professors who were swiftly joined by members of the German Sociological Association in a refusal to supply data to the CHE rankings agency (Schmidt 2013).

As mentioned earlier, there has been a turn in the UK towards responsible metrics with the publication of *The Metric Tide* report (Wilsdon *et al* 2015). In the concluding chapter we discuss the impact of similar initiatives such as the Leiden Manifesto (Hicks *et al* 2015) and the San Francisco Declaration on Research Assessment (DORA) which continues to accrue signatories in the UK.

Such cautionary restraints are necessary in the face of institutional pressures to fulfil metric-based targets. It is heartening, if somewhat ironic, to see that the next REF 2021 incorporates a robust interdiction against selecting staff outputs on the basis of citations and journal impact factors. Indeed, in an attempt to blunt gaming, REF 2021 will require that all active researchers be submitted to the audit (Kernohan 2018). Predictably, university managers are already acting to subvert this prescription by moving some staff to teaching-only contracts (Bothwell 2018) and by fudging their own highly variable definitions of 'research active'.

There is also research which discusses what responsible performance management might look like in the context of universities (Franco-Santos *et al* 2014). This work distinguishes between stewardship and agency approaches to performance management, and urges universities to consider a more judicious application of these when considering what is appropriate for the type of work employees engage in. Stewardship approaches 'focus on long-term outcomes through people's knowledge and values, autonomy and shared leadership within a high trust environment'. By contrast, 'agency approaches focus on short-term results or outputs through greater monitoring and control' (Franco-Santos *et al* 2014: 7). In the past decade, the teleological pull of the REF has ensured that the latter, short-term approach has determined progress and promotion for most academics in the UK. Unquestionably, institutions with a mission that is focussed on 'long-term and highly complex goals, which are difficult or very costly to measure (e.g., research excellence, contribution to society)' (Franco-Santos *et al* 2014: 7) are more likely to benefit from developing a stewardship approach to performance management. However, perhaps because leadership training fails to incorporate management research (Harley 2018), or because managerialism itself is predicated on tight control of activity and ethos, there has been a failure to align complexity of mission with a more considered implementation of performance management.

As linguists we have made the case in this and previous chapters that discourse is revealing of culture and identity, and also a medium for enacting change. There are counter-narratives which can be explored and elaborated in the cause of resistance to the more damaging structures of managerialism. Moore *et al* (2017) recommend that we retrain ourselves to evaluate our academic endeavours in terms of soundness and capacity, whilst Robeyns (2016) wishes to reclaim the notion of capability. In earlier decades, the essence of capability was about developing talents, equality, social justice and overall well-being. This has been inverted in an era of weakened workers' rights to refocus on 'incapability', defined as failure to perform the duties of the post to the standard required by the employer. Evidently, if the targets that delineate that standard are unattainable, then there is a risk that any otherwise capable member of staff can be disparaged.

Just as accountability has been demanded of employees, it has demonstrably failed to exercise discipline over the managerial class. Lorenz (2012: 609) recounts that all the recent world scandals including the banking crisis, Lehman Brothers and Enron have occurred in spite of constant audits. Most recently in the UK, the building and services contracting firm Carillion faced liquidation in January 2018. This suggests the need for a new narrative for accountability, and we suggest it can be rehabilitated if it can be returned to another meaning of 'being responsible' (Lorenz 2012: 617–618), but this does not need to be metricised or to exclude narratives of trial and error.

The UK university has become the space for an experiment in managerial fundamentalism. This has demanded that we submit ourselves to the logic of neoliberalism with its belief that markets, competition, winners and losers will deliver progress and efficiency. Ultimately it will be students who are fated to be the losers. When metrics dictate what and whom might be submitted to the REF research audit, then this defines what counts as research. Universities are now reviewing the status of any staff who are not deemed 'research active' under these criteria and they are likely to be transferred to a 'teaching-only pathway' in many HEIs. The feature of UK higher education which has made it outstanding, and was for many years incentivised by QAA inspections, namely research-led teaching, will decline, along with the cross-fertilisation of teaching and research. This is a recipe for a divided and alienated profession.

References

Bendix Petersen, E. and Davies, B. 2010. In/difference in the neoliberalised university. *Learning and Teaching in the Social Sciences* 3 (2): 92–109.

Berg, L., Huijbens, E. and Larson, H. 2016. Producing anxiety in the neoliberal academy. *The Canadian Geographer* 60 (2): 168–180.

Bishop, D. 2013a. Journal impact factors and REF 2014. *BishopBlog*. http://deevybee.blogspot.com/2013/01/journal-impact-factors-and-ref-2014.html (Accessed 6 June 2018).

Bishop, D. 2013b. The academic backlog. http://deevybee.blogspot.com/2013/05/the-academic-backlog.html (Accessed 21 July 2018).

Bishop, D. 2013c. High-impact journals: Where newsworthiness trumps methodology. http://deevybee.blogspot.com/2013/03/high-impact-journals-where.html (Accessed 21 July 2018).

Bishop, D. 2014. Why evaluating scientists by grant income is stupid. http://deevybee.blogspot.com/2014/12/why-evaluating-scientists-by-grant.html (Accessed 21 July 2018).

Bishop, D. 2016. There is a reproducibility crisis in psychology and we need to act on it. http://deevybee.blogspot.com/2016/03/there-is-reproducibility-crisis-in.html (Accessed 31 July 2018).

Bothwell, E. 2018. Don't get comfortable: The rise of the precarious academy. *Times Higher Education*. www.timeshighereducation.com/features/dont-get-comfortable-the-rise-of-the-precarious-academy (Accessed 28 August 2018).

Brady, A. 2018. Bind me – I can still sing. *Still Point Spaces blog*. https://blog.stillpointspaces.com/2018/07/bind-me-i-still-can-sing/ (Accessed 29 August 2018).

Burrows, R. 2012. Living with the h-index? Metric assemblages in the contemporary academy. *The Sociological Review* 1 (2): 355–372.

Butler, N. and Spoelstra, S. 2014. The regime of excellence and the erosion of ethos in critical management studies. *British Journal of Management* 25: 538–550.

Carrigan, M. 2015. Life in the accellerated academy. *LSE Impact* blog. http://blogs.lse.ac.uk/impactofsocialsciences/2015/04/07/life-in-the-accelerated-academy-carrigan/ (Accessed 3 July 2018).

Colquhoun, D. 2012. Is queen Mary university of London trying to commit scientific suicide? *DC's Improbable Science* blog. www.dcscience.net/2012/06/29/is-queen-mary-university-of-london-trying-to-commit-scientific-suicide/ (Accessed 21 July 2018).

Colquhoun, D. 2016. More on bullying at Imperial College London: What's being done? www.dcscience.net/2016/12/21/more-on-bullying-at-imperial-college-london-whats-being-done/ (Accessed 6 June 2018).

Cooper, V. and Whyte, D. 2017. *The Violence of Austerity*. London: Pluto.

Davies, B. 2006. Subjectification: The relevance of Butler's analysis for education. *British Journal of Sociology of Education* 27 (4): 425–438.

Davies, B. and Bendix Petersen, E. 2005. Neo-liberal discourse in the academy: The forestalling of (collective) resistance. *Learning and Teaching in The Social Sciences* 2: 77–98.

Davies, W. 2014. Governing through unhappiness. http://potlatch.typepad.com/weblog/2014/12/governing-through-unhappiness.html (Accessed 29 August 2018).

Deem, R., Hillyard, S. and Reed, M. 2007. *Knowledge, Higher Education and the New Managerialism: The Changing Management of UK Universities*. Oxford: Oxford University Press.

Docherty, T. 2016. On critical responsibility and criminal irresponsibility: The managed university. Lecture given at the University of Wolverhampton, 2nd February 2016.

DORA. San Francisco Declaration on Research Assessment. https://sfdora.org/ (Accessed 17 July 2018).

Edwards, M. and Roy, S. 2017. Academic research in the 21st century: Maintaining scientific integrity in a climate of perverse incentives and hypercompetition. *Environmental Engineering Science* 34 (1).

Evans, M. 2010. Coercion and consensus in higher education. *Learning and Teaching in the Social Sciences* 3 (2): 39–54.

Flaherty, C. 2015. Refusing to be evaluated by a formula. *Inside Higher Education*. www.insidehighered.com/news/2015/12/11/rutgers-professors-object-contract-academic-analytics (Accessed 25 July 2018).

Foucault, M. 2007. *Security, Territory, Population: Lectures at the Collège de France, 1977–1978*. (Trans. G. Burchell). Basingstoke: Palgrave.

Franco-Santos, M. and Doherty, N. 2017. Performance management and well-being: A close look at the changing nature of the UK higher education workplace. *The International Journal of Human Resource Management* 28 (16): 2319–2350.

Franco-Santos, M., Rivera, P. and Bourne, M. 2014. *Performance Management in UK Higher Education Institutions*. London: Leadership Foundation for Higher Education.

Gabriel, Y. 2012. Organizations in a state of darkness: Towards a theory of organizational miasma. *Organization Studies* 33 (9): 1137–1152.

Galtung, J. 1969. Violence, peace, and peace research. *Journal of Peace Research* 6 (3): 167–191.

Gill, R. 2009. Breaking the silence: The hidden injuries of neo-liberal academia. In R. Flood and R. Gill, eds. *Secrecy and Silence in the Research Process: Feminist Reflections*. London: Routledge. 228–244.

Grove, J. 2015. Stefan Grimm inquest: New policies may not have prevented suicide. *Times Higher Education*. www.timeshighereducation.com/news/stefan-grimm-inquest-new-policies-may-not-have-prevented-suicide/2019563.article (Accessed 29 August 2018).

Grove, J. 2018. Half of UK academics 'suffer stress-linked mental health problems. *Times Higher Education*. www.timeshighereducation.com/news/half-uk-academics-suffer-stress-linked-mental-health-problems (Accessed 29 August 2018).

Hall, R. 2018. *The Alienated Academic. The Struggle for Autonomy Inside the University*. London: Palgrave.

Hall, R. and Bowles, K. 2016. Re-engineering higher education: The subsumption of academic labour and the exploitation of anxiety. *Workplace: A Journal for Academic Labour* 28: 30–47.

Harley, B. 2018. Confronting the crisis of confidence in management studies: Why senior scholars need to stop setting a bad example. *Academy of Management Learning and Education* 17 (3).
Hicks, D., Wouters, P., Waltman, L., de Rijcke, S. and Rafols, I. 2015. The Leiden manifesto for research metrics. *Nature* 23: 429–431.
Holmwood, J. 2011. TRACked and FECked: How audits undermine the arts, humanities and social sciences. *Exquisite Lives Research* blogs. http://exquisitelife.researchresearch.com/exquisite_life/2011/03/tracked-and-fecked-how-audits-undermine-the-arts-humanities-and-social-sciences.html (Accessed 29 August 2018).
Holmwood, J. 2014. Turning the audit screw: The degradation of higher education. *Global Dialogue* 4 (4).
Jones, S. and Oakley, C. 2018. The precarious postdoc. www.workingknowledgeps.com/wp-content/uploads/2018/04/WKPS_PrecariousPostdoc_PDF_Interactive.pdf (Accessed 29 August 2018).
Kallio, K., Kallio, T., Tienari, J. and Hyvönen, T. 2015. Ethos at stake: Performance management and academic work in universities. *Human Relations* 69 (3): 1–22.
Kernohan, D. 2018. What we now know about REF2021. https://wonkhe.com/blogs/what-we-now-know-about-ref2021/ (Accessed 23 July 2018).
Knights, B. 2013. Politics and enhancement: The English Subject Centre. In D. Philips and K. Shaw, eds. *Literary Politics: The Politics of Literature and the Literature of Politics*. Basingstoke: Palgrave. 181–193.
Krause, G. 2018. We must confront the culture of overwork to tackle academia's mental health crisis. *Times Higher Education*. www.timeshighereducation.com/blog/we-must-confront-culture-overwork-tackle-academias-mental-health-crisis (Accessed 29 August 2018).
Landau Law Soliciors. https://www.landaulaw.co.uk/ (Accessed 17th July 2019).
Lilienfeld, S. 2018. The neglected implications of grant culture. *Inside Higher Education*. www.insidehighered.com/views/2018/07/02/ethical-issues-surrounding-academes-grant-culture-opinion (Accessed 15 August 2018).
Lorenz, C. 2012. If you're so smart, why are you under surveillance? Universities, neoliberalism, and new public management. *Critical Inquiry* 38 (3): 599–629.
Lynch, K. 2010a. Carelessness: A hidden doxa of higher education. *Arts and Humanities in Higher Education* 9 (1): 54–67.
Lynch, K. 2010b. Neoliberalism and marketization: The implications for higher education. *European Educational Research Journal* 5 (1): 1–17.
Michalek, A.M., Hutson, A.D., Wicher, C.P. and Trump, D.L. 2010. The costs and underappreciated consequences of research misconduct: A case study. *PLoS Medicine* 7: e1000318.
Moore, S., Neylon, C., Eve, M., O'Donnell, D. and Pattinson, D. 2017. 'Excellence R Us': University research and the fetishisation of excellence. *Palgrave Communications* 3 Article 16105.
Moriarty, P. 2014. The vacuity of excellence. http://physicsfocus.org/philip-moriarty-vacuity-excellence/ (Accessed 18 May 2015).
Morozov, E. 2014. The rise of data and the death of politics. *The Observer*. www.theguardian.com/technology/2014/jul/20/rise-of-data-death-of-politics-evgeny-morozov-algorithmic-regulation (Accessed 29 August 2018).
Morrish, L. 2014. Against REFonomics: Quantification cannot satisfy the demands of rationality, equity and tolerability. http://blogs.lse.ac.uk/impactofsocialsciences/2014/12/22/refonomics-and-reformations/ (Accessed 1 July 2018).

Morrish, L. 2015. Raising the bar: The metric tide that sinks all boats. Academic Irregularities Blog. https://academicirregularities.wordpress.com/2015/11/26/raising-the-bar-the-metric-tide-that-sinks-all-boats/ (Accessed 25 July 2018).

Morrish, L. 2016. The rise of the Trump academic. *The Sociological Review*. www.thesociologicalreview.com/blog/the-rise-of-the-trump-academic.html (Accessed 21 July 2018).

Morrish, L. 2019a. The accident of accessibility: How the data of the TEF creates neoliberal subjects. *Social Epistemology*. https://doi.org/10.1080/02691728.2019.1638991

Morrish, L. 2019b. Universities and staff mental health – A toxic environment? *Higher Education Policy Institute*. Occasional Paper 20, https://www.hepi.ac.uk/2019/05/23/pressure-vessels-the-epidemic-of-poor-mental-health-among-higher-education-staff/

Morrish, L. and. O'Mara, K. 2011. Queering the discourse of diversity. *Journal of Homosexuality* 58 (6–7): 974–990.

Morrish, L. and Sauntson, H. 2016. Performance management and the stifling of academic freedom and knowledge production. *Journal of Historical Sociology* 29 (1): 42–64.

Morrissey, J. 2013. Regimes of performance: Practices of the normalised self in the neoliberal university. *British Journal of Sociology of Education* 36 (4): 614–634.

Nussbaum, M. 1995. Objectification. *Philosophy and Public Affairs* 24 (4): 249–291.

Oswald, A. 2018. Middle-aged academics are at greater suicide risk than students. *Times Higher Education*. www.timeshighereducation.com/opinion/middle-aged-academics-are-greater-suicide-risk-students (Accessed 29 August 2018).

Parker, M. 2014. University, Ltd: Changing a business school. *Organization* 21 (2): 281–292.

Peck, J. and Tickell, A. 2002. The urbanization of neoliberalism: Theoretical debates on neoliberalizing Space. *Antipode* 34 (3): 380–404.

Pells, R. 2018. Cardiff plans review after suicide of 'overworked' lecturer. *Times Higher Education*. www.timeshighereducation.com/news/cardiff-plans-review-after-suicide-overworked-lecturer (Accessed 3 August 2018).

Peseta, T., Barrie, S. and McLean, J. 2017. Academic life in the measured university: Pleasures, paradoxes and politics. *Higher Education Research and Development* 36 (3): 453–457.

Petersen, E. B. 2016. The impact of managerial performance frameworks on research activities among Australian early career researchers. In K. Trimmer, ed. *Political Pressures on Educational and Social Research: International perspectives*. New York: Routledge. 104–115.

REF 2021. Decisions on staff and outputs. www.ref.ac.uk/media/ref,2021/downloads/REF%202017_04%20Decisions%20-%20updated%2011.04.2018.pdf (Accessed 24 July 2018).

Robeyns, I. 2016. The capability Approach. In E. Zalta, ed. *The Stanford Encyclopedia of Philosophy*. Stanford, CA: CSLI.

Sangaramoorthy, T. 2015. A hockey mom seeks tenure. *Chronicle of Higher Education*. http://chronicle.com/article/A-Hockey-Mom-Seeks-Tenure/229193/ (Accessed 24 July 2018).

Sauntson, H. 2013. Sexual diversity and illocutionary silencing in the English national curriculum. *Sex Education: Sexuality, Society and Learning* 13 (4): 395–408.

Sayer, D. 2015. *Rank Hypocrisies: The Insult of the REF*. London: Sage.

Schmidt, F. 2013. German academics boycott CHE ranking system. *Times Higher Education*. www.timeshighereducation.com/news/german-academics-boycott-che-ranking-system/2002595.article (Accessed 2 August 2018).
Shore, C. 2008. Audit culture and illiberal governance: Universities and the politics of accountability. *Anthropological Theory* 8 (3): 278–298.
Shore, C. and Wright, S. 2015. Audit culture revisited: Rankings, ratings and the reassembling of society. *Current Anthropology* 56 (3): 421–444.
Sparkes, A. 2007. Embodiment, academics and the audit culture: A story seeking consideration. *Qualititative Research* 7 (4): 521–550.
Stern Review. 2016. REF Review: Building on Success and Learning from Experience. July 28. www.gov.uk/government/publications/research-excellence-framework-review (Accessed 28 September 2018).
Strathern, M. ed. 2000. *Audit Cultures: Anthropological Studies in Accountability, Ethics and the Academy*. London: Routledge.
Taberner, A. 2018. The marketization of the English higher education sector and its impact on academic staff and the nature of their work. *International Journal of Organizational Analysis* 26 (1): 129–152.
Thorpe, C. 2008. Capitalism, audit and the demise of the humanistic academy. *Workplace* 15: 103–125.
Tokumitsu, M. 2014. In the name of love. *Jacobin Magazine*, 13. https://jacobinmag.com/2014/01/in-the-name-of-love (Accessed 24 July 2018).
Vinkers, C., Tijdink, J. and Otte, W. 2015. Use of positive and negative words in scientific PubMed abstracts between 1974 and 2014: Retrospective analysis. *British Medical Journal* 351: h6467.
Wilsdon, J. et al. 2015. *The Metric Tide: Report of the Independent Review of the Role of Metrics in Research Assessment and Management*. London: HEFCE.
Žižek, S. 2009. *Violence: Six Sideways Reflections*. London: Profile Books.

5 Language and audit culture 2

The case of the Teaching Excellence Framework

Context

The 2016 *Success as a Knowledge Economy* (SKE[1]) white paper mentioned in previous chapters ushered in a new period of uncertainty in regulation and funding for universities in the UK. It came at a very inopportune time. The EU Referendum result had already created insecurity regarding the future of much of UK higher education research funding. Even Universities UK seemed overwhelmed and asked for the government to press the pause button on HE reform. This was destined not to happen. The bill met resistance as it made its way through parliament, particularly from the House of Lords, but Jo Johnson's, the then minister of state for universities, science, research and innovation (i.e. higher education), ideological framework remained intact.

On 4 November 2016, *The Times* headlined a story on 'new providers' of higher education in the UK which echoed the title of the white paper: *Dyson University Is a Wake-Up Call for Higher Education: Reforms Will Hold the Key to Our Success as a Knowledge Economy.* Dyson, we remind readers, is a British company renowned for innovative and attractively designed home appliances. Its founder, James Dyson, although himself a graduate of art schools, has often bemoaned the lack of engineering graduates in the UK. To remedy this, through the James Dyson Foundation, he has donated to universities in the UK such as the University of Cambridge and Imperial College, London, in order to support the education and training of engineers. The story in *The Times* was announcing a new venture – the Dyson Institute of Technology – that the benefactor hopes will address the perceived shortage of technically skilled graduates. The announcement was welcomed by Johnson, and his hope was it would send a message of a change through the higher education sector:

> Today's announcement that the company will set up its own higher education institution is emblematic of its far-sighted approach. The new Dyson Institute of Technology will help to tackle the chronic

> shortages of engineers that have long held our economy back [. . .] At a time when students are crying out for new ways of studying, the market share of the traditional three-year degree programme has increased from 65 per cent to 78 per cent over the past five years. Our reforms will change that. We will strip existing universities of the power to act like bouncers, deciding who should and should not be let into the club.
>
> (Johnson 2016)

This announcement had been foreshadowed in a widely reported speech from 2015 at the University of Surrey. In it, Johnson made claims of there being 'lamentable teaching' in universities, and offered one anecdote about a student who claims not to have seen his personal tutor for two years. The solution he offered was to level the playing field for new providers of higher education, stating, 'Success in higher education should be based on merit, not on incumbency'. Johnson envisaged a more rapid pathway to degree-awarding powers and to the award of the title of university. The most inflammatory part of the speech was his anticipatory retort to critics of this policy. He answered with this: 'The requirement for new providers to seek out a suitable validating body from amongst the pool of incumbents is quite frankly anti-competitive. It's akin to Byron Burger having to ask permission of McDonald's to open up a new restaurant'.[2]

It was clear to those in the traditional university sector that Johnson was wanting to kick in some doors. Ball (2003) voices a concern over the rush to make universities replicas of the entrepreneurial business with high risk, short-term, fast moving, disruptive models of acting. What academics found most offensive, however, was the suggestion that universities can somehow be compared to fast food franchises, and that, having complied for decades with government and regulatory bodies' standards and procedures for quality assurance, they are now being derided and cast once more as deficient and failing. The issues of competition and economic enhancement were presented in a discourse which was bereft of any associations with academia. This was deliberate. In this chapter, by focusing on an analysis of SKE, we examine current linguistic manifestations of neoliberal discourse as it continues to be introduced into university teaching.

It is important to mention that the bill underwent several important amendments during its passage through the House of Lords, which changed its shape and the function of some of its key elements, namely the TEF. In this chapter, we are referring to the text of SKE, with particular reference to Chapter 2.

The changes proposed by SKE were widely regarded as bringing about disruption to universities, not least by the minister who jubilantly embraced the concept. Amongst the key planks of SKE was an invitation to new private 'challenger institutions' who may be granted degree-awarding powers more quickly than previous regulation allowed. Other changes were proposed to governance, academic freedom and protections against arbitrary dismissal which appear to infringe the historic autonomy that universities enjoyed from government. A critique of the proposed changes can be found in an alternative white paper, authored by a group of concerned academics (Holmwood *et al* 2016) can be found at https://heconvention2.wordpress.com/alternative/.

The most significant proposal was for a TEF to mirror the REF which we discussed in Chapter 4. The new audit of teaching was proposed to correct supposedly 'lamentable' teaching which Johnson referred to. The paragraphs which outline how the TEF will work display some baffling logical linkages. Below are listed some of the assertions made in the paragraphs which outline the justification for the TEF:

- higher education leads to better employment outcomes, but these outcomes are not consistent;
- there is considerable variation in employment outcomes and employability amongst subjects and across institutions;
- students often enter HE with little information to guide their choices;
- students often say they would have chosen a different course;
- the importance of students having access to a wide array of work experience opportunities;
- a recent IFS study also found huge variance in graduate earnings depending on choice of subject and institution, as well as background;
- higher average earnings mean that graduates make an important contribution to society through their tax revenues;
- employers and HE providers working together on curriculum design, and graduates having the 'soft skills' they need to thrive in the work environment.

(SKE: 42)

Johnson was resolutely convinced that the answer to all of these was the TEF, a new OfS and the entry of private challenger institutions which the government claimed would help raise teaching standards. From 2018/19, an award of excellent or outstanding would permit an HEI to increase its fees in line with inflation. Others, even those meeting expectations, would be likely to suffer various degrees of attrition and their students condemned to a 'choice' of an educational resource eroded by inflation. The idea, though, was that students should exercise their choice by avoiding those institutions. Their fate would be requiring institutions to draw up plans for 'market exit' (SKE: 38).

Almost alone amongst their peers, the vice-chancellors of Nottingham Trent and Exeter universities argued for forging ahead with reform and the implementation of the TEF. By contrast, a poll by *THE* shows only

4% of academics thought the TEF would provide an authentic and accurate measure of teaching quality.[3]

Nevertheless, the government remained confident that good teaching could be measured on an institutional basis. Perhaps the first point to emphasise is that these measures are, as SKE admits, proxies rather than actual measures of the good teaching that transpires in classrooms and other learning contexts.

> Such things can be measured: students assess their satisfaction with their courses, retention rates are a good proxy for student engagement, contact hours can be measured, employers choose to sponsor some courses, or work with some institutions, because of the industry-relevance of their offerings, and employment rates can be measured. Some of these metrics are of course proxies – but they directly measure some of the most important outcomes that students and taxpayers expect excellent teaching to deliver. And we recognise that metrics alone cannot tell the whole story; they must be benchmarked and contextualised, and considered alongside the additional narrative that can establish a provider's case for excellence.
>
> (SKE: 46)

Secondly, nowhere in SKE is there any evidence of so-called lamentable teaching. In fact the published NSS figures show the opposite. Nevertheless, taken nationally, the average satisfaction figure is extremely high at 87% (England 2016 NSS results) with a rather narrow range of scores. So why, asks Bishop (2016), is there any need for a TEF? It is ironic that opponents of the TEF feel bound to seize on NSS scores, underpinned by metrics they feel to be unreliable, to verify that there is little wrong with university teaching (Morris 2017). There are some managers in the sector who think the TEF is probably their best defence against unsubstantiated claims such as Johnson's.

Other critics, such as Johnston, dispute the pedagogical premises of the TEF:

> If a university is about the creation of self-directed independent learners then the discourse of 'teaching' as opposed to 'educating' needs to be unsettled. If a university's value proposition is an experience of education that is highly distinct from secondary and further education then TEF is broadly irrelevant,[4]

It is not inappropriate to mention a similar experience of Johnston's:

> I recall being described on a module comments form as 'confused' because I couldn't tell the student which of the two meanings of the term 'marketing' was the correct one: marketing as a management

> principle or management function. The student protested further, 'if you don't know then what chance have I got'.

Anyone who teaches undergraduates who are encouraged to expect gratification in place of learning will recognise the student's attitude, and it is documented by Nixon *et al* (2016).

Just as there have been differences of perspective over questions of assessment of teaching, we must also recognise that there is likely to be a shift in the direction with regard to graduate outcomes. These could legitimately be taken to encompass student achievement in their degrees, satisfaction with the experience or learning gain. However, SKE is clear that the framework of the TEF will prioritise graduate earnings, and this is one of the proposed measures as the TEF moves towards 'a more granular and informative assessment of graduate outcomes' (SKE: 48). This view was endorsed by just one vice-chancellor (Peck 2015).

Possibly the best exposé of this misguided proxy measure was the study published by the Institute of Fiscal Studies (Britton *et al* 2016). It demolishes graduate salary as a metric, with its finding that 'graduates from richer family backgrounds earn significantly more after graduation than their poorer counterparts, even after completing the same degrees from the same universities'. Although this study is acknowledged in SKE, the logic is not absorbed. We can also predict that a later study (Belfield and Britton 2018) which advises against using graduate salaries to evaluate universities will be similarly discounted. If we can assume that excellent teaching will not be restricted to more socially advantaged students, what relevance is there to measuring graduate earnings? We can detect an implicit threat in SKE that the government may seek to pressure universities to close courses which do not deliver the right 'outcomes' – i.e. graduates who are able to earn enough to pay back the cost of their student loans. This reasoning exposes the real purpose of this metric as purely ideological; it is designed to incentivise universities to consider the scenario that if their graduates do not pay back their fee loans, the implicated course may be closed. At this point, it should also be mentioned that the correspondence between university course and graduate salary can be achieved since the implementation of the Small Business, Enterprise and Employment Act (2014). This legislation enables mining of tax records for integration with student loan and university degree records. After all, why would a government fail to deploy a happy accident of data availability when it might validate their preference to judge universities by their visible contribution to personal wealth accumulation?

Despite any evidence of need or indeed any direct measures of teaching quality, the TEF went ahead even before the Higher Education and Research Bill made its way through Parliament. In 2017/18 the TEF was run on a voluntary basis and a 'provider' was permitted to opt in, presumably if it wished to establish a good reputation for teaching. The second iteration was intended by Jonson to have financial implications, and a complex architecture of metrics, benchmarks and 'flags' would be pegged to limited fee increases (Bagshaw and Morris 2016).

Throughout the debates in parliament, and in response to scepticism from higher education sector leaders, the government maintained its stance that the TEF was needed to ensure high teaching quality in universities. A mock league table of benchmark-adjusted metrics published by *THE* showed that the Russell Group universities were eclipsed by a Midlands triangle of Loughborough, Aston and De Montfort universities. It is worth considering whether this outcome was itself part of the plan to create the conditions whereby the Russell Group reject participation in the TEF and follow the incentives towards privatisation. For some years, the Russell Group has been considering the advantages of going private in order to escape a government-imposed fee cap. So, perhaps the ultimate goal is to incentivise privatisation of an elite tier of universities, and possibly, the closure of a few universities which have widened participation, but failed to compensate for the unequal distribution of wealth which has been part of the neoliberal project. This insight is articulated by Woodstock and Toscano (2016) who ask:

> What are we to make of the White Paper's suggestion, to wit that it is teaching quality that produces inequality? This exorbitant claim – designed among other things to dress up the principal aim, which is financial disciplining, deregulation and stratification of the sector.

Government policy seemed to be guiding the elite universities of the UK to follow their counterparts in Australia and start charging variable fees which have little to do with teaching quality and everything to do with accrued reputation – something which SKE claims it wishes to dismantle. Rather than providing concrete information on which students can base their choices, this uninformative snapshot will leave students confused between choosing between placing their trust in established reputation or the unsubstantiated proxies of the TEF. This appears to illustrate what Woodstock and Toscano (2016) call 'the mendacious mantra of "student choice", which was already a centrepiece of the *Browne Review* commissioned by the previous Labour government'.

There was, of course, a great deal of argument and evidence assembled by critics of the TEF. The Convention for Higher Education ran several conferences and also organised the writing of an alternative white paper (Holmwood *et al* 2016). A cost-benefit analysis of the TEF was provided by Bishop (2016) who argued that the TEF will do nothing to increase good teaching, curtail bad teaching or provide students with any more guidance than they already have. Those critics of the REF who have seen escalating costs and a scale of wastage when universities engage in gaming the system, rather than supporting research, predict the same scenario for the TEF.

It is hard to see how the TEF could seriously be held up as a protective mechanism for teaching quality. As we have already pointed out, the metrics proposed are mere proxies for teaching quality, remote from actual classroom practices. There are many factors influencing successful teaching and student engagement and satisfaction: students may be very satisfied with individual teachers, whilst perceiving elements of the course to be disappointing, funding to be inadequate, accommodation too expensive or the claims of family or paid employment to be stronger. Academics have limited agency to affect outcomes such as retention, student satisfaction and employment. Even as incentives the metrics fail. Although universities now have the tools to immediately individualise TEF scores of student satisfaction, nobody is going to be poached by an HEI for their superior teaching scores. Similarly, it is likely that few academics will be to be tempted to move to a stronger teaching department to improve their status.

With regard to the long-standing audit of UK research in the form of the REF (and previously the Research Assessment Exercise, RAE), universities have gone along with it because (up to now at least) there were reputational, even if few financial, gains to be won. However, if the Lords' 2017 amendment on denying fee rises to TEF standing goes ahead, there will be little gain in either dimension, and, in fact, there could be many reputational risks particularly amongst the elite of the sector. There are also alarm bells sounding as we write about the status of a deeper layer of subject-level TEFs, which may deliver less favourable results than a previously assured institutional ranking. Universities are left wondering what would be the gain in entering such an audit. The TEF might be about to repeat some of the mistakes of the early QAA subject reviews which denounced some subjects as failing, and, with its ministerial boast of being a 'game changer', may well bring about serious reputational blowback.

Given the evident success of the UK higher education sector, many academics and commentators were perplexed about why a government would wish to introduce more financial and regulatory uncertainty. Davies (2016) quotes McGettigan: 'This is a document that bristles with resentment towards the established university sector'. It raises a question of why does the government, and clearly parts of the media, hate universities so much?

For universities, the TEF is another hurdle to be surmounted. For the government, if there is a market-oriented ideological purpose, then another costly regulatory system is deemed worth paying for if the desired outcomes are achieved. New staff will be deployed to manage the process, and so even if the promised tuition fee rise in line with inflation is allowed, it will be quickly consumed in the race to enhance the institutional image. Woodstock and Toscano (2016) argue that the additional consumer mechanisms will serve as a disciplinary tool, and possibly as licence for university closure. Given that the first chapter of SKE is entitled 'Competition', and 'Market Exit' is the title of a section, this is entirely probable. The Darwinian discourse is confirmed by the requirement for all 'providers' to have a plan for such a market exit in case that should be their 'choice':

> Those who believe that stability and durability are positive features of such institutions will have to think again, as the government works to impose what it proudly calls a 'history-blind' system.
>
> (Woodstock and Toscano 2016)

This can be interpreted that no reputation accrued over years, or centuries, can be taken into account. It is Year Zero for universities, and the goals for recognition are the ones being shakily erected by government.

Within the context outlines discussed earlier, we present a systematic analysis of Chapter 2 of SKE. Jones *et al* (2016) discuss the nature of the discursive intervention that propels higher education closer to an alignment with neoliberal values and invite a challenge to that intention. Key to their argument is that discursive framing is crucial to reception, and our discussion of SKE is a case study in how to do this. We build on the work of Jones *et al* by conducting a more detailed and systematic linguistic analysis to show the precise discursive mechanisms through which neoliberal values are legitimated, perpetuated and normalised.

Jones *et al* (2016) also posit several other assumptions encoded in SKE which are that teaching and research need rebalancing, and that value for money is seen as a problem by students. In the right wing press, universities themselves are constantly problematised with assumptions of poor teaching, the offering of 'pointless degrees', and the dissatisfaction of employers with graduates. All of these myths can be falsified by reference to data published in annual reports by UUK, QAA, NSS, HESA (employment statistics); nevertheless this undermining thread is echoed in the discourse chosen throughout SKE, and, it must be said, in unsympathetic media portrayal. In Case Study 7, we discuss each of these and several other emergent features of neoliberal discourse in SKE.

Case study 7: TEF white paper – Success as a Knowledge Economy (SKE)

Corpus analysis

As in the other case studies, we start by presenting a keyword analysis to identify themes and discursive priorities in SKE (the paper is 31,609 words). The top 50 keywords in SKE are presented in Table 5.1.

Table 5.1 Keywords in SKE

1. providers	2. TEF	3. students	4. higher	5. research
6. UKRI	7. funding	8. education	9. DAPS	10. quality
11. HEFCE	12. innovation	13. provider	14. sector	15. teaching
16. student	17. innovate	18. ensure	19. institutions	20. outcomes
21. access	22. UK	23. regulatory	24. participation	25. disadvantaged
26. system	27. excellence	28. RDAPS	29. councils	30. review
31. widening	32. metrics	33. choice	34. regulator	35. consultation
36. universities	37. data	38. fee	39. functions	40. apprenticeships
41. deliver	42. future	43. competition	44. university	45. backgrounds
46. cap	47. QAA	48. probationary	49. BIS	50. framework

Examining the semantic environments of some of the keywords (especially those that function as SDS) can be useful for revealing some of the prevalent underlying ideologies reinforced through the text. In the next section, we continue to use corpus tools to explore the semantic environments of some key SDS in the document.

SDS analysis

In Table 5.1, *provider**, as the top keyword, has over 50 mentions, whereas *university* has just 2. It is clear that the focus of SKE is higher education, but *provider* is a motivated choice which permits the contemplation of HEIs other than traditional universities. This discursive shift is necessary if traditional universities are to be challenged by newly credentialed private institutions. *Provider** is also an SDS which permits slippage over what may constitute a HE provider. It also implies a uni-directional practice in which the institution simply gives/provides to its 'consumers' in exchange for money. *Provider** is therefore a keyword which reflects and reinforces the neoliberal 'exchange of goods and services' ideology pervading the document.

High on the keyword list is *innovation* (and *innovate*). The keyness of these terms suggest that they are primary concerns of the TEF. However, as SDS, they are almost impossible to define and, importantly for the TEF, quantify for the purpose of producing metrics.

The keyword list contains words which signify a strong concern with constructing HEIs as commercial and financial enterprises. Such words include *funding*, *HEFCE*, *fee* and *cap*. *Regulatory* and *regulator* also appear in the 23rd and 34th position, respectively. In conjunction with the finance-related words, they suggest a strong emphasis on the role of the TEF as regulatory/policing (of academic staff) and as financially motivated. These are the key neoliberal driving forces behind the TEF.

We find that a further SDS revealed through the keyword list is *excellence* (mentioned 11 times), for example:

- for the first time bring sector-wide rigour to the assessment of teaching excellence
- the potential for TEF to drive innovation in teaching excellence if it is applied more widely

This theme encodes a number of presuppositions, some of which conflict with the evidence. *Excellence* is arrived at via 'choice' and 'competition' – the conjoined twins of neoliberalism. The first presupposition is that there is a lack of excellence, particularly in teaching. No evidence is presented for a problem with quality or teaching in universities; however, merely the assertion of 'patchy' or 'lamentable' teaching embeds a presupposition that this situation exists.

Excellence itself is a problematic term which receives critical attention from Moore *et al* (2017) who recognise that 'the evaluation of 'soundness' is based in the practice of scholarship, whereas 'excellence' is a characteristic of its objects (outputs and actors)'. As an alternative, they recommend instead a rhetoric around *soundness*, *capacity* and *credibility*. This, they point out, would essentially be an evaluation of process, which is what current quality assurance already delivers. Importantly, 'soundness' can be objectively recognised with criteria and benchmarking with 'appropriate standards of description, evidence, and probity rather than flashy claims of superiority – presents an alternative to the existing notions of 'excellence'' (Moore *et al* 2017).

Choice also emerges as a keyword. The unambiguous presupposition underlying the use of *choice* within the text is that choice has not existed previously in higher education, for example:

- This starts when students cannot make informed choices.

This ideological assumption is used throughout as it is a key justification for the TEF. In fact, students have access to a wealth of information about the quality and ranking of courses, from league tables of university rankings, to Unistats to HEFCE and QAA reports, DLHE and NSS results. Universities themselves provide information about courses and graduate destinations on their websites, and open days have become much more frequent and professional events. The reality is that there *has* always been choice in higher education. But all HEIs have entry criteria which *do* restrict individual choice. In the next example, use of the verb *introduce* again implies that choice is something new that students have not previously had:

- introduce high-quality choices for students in a competitive market

It is not immediately clear from this phrase what is meant by a high-quality choice – whether this be the TEF metrics, or the assumed improvements in university teaching themselves which will constitute high-quality choices, but this sentence clarifies that the emphasis is on providing accurate metrics and hints at graduate employment outcomes:

- We need to make sure that students have access to the best possible information to make choices about what they study, and the benefits that they can expect to gain from those choices.

It is assumed that the TEF will be a mutually beneficial arrangement, since 'the reputational advantage that will accrue to providers achieving the highest TEF ratings will be substantial, particularly given this Government's removal of student number controls' (SKE 2.19). The government is making the assumption that it is TEF scores which will influence students' choices/undergraduate recruitment, and that this information will override any historical reputation or enduring status which may have influenced student choice previously. A point which is overlooked in this analysis is that TEF rankings will be temporary so that a student may enrol in a gold-starred course, and graduate from one awarded a bronze (and vice versa).

The two strongest lexical collocates of *choice* in the document are *quality* and *competition*. The semantic alignment of *choice* and *quality* means that choice accrues an overwhelmingly positive meaning. This is further reinforced through co-occurrences with words such as *gain*, *best*, *high [quality]* and *promote*, as in the following examples:

- our ambitions to introduce high quality choice for students
- The system needs to have informed choice and competition
- we will improve quality and enable choice for all students, particularly those
- that they can expect to gain from those choices. We take a broad view
- should be able to make the best choices to fit their own individual
- give the OfS an explicit duty to promote choice and competition, which will

Collocates such as *increasing*, *more* and *expanding* also reinforce the positive meaning of choice created in the document, and the underlying assumption that more choice, rather than less choice and greater specialisation, is better.

- flexibility into the HE system, increasing choice for students and promoting
- within the market, and expand the choices available to students.

- high quality entrants and increased choice for students, our primary goal
- there is more choice in where and how students can
- on student numbers to allow greater choice and help competition
- We will increase choice and flexibility in the sector

The collocation of *choice* and *competition* creates a semantic relationship between the two terms, thus implying that choice creates competition, and vice versa, and that both of these processes are beneficial to students and to the sector.

- individuals with experience of fostering choice and competition
- To have regard to promoting choice and competition
- to play in the HE sector. By promoting choice and competition and ensuring
- For the first time, competition, choice and the student interest will be

There is something of an irony in fetishising 'choice' when the government has engineered a funding context in which many more students feel obliged to study at a university close to their domicile. Inevitably, in order to avoid accruing debt, some students will seek to save money by remaining in the parental home. The traditional UK 'boarding-school' model then becomes the provenance of the more fortunate, whilst less privileged students have their choice restricted to the local university, regardless of TEF scores. It is disingenuous to place the blame for inequality of outcomes onto fictitious flaws in university provision and quality of teaching. Woodstock and Toscano (2016) write:

> The regulatory congeries of the TEF, combining deeply flawed feedback mechanisms (the NSS) with an invidious and hypocritical use of employment statistics, has no chance whatsoever of either giving students any real power (which can only be collective, not individual), nor to reverse the government's own responsibility for worsening the social conditions of BME and working-class students.

Outcomes is a high keyword (20th in the list). *Outcomes*, like many of the keywords discussed so far, is another SDS. The presupposition that good quality teaching leads inevitably to good *outcomes* is repeated throughout. The precise definition of *outcomes* is ambiguous, however, and seems to shift frequently. For example:

- However the outcomes that we observe from English higher education are not consistently strong. This starts when students cannot make informed choices.

- Great teaching increases the likelihood of good <u>outcomes</u>.

The second example is also a bare assertion which does not attempt to explain how or why teaching and good outcomes are linked; the correlation is just assumed as it is in the next quotation:

- There are providers where employment outcomes are significantly above the sector-accepted benchmark and others that are significantly below the benchmark. Clearly, good quality teaching makes a difference.

There is uncertainty whether *outcomes* refers to the challenge of learning, value for money, employment or satisfaction with the experience. It is clear there is some instability of reference, as in this next example:

- Most students stay locked into their course even if it is not right for them. This leads to dissatisfaction and poor outcomes: the consumer organisation *Which?* has found that three in ten students think that the academic experience of higher education is poor value, and the issues raised by students in that research included the amount, and quality, of teaching they received, and the extent to which they are academically challenged.

This example ignores that fact that it is expensive to change courses. And there continue to be limited choices for students because each individual course comes with its own entry criteria and requirements. The figure mentioned in the previous example also refers to a 2014 *Which?* survey whose related press release actually cites a figure of 18% of students dissatisfied with value for money.[5] The report itself cites, 'Three in ten undergraduates thought that their experience was poor value', but this bald statistic is complicated by this comment:

> When students got to university, as undergraduates, they often spoke passionately about the wider personal and social benefits of university: the experience of living independently, meeting new people and developing a sense of identity. This 'transformative' element of the university experience meant that while students might identify aspects of the academic experience, or the accommodation as poor value, this was often overshadowed by the wider benefits.
>
> (http://press.which.co.uk/wp-content/uploads/2014/11/Which-A-degree-of-value-Nov-2014.pdf)

This misleads the reader into believing that 30% of students are dissatisfied with their course, feel they are stuck with it, despite poor teaching and poor value for money. Even if it were not an abuse of statistics, it is, in any case an empty notion, according to Collini (2016). Discussing the related Green Paper of November 2015, he maintains that 'it says nothing about what you should get or how much you should pay for it. It is empty too because no one, presumably, is in favour of not getting value for money' (www.lrb.co.uk/v38/n02/stefan-collini/who-are-the-spongers-now). In actual fact, a recent HEA/HEPI report (Neves and Hillman 2016) indicates that value for money only becomes an issue in 2012, in concert with the raising of the tuition fee to £12,000. More significantly, the 'issues raised' which are taken to drive judgements of value for money are, of course, those surveyed by the report's authors, and the correlation of each of those issues mentioned is only weakly correlated with value for money judgements (between +0.38 and −0.35), as shown in Figure 5.1.

In the same report, student rates of satisfaction with their course are quoted at 85%.[6] It is not just a misleading interpretation of weak correlation that challenges the reporting of the student-as-consumer experience – these faulty linkages continue to be asserted and established discursively throughout SKE. It is a three-pronged approach: selective use of questions, cherry-picking statistics and insistent repetition of misleading discourse.

In the next quote, there is no ambiguity about the meaning of *outcomes* – it refers to employment after graduation:

- looking at graduate employment outcomes for STEM subjects and computer sciences, respectively. These reviews found considerable variation in employment outcomes and employability amongst subjects and across institutions and both point to a range of factors that need to be considered in strengthening outcomes

The notion of *outcomes* continues to be enmeshed with the idea of economic value, emphasised with the repetition of *investment*:

- the 'soft skills' that employers consistently say they need. These include capacity for critical thinking, analysis and teamwork, along with the vital development of a student's ability to learn

And here:

- These decisions are significant factors in determining a student's future life and career success, so it is crucial that they represent sound investments. We need to make sure that students have access to the best possible information to make choices about what they study, and the benefits that they can expect to gain from those choices.

3.2 Analysis: What drives value for money perceptions?

As with overall satisfaction, Pearson correlation analysis was conducted across a range of questions in the survey to assess which aspects of the student experience are the greatest drivers of value-for-money perceptions.

Top-ten correlations with good/very good value for money

Measure	*Pearson correlation value*	*Strength of correlation with overall satisfaction*	*% agree score*
Experience has marched expectations	0.386	Moderate	76
If you knew what you Co nova, would you have chosen a different course	•0.35	Moderate	33
Teaching staff were helpful and supportive	0.348	Moderate	65
Teaching staff motivated you to Co your best work	0.33	Moderate	51
I am satisfied with the amount of Brno-tabled sessions 1 ha. a had	0.325	Moderate	64
Teaching staff made their subjects interesting	0.324	Moderate	54
Teaching staff were poor ac exploring things	•0.303	Moderate	0
Teaching staff maintain and Improve their teaching suits on a regular basis	0.294	Weak	56
Teaching staff gave you useful feedback	0.293	Weak	53
Teaching staff maintain and Improve their subject knowledge on a regular basis	0.293	Weak	78

Figure 5.1 Value-for-money correlations

There is direct discursive linkage here between higher education courses, and the conviction that students go to university to enhance their economic position and future employment. Proximity between the mention of economic benefits and the reference to 'outcomes' leads to an assumption that 'outcomes' of HE are synonymous with graduate salaries and successful employment in internationally competitive industries. The use of 'return on investment' is new to discussions of university outcomes and is presented as being in the interests of both students and employers. However, trust in this claim is weakened when we reflect that it is only students who are required to pay the costs of higher education. Investment can be considered a polysemic term which is used variously to reference both economic capital and emotional/intellectual capital. Similarly, the referent for *value for money* shifts throughout SKE from contact hours to return on investment.

- What we expect though, is that excellent teaching, whatever its form, delivers excellent outcomes. There is of course more to university than financial gain, but the idea that excellent teaching occurs in a vacuum, independent of its impact on students' future life chances, is not one we can or should accept.

Whilst it is good to see an affirmation of other justifications of HE, we see once again a confirmation of the co-reference of outcomes with financial gain. Similarly, there is a naïve assumption that excellent teaching can be expected to lead to financial gain. Anyone can think of courses which may feature excellent teaching, and which are research-led courses of the highest quality, but which have little chance of high return on investment. Nursing is often suggested as one such course. It has high economic necessity, but economic outcomes are low in comparison to, for example, courses in business and finance. And there are many such courses offered at universities.

Outcomes, *competition* and *choice* are all discursively linked. This is demonstrated in this quote:

- We need to ensure that our higher education system continues to provide the best possible outcomes. These come from informed choice and competition.

There is no essential logical relationship to them, but the presuppositions that are encoded cement an ideological connection so that return on investment is assumed to arise from informed choice and competition, rather than, alternatively, cooperation between institutions. In a similar way, competition and quality are also discursively linked leading to presupposition that they are in a causal relationship (Davies 2016). It is significant that alternative routes to successful outcomes for degree students are never considered. Only tangentially is cooperation addressed in SKE – it is hoped that the TEF will incentivise students to transfer between universities during the course of their degree, further enhancing *competition* and *choice*.

Investment and *teaching quality* are linked discursively to justify the assertion of information about the latter translating into a guarantee of the former: 'The quality of teaching should be among the key drivers of a prospective student's investment' (SKE 2.8). In fact, a recent Institute for Fiscal Studies report (Britton *et al* 2016) shows that parental income is the best predictor for graduate earnings (the likely meaning of *investment* here). This reference to social class and entrenched advantage as a ladder for social mobility would not be preferred by the government. SKE prefers the prospective student to think that their choice, informed by TEF rankings, will map directly to their future income. But the evidence suggests otherwise.

Critical metaphor analysis

The metaphors which occur throughout the document fall mainly into the domains of sport, war, engineering (universities as machines), trade and commerce and nature (in terms of growth). These domains are the same as those occurring in the other document sets analysed throughout this book, suggesting that a fairly restricted set of metaphors are a key discursive means of constructing neoliberal discourses around higher education. Sport and war are, of course, competitive arenas in which there are always 'winners' and 'losers'. The use of such metaphors pits universities against each other and precludes the possibility of any mutual cooperation and collegiality in terms of their function and operation. Common sport metaphors in SKE include references to *track records*, *goals*, *setting a high bar*, *tackling*, *raising the game*, *gaming*, *champions* and *baselines* as in the following typical examples:

- Competition between providers in any market incentivises them to <u>raise their game</u>
- whether a provided has a long-established <u>track record</u>
- we consider that the <u>track record</u> requirement is necessary
- HEFCE has a very successful <u>track record</u> of collaborative working
- We will continue to <u>set a high bar</u> on quality
- for all providers that can meet our <u>high</u> quality <u>bar</u>
- This will ensure that we maintain a high and rigorous <u>bar</u> for entry into the system
- we expect significant progress on these two <u>goals</u>
- The Prime Minister has set two specific, clear <u>goals</u> for this area of higher education
- the Prime Minister's ambitions for higher education and other <u>goals</u> set out in the Green Paper
- The Government will set strategic <u>goals</u> and outcome measures
- The Teaching Excellence Framework (TEF) will build on that <u>baseline</u>
- provided they meet the <u>baseline</u> quality threshold
- will continue to be aligned with successfully achieving the <u>baseline</u> quality threshold

- compliance with consumer law will be fully integrated into the base-line requirements for quality assurance
- This will make an important contribution to tackling the long-term decline in part-time student numbers
- how providers are tackling grade inflation
- Rather than implementing crude metrics that could easily be gamed
- to prevent the TEF being gamed
- act as a champion for the UK's world class system
- It will be required to have diverse representation on the board to champion the student interest

A further common sport metaphor used is that of the level *playing field*:

- Stakeholders pointed to the importance of a level playing field across the sector
- Levelling the playing field through deregulation
- thereby creating a more level playing field
- where anyone who demonstrates they have the potential to offer excellent teaching and clears our high quality bar can compete on a level playing field
- to provide assurance for students and establish a level playing field

An underlying supposition which is conceptually related to the source domain of a 'level' playing field is that the arena in which the sporting competition takes place is equal and does not give an unfair advantage to one team or to certain competitors (i.e. no one is having to play uphill). Thus, the repeated use of this metaphor creates the illusion that all HEIs have an equal chance of scoring highly in the metrics which underlie the TEF and other regulatory mechanisms.

The militaristic war metaphors function in a similar way to the sport metaphors in that they discursively construct universities as aggressively competitive arenas in which there are victors and losers. We contend that the use of such war metaphors is insensitive, hostile and threatening. Typical examples include the following:

- detailed quality reviews will be triggered in a number of ways
- Equivalent reviews may be triggered in the areas of financial sustainability, management and governance, each triggered in a similar way to a quality review. Where a review visit has been triggered by a specific concern
- help build an intelligence base and act as an early warning mechanism to understand whether and how students are being protected
- Launching a call for evidence on flexible learning

- will continue to have a role in agreeing Access and Participation Agreements with providers but will not themselves set targets

When universities are not being discursively constructed as sporting arenas and battlegrounds, they are frequently being constituted as machines through the use of engineering metaphors. The concept of a university being a dehumanised mechanical system is reinforced through metaphors such as *controls*, *operating model*, *tools*, (performing) *functions*, *system*, *engine*, *fuel* and *driver* amongst others. Typical examples are included below:

- Among its range of compliance controls, student number controls will remain an important tool
- All providers will be able to choose their operating model
- to suit a wider range of provider operating models
- the regulation of higher education will be restructured, shifting from an outdated top-down model of a funding agency to a market regulator clearly focused on the student interest
- but will otherwise remain an important tool to ensure students
- in a format that is suitable for their development of information tools
- the external examining system is functioning properly
- how well that body is performing its functions
- This is a significant improvement on the current system
- So we will commit to the dual support system within England
- supportive of the Government's commitment to retaining the dual support system
- It will also help to deliver simplified systems and processes for funding recipients
- for our university system to fulfil its potential as an engine of social mobility, a driver of economic growth
- They generate the know-how and kills that fuel our growth
- with formula-based quality-related research funding
- better mechanisms for the sharing of expertise and best practice

The repeated construction of universities as mechanic rather than organic through this source domain encourages them to be conceptualised as controllable and predictable. Moreover, machines are controlled by *someone* – they are not self-controlling, interactive or adaptable to environments. Their capacities are limited by how they have been built and programmed. They are susceptible to malfunction and are in constant need of 'upgrading' (unlike organic systems which naturally adapt to changing environments). Interestingly, the TEF document does also contain a number of metaphors which reference natural phenomena in some way. Some co-occur with the machine metaphors whilst others tend to refer to the higher education *environment* (or *landscape*) more broadly whereas the machine metaphors are used more in relation to the operation of universities as individual entities competing against each other. Metaphorically, the HE 'sector' is referred to in terms of *growth* and as a *landscape* as in the following examples:

- They generate the know-how and kills that fuel our growth
- drive economic growth and be a catalyst for social mobility
- The growth in FE colleges and alternative providers
- includes nurturing high-growth potential SMEs
- The higher education landscape has changed fundamentally
- we will simplify the regulatory landscape
- We will put the interests of the student at the heart of our regulatory landscape
- to ensure that they remain truly representative of the changing landscape
- The regulatory and funding landscape is complex and inefficient
- Reforming the funding landscape to meet tomorrow's challenges
- improved quality of evidence on the UK's research and innovation landscape

The idea of a 'lifecycle' is also present, with *cycle* referring to regulatory practices and metric systems such as the REF and TEF, and *lifecycle* referring exclusively to 'disadvantaged students'.

- up by 4% from the previous cycle
- We expect to have established a regular cycle of publications
- continue to cover the whole lifecycle for disadvantaged students
- duty to cover equality of opportunity across the whole lifecycle for disadvantaged students

Other nature metaphors include *blue skies* and *bedrocks* although these do not occur frequently:

- described by Sir Paul Nurse, as 'one of the bedrocks of UK research'
- ensuring a strategic focus at the head of the organisation that spans blue skies research and business-led innovation
- to identify opportunities arising from blue skies research

Perhaps unsurprisingly, a final metaphorical field which is prevalent throughout the document is that of trade and commerce. Higher education is repeatedly referred to as a *market/marketplace* and universities and education as *products* and *assets* as in the following examples:

- has significantly changed the marketplace
- Our universities rank among our most valuable national assets

- to ensure students are protected if providers exit the market
- We want a globally competitive market
- these measures will stimulate institutional competition within the market
- But we have not yet made a decisive enough move to open the higher education market
- innovation infrastructure and supporting open competitive markets
- offering consumers a greater choice of more innovative and better quality products and services at lower cost
- resource for the delivery of vital higher education products including data for the Unistats website
- we will introduce an alternative student finance product for the first time

In the previous examples, *market* and similar terms co-occur with references to competition. *Products* are not just university courses – interestingly, higher education products now also include 'data' and 'student finance'. References to international recruitment have been replaced with the trade metaphor of *export*.

- higher education is a key export sector
- help contribute towards boosting education exports

As in many other HE-related documents explored throughout this book and elsewhere, students are metaphorically constructed as *consumers* within the HE marketplace, which further consolidates the illusion of choice, autonomy and consumer capital.

- requirements regarding students' rights as consumers
- strengthen the consumer interface of the research and innovation funding landscape

Other finance and commerce metaphors are signalled through lexical items such as *premium*, *procure*, *investments*, *market returns* and *value for money*:

- as demonstrated by the strong graduate premium
- the requirement to procure creates unhelpful uncertainty
- so it is crucial that they represent sound investments
- to have a better picture of the labour market returns likely to result from different institution and course choices
- we will increase quality, efficiency and value for money through better informed choices and competition

The newly established OfS is described in commercial terms as a *market regulator* with no reference to any other potential functions other than a monetary one.

- We will establish a single market regulator
- The OfS will be a consumer focused market regulator

Discussion

The analysis presented earlier reveals discursive themes in SKE of choice, competition, excellence and 'value for money'. These themes resonate with arguments about the purpose of a university, and they have gained energy since the turn of the millennium (Barnett 2015, 2016; Collini 2016; Evans 2004). Collini (2016) views their purpose as protection of disinterested enquiry and the transmission of a cultural and intellectual inheritance, and as institutions central to the defence of a democratic society. But as Rammell (2016) points out, it is the notion of public interest itself which is being contested. The view that has gained strength during an era of neoliberal reforms is that universities have a responsibility to create human capital to advance an internationally competitive economy, rather than them being to understand and protect the world. Charles (2017) argues that the origins of TEF lie in human capital theory (Becker 1964; Schultz 1972). Hall (2017) agrees, tracing the move from higher education as civic good, to economic justification:

> Moreover, where the funding for education has shifted from the State to the individual, student debt is related both to performance and to academic value. Or rather academic performance and outcomes that are recalibrated through their relation to future earnings and employability become a justification for debt. As a result, education is increasingly seen as a positional, economic good framed through human capital theory or total factor productivity, rather than as a service or a civic good.
>
> (Hall 2017: 186–187)

Citing Schultz, and Becker, Charles (2017: 4) defines human capital as:

> the useful skills and knowledge acquired through education and training should be conceptualized as a form of capital with economic value, in which we consciously invest in order to enhance our capacities to do productive work and, as a consequence, increase our future earnings.

From the conservative side, the purpose of universities is cast as supplying the engine of the nation's economic competitiveness. It was therefore inevitable that the government might seek to enhance the role of teaching, and particularly research-led teaching in order to develop the high-level skills it judged vital for international competitiveness. It is not incompatible with the values of teaching and research that many academics would espouse. It is ironic, however, that the obvious linkage of human capital theory and the view of many academics of higher education for the public good (Barnett 2015; Rammell 2016), is not a theme in SKE. Instead, the focus is squarely on individual return on investment, as if universities were somehow devoid of wider public purpose.

The UK government has appropriated a stance of defender of the student interest and has sought to position students as informed and rational consumers. As Davies (2016) writes of SKE, 'Its unthinking certainty that progress is found via "choice" and "competition" repeats the excesses of 20th century rationalist planning'. Their proposed vehicle is an invitation to new private providers, and the deployment of the TEF which apparently will enable student choice. The presupposition (false) is that data on quality of courses does not already exist, and that the proposed metrical assemblage will resonate with students. There is a contradiction between the government's posturing and the reality. Students are not just raw human capital, waiting to be developed in their own 'return on investment' interest. The corollary of the post-*Browne Review* financial pact (foreshadowed as far back as the Thatcher Government) is that money follows the student. In this model, students are also assets to be sweated (Davies 2016).

The government, though, would deny any explicit agenda of privatising, financialising or marketising higher education. As Hillman (2017) points out, there has been a strategic evolution of government choice of discourse which has moved from 'private providers' to 'alternative providers' to 'challenger institutions' to emphasise the focus on competition which is positioned as a benefit to students.

However, none of this has been able to obscure some inconvenient realities such as widespread concern about the apparent relaxing of regulations regarding the entry of new higher education providers, and the speedier progress towards degree-awarding powers that the white paper sets in place. Evans (2016) critiques the key assumptions that such 'competition' from private institutions would offer value for money (when several have been found to be committing fraud), create diversity in the sector (they offer a narrow range of courses), or offer better teaching (given their reliance on contingent staff and high staff-student ratios). There is also the possibility that such HEIs might offer courses such as complementary medicine, which would not always meet the criteria for academic rigour demanded by established universities.

There is no shortage of commentaries which distil the problems of a student as consumer model and higher education positioned as service industry (Collini 2016; Molesworth *et al* 2011; Nixon *et al* 2016). Possibly the most disquieting of these critiques is that it creates conservative learners (Nixon *et al* 2011) and that it reproduces a subjectivity of narcissism. Even in traditional universities, if student choice is the key driver of provision, then some counter-productive consequences are likely to emerge. In the UK, some chemistry departments (e.g. Kings College, closed 2003, reopened 2011, Swansea closed in 2004, reopened 2017; Exeter, closed in 2006) were closed, downsized or merged as student numbers declined.

The nature of university research and academic specialisation means that they will not always be able to respond to a consumerist desire, and world-class research will only be afforded by stability and predictability of income. As Marginson (2013) argues, when universities are positioned as competing in a quasi-market, this engenders an inauthentic narrative which creates unrealisable expectations about higher education. Collini (2016) would agree, pointing out that student satisfaction seems to favour low staff-student ratios, which have risen from 1:8 to more like 1:19 in the face of government cuts. It is simply not possible to provide 'personalisation' with this kind of workload. But in what Collini calls 'a neat trick', the interests of students have been aligned with those of taxpayers and the government. This deflects attention from the government which has increased student debt and instead shifts the responsibility to those who are blamed for 'lamentable teaching'.

SKE and plans for the TEF have emerged at a time when universities have occupied the media headlines, and often not with sympathetic treatment. The government and media seem to regard academics and universities (and, increasingly, other public services such as schools and the NHS) as being responsible for a whole host of social ills. Universities are apparently failing to produce employable graduates, and employers are unhappy with the skills and knowledge of graduates. Neither of these propositions is true according to the reports referred to earlier, but it has not impeded the flow of stories about lack of social inclusion, failure to widen participation, to tackle sexual harassment on campus, to protect free speech, address the gender pay gap, and lower attainment by BME students. Evidently, academics and the representatives of management – Universities UK – have failed to make the case for the success, and the necessity of strong, autonomous universities. Rammell (2016) has reinvigorated the case for the defence of the public interest in higher education, both in defining the notion more explicitly and in strengthening its oversight in policy making. He fears that the legislation emerging from SKE will result in weakening of universities as in the public interest unless it is amended. As we wrote, the progress of the Higher Education and Research Bill was making its way through the stages of parliamentary scrutiny. At one point, the Lords seemed inclined to add amendments which include a specification on the nature and purpose of a university, and opposition to any link between TEF ranking and fee rises. These amendments were rejected by the government (25 April 2017).

The TEF has been promoted by its adherents as strengthening the position of students. It does not – and the NUS has voted to disengage from TEF. Most university student union branches are aligning with this position because of the link with fee rises, but also in the light of evidence that shows that the student as consumer framework is damaging to educational experience (Bunce *et al* 2016; Molesworth *et al* 2009; Naidoo and Jamieson 2005). Students are aware that the TEF is the vehicle by which students are pitted against the staff who are trying to serve them.

If a case is to be made, and public opinion influenced, it is clear that critical voices within universities will need to challenge the discourse in order to challenge the ideological appropriation of the government. Jones *et al* (2016) ask whether universities could learn from the TEF's advocates how better to influence public discourses. The authors write that in an era where universities are awash with metrics, the new TEF is a hard sell, so in coordinating resistance, opponents need to learn lessons about framing the argument discursively. So, for example, on the value for money question, they concede that 'only 37% of undergraduates now report that their degree represents good value for money, down from 53% just four years ago'. However, they allude to two arguments against this framing. Firstly, it positions universities as narrowly commercial, so individual value for money as opposed to general public good, and secondly, large fee increases mean that university is bound to be seen as exploitatively expensive by students. This does not mean they are dissatisfied with their courses or teaching quality; in fact, the NSS indicates they are satisfied (HEFCE 2016).

Charles (2017) offers a more optimistic view, and declares that the very fact that the TEF is flawed and manifestly fails to measure teaching quality, offers its own possibilities for reimagination. Conceptualisations of university teaching may be re-worked in ways which are productive for both teacher and student, but which can sit outside of arguments originating with economic rationalities. Perhaps the best way forward is through a reconceptualisation of pedagogy. It is a view of research which is primarily animated by the practice of teaching the discipline. In a discussion of such teaching-led research, Charles (2017: 12) looks forward to all teachers and students becoming researchers so that 'the contours of a notion of teaching-based, teaching-informed and teaching-led research outlined here are intended to critically intervene within the educational discourse of teaching excellence and research-led teaching in order to reimagine the teaching-research nexus anew'.

It seems, though, that in higher education we are doomed to reject forward-thinking and progressive moves which embody the values of those who work in higher education. Knights (2013) documents the demise of subject centres in the UK, in which the 'fertile educational experiment' was supplanted by surveillance and the absurd proxy metrics of New Public Management. This prefigures the imagining of the TEF and debates about learning gain, as these are entirely consonant with a culture where 'reporting in detail at every stage on outcomes easily turns into a symbolic substitute for actual work in the field' (Knights 2013: 184).

There are indeed attendant risks of escalation of audit culture. Stoten (2013) and Mather and Seifert (2014) report on morale amongst further education lecturers in a context of NPM, and find that intrusive surveillance leads to deskilling, de-professionalisation and demoralisation inducing 'worker reactions including dull compliance, fear and resilience' (Mather and Seifert 2014: 108). Another paradox is identified by Morrish (2017) who points out that innovation in pedagogy is inadvertently deterred by attempts to surveil it.

If teaching has not yet been fully transformed from 1990s patterns, it is less because university staff are resistant to change, but more because students are conventional in their learning preferences. When staff appraisals and university league tables hinge on the results of the NSS, we are forced to pay attention to feedback that expresses a preference for 'a good set of notes' over more challenging exercises in group work and problem-solving. University managers may well make noises about disrupting student expectations of learning and teaching, but will hold individual lecturers responsible for any drop in satisfaction scores. The accountability demanded by the TEF will actually incentivise conservatism.

Nevertheless, what HE professionals are reporting (e.g. in blogs and social media) is a perception of university leadership which is entirely without connection to practitioners and their purpose. Knights makes clear that at its inception, the project of the subject centres was a worthy and valuable one which worked hard to gain the trust of academics. But this affinity between practitioner and subject centre rendered them the object of suspicion as the centres became absorbed into the Higher Education Academy. It was a relationship which mirrored the relationship of academic department to university management in many cases (Knights 2013). It is not lost on us that this suspicion of academics and the disciplines is manifest by government ministers, who now turn to the TEF to evidence their suspicions, and remedy the supposed deficits. What none of the legislation, or opposition to it, does is to make the case for diversity of provision in the sector, and certainly not for diversity of teaching methods. This remains unlikely when a kind of overarching template is envisioned by government, and acceded to by sector leaders who, after 30 years of placatory acquiescence, have lost their sense of direction and autonomy. Presently, autonomy and innovation led by professional judgement and collaboration, seem lost to us, but as the early subject centres prove, it could still be resurrected, with the trust of academics if imbued with academic credibility.

The case for an agreeable regulation of universities and teaching quality is still being made in Parliament, but is the government listening?

Notes

1. Throughout this chapter, we refer to the white paper as 'SKE' for the purpose of brevity.
2. www.gov.uk/government/speeches/higher-education-fulfilling-our-potential

3. www.timeshighereducation.com/features/the-teaching-survey-2017-results-and-analysis
4. Comment posted to blog: https://academicirregularities.wordpress.com/2016/07/21/tef-times-2nd-reading-of-the-he-bill/]. In an atmosphere where anecdote is deemed sufficient to drive policy-making http://cdbu.org.uk/governments-letter-to-the-lords-re-tef-a-reply/
5. https://press.which.co.uk/whichpressreleases/higher-education-needs-to-deliver-value-for-money/
6. www.hepi.ac.uk/wp-content/uploads/2016/06/Student-Academic-Experience-Survey-2016.pdf

References

Bagshaw, A. and Morris, D. 2016. Fun with flags: How metrics will work in TEF outcomes. *Wonkhe*. http://wonkhe.com/blogs/policy-watch-fun-with-flags-the-role-of-metrics-in-tef-outcomes/ (Accessed 23 April 2017).

Ball, S. 2003. The teacher's soul and the terrors of performativity. *Journal of Education Policy* 18 (2): 215–228.

Barnett, R. 2015. In search of a public: Higher education in a global age. In O. Filippakou and G. Williams, eds. *Higher Education as a Public Good: Critical Perspectives on Theory, Policy and Practice*. Oxford: Peter Lang.14–27.

Barnett, R. 2016. *Understanding the University*. London: Routledge.

Becker, G. 1964. *Human Capital: A Theoretical and Empirical Analysis with Special Reference to Education*. Chicago, IL: University of Chicago Press.

Belfield, C. and Britton, J. 2018. Using graduate earnings to assess universities. *Institute for Fiscal Studies*. 11 June. www.ifs.org.uk/publications/13059

Bishop, D. 2016. Cost-benefit analysis of the teaching excellence framework. http://deevybee.blogspot.co.uk/2016/07/cost-benefit-analysis-of-teaching.html (Accessed 23 April 2017).

Britton, J., Dearden, L., Shephard, N. and Vignoles, A. 2016. What and where you study matter for graduate earnings – but so does parents' income. *Institute for Fiscal Studies*. www.ifs.org.uk/publications/8235 (Accessed 23 April 2017).

Bunce, L., Baird, A. and Jones, S. 2016. The student-as-consumer approach in higher education and its effects on academic performance. *Studies in Higher Education* 42 (11): 1958–1978.

Charles, M. 2017. Teaching, in spite of excellence: Recovering a practice of teaching-led research. *Studies in Philosophy and Education*: 1–15.

Collini, S. 2016. Who are the spongers now? *London Review of Books* 38 (2): 33–37. www.lrb.co.uk/v38/n02/stefan-collini/who-are-the-spongers-now

Davies, W. 2016. The higher education white paper: Euphemisms for destruction. *The Sociological Review*. www.thesociologicalreview.com/blog/the-higher-education-white-paper-euphemisms-for-destruction.html?utm_content=buffered9ffandutm_medium=socialandutm_source=twitter.comandutm_campaign=buffer (Accessed 17 July 2016).

Evans, G.R. 2016. Alternative providers of higher education: What are the risks? *Higher Education Review* 49 (1): 5–25.

Evans, M. 2004. *Killing Thinking: The Death of the Universities*. London: Continuum.

Hall, R. 2017. Performance information and data-driven academic anxiety. In L. da Silva Rosado and G. dos Santos Ferreira, eds. *Education and Technology: Critical Approaches*. Rio de Janeiro: University Estácio de Sá Press. 185–205.
HEFCE. 2016. National Student Survey. https://webarchive.nationalarchives.gov.uk/20160702155722/http://www.hefce.ac.uk/lt/nss/ (Accessed 18th July 2019)
Hillman, N. 2017. Why we must protect the university autonomy. Speech to the inaugural G20 meeting at the University of Buckingham. www.hepi.ac.uk/2017/04/03/4014/ (Accessed 23 April 2017).
Holmwood, J., Hickey, T., Cohen, R. and Wallis, S. 2016. The alternative white paper for higher education: In defence of public higher education – Knowledge for a successful society: A response to 'success as a knowledge economy'. https://heconvention2.files.wordpress.com/2016/06/awp1.pdf (Accessed 23 April 2017).
Johnson, J. 2016. Dyson university is a wake-up call for higher education. *The Times*, November 4. www.thetimes.co.uk/article/dyson-university-is-a-wake-up-call-for-higher-education-gjgnz5gls (Accessed 28 September 2018).
Jones, S., Courtney, S. and McGinity, R. 2016. Could universities learn from the TEF's advocates how better to influence public discourses? www.thesociologicalreview.com/blog/could-universities-learn-from-the-tef-s-advocates-how-better-to-influence-public-discourses.html (Accessed 23 April 2017).
Knights, B. 2013. The politics of enhancement: The last days of the English subject centre. In D. Philips and K. Shaw, eds. *The Politics of Literature and the Literature of Politics*. Basingstoke: Palgrave Macmillan. 181–193.
Marginson, S. 2013. The impossibility of capitalist markets in higher education. *Journal of Education Policy* 28 (3): 353–370.
Mather, K. and Seifert, R. 2014. The close supervision of further education lecturers: 'You have been weighed, measured and found wanting'. *Work, Employment and Society* 2 (1): 95–111.
Molesworth, M., Nixon, E. and Scullion, R. 2009. Having, being and higher education: The marketisation of the university and the transformation of the student into consumer. *Teaching in Higher Education* 14 (3): 277–287.
Molesworth M., Nixon, E. and Scullion, R. eds. 2011. *The Marketisation of UK Higher Education and the Student as Consumer*. London: Routledge.
Moore, S., Neylon, C., Eve, M. P., O'Donnell, D. P. and Pattinson, D. 2017. 'Excellence R Us': University research and the fetishisation of excellence. *Palgrave Communications* 3: 161–165.
Morris, D. 2017. http://wonkhe.com/blogs/here-to-stay-the-politics-behind-tef-wonkery/ (Accessed 23 April 2017).
Morrish, L. 2017. The wonkers and the wonked. https://academicirregularities.wordpress.com/2017/02/27/the-wonkers-and-the-wonked/. (Accessed 23 April 2017).
Naidoo, R. and Jamieson, I. 2005. Empowering participants or corroding learning? Towards a research agenda on the impact of student consumerism in higher education. *Journal of Education Policy* 20 (3): 267–281.
Neves, J. and Hillman, N. 2016. *The 2016 Student Academic Experience Survey*. HEPI/HEA report. www.hepi.ac.uk/wp-content/uploads/2016/06/Student-Academic-Experience-Survey-2016.pdf (Accessed 24 April 2017).
Nixon, E., Scullion, R. and Hearn, R. 2016. Her majesty the student: Marketised higher education and the narcissistic (dis)satisfactions of the student consumer. *Studies in Higher Education*: 1–21.

Nixon, E., Scullion, R. and Molesworth, M. eds. 2011. How choice in higher education can create conservative learners. In M. Molesworth, E. Nixon and R. Scullion, eds. *The Marketisation of UK Higher Education and the Student as Consumer*. London: Routledge. 196–208.

Peck, E. 2015. Finding new ways to measure graduate success. *Wonkhe*. http://wonkhe.com/blogs/finding-new-ways-to-measure-graduate-success/ (Accessed 21 April 2017).

Rammell, B. 2016. Protecting the public interest in higher education. *HEPI Occasional Papers* 15.

Schultz, T. 1972. Human capital: Policy issues and research opportunities. In T. Schultz, ed. *Economic Research: Retrospect and Prospect. Volume 6: Human Resources*. Cambridge, MA: National Bureau of Economic Research.

Stoten, D. 2013. Professionalism, identity and the self: The de-moralisation of teachers in English sixth form colleges. *Research in Post-Compulsory Education* 18 (4): 365–376.

Woodstock, J. and Toscano, A. 2016. On the poverty of student choice. *The Sociological Review*, 19 July. www.thesociologicalreview.com/blog/on-the-poverty-of-student-choice.html (Accessed 28 September 2018).

6 Colonising the corporate academic

Context

Are universities businesses? In many universities, if you ask the vice-chancellor and the 'senior management team' of pro vice-chancellors, you will find that *business* is their preferred designation for the institution, with *university* acknowledged only on ceremonial occasions. This is particularly true, paradoxically, of those universities in the UK which fought so hard to obtain university status in 1992. Outside of a small group of managers, however, you are likely to meet great hostility to the proposition. Indeed, aligning oneself with the idea of universities as businesses is almost diagnostic of managerial aspirations.

Whereas once the university was conceived of as a refuge from market values in its tolerance of venture and failure, they now largely reward entrepreneurial, self-governing and competitive subjects, who are happy to function within the limits and discourse set for them by the managerial project. As we have moved forward in this vein, the idea of universities as places where scholars may take intellectual risk has largely been lost. Instead, we must reproduce nothing but success and certainty, with consequent 'impact'. We must be personally responsible for making the right choices to ensure our advancement within a framework of academic Darwinism.

This state of affairs is consistent with the analysis of academic capitalism, defined by Slaughter and Leslie (1997) as the imposition of markets and market-like behaviours on universities. Morrissey (2013) astutely observes that the language by which academics are brought within the control of the managerial regime echoes the language of the economic crisis. As Chapters 2 and 3 have shown, both students and the university's 'products' have been monetised and commercialised.

In managerially dominated universities we observe a culture of the 'corporate boast', with markets and competition espoused as priorities, and this is staged via the university mission statement (discussed in Chapter 3). In universities, the conflict between managerial and academic values is primarily a struggle over discourse and the symbolic. It works by forcing the academic to cite discourse which redefines their subjectivity in terms of managerial values (Davies 2003; Davies and Bendix Petersen

2005). In supporting this assumption, we invoke the Foucauldian notion of 'governmentality'. The relevance for neoliberal universities in the 21st century will be apparent to those who labour within them. As Foucault (2008: 323), has argued, the scope of neoliberalism has now extended into domains which are not primarily economic. Higher education is one such domain. The project of neoliberal governmentality is for universities to engender a new kind of subject formation – one which embodies and responds to the increased corporatisation of universities. (Morrissey 2013). Davies and Bendix Petersen (2005: 79) write that neoliberalism works on our subjectivities 'taking us over with or without our consent'. The new subject formation is imposed as managers achieve a destabilisation of established academic practices, and a superseding of existing values of cooperation, collective governance and democracy. Indeed, control over academics is the symbolic capital over which other areas of the university vie to exert dominion: estates, human resources, 'quality', professional development – even car parking.

As an example, one popular managerial tactic has been to impose open-plan offices on academics. The case is usually made by appeal to the unproven but ideologically rooted notions of greater productivity and 'sustainability' (Baldry and Barnes 2012). This justification is weakened, however, as most senior staff who advocate the policy retain private office space. All the while, the fiction is maintained that 'space is allocated to task, not to a person or to status' (University Estates website). In reality, the imposition has more to do with a manipulation of the symbolic resources of institutional space. The academic's desire for some control and personalisation of the space is subordinated to the facilities manager's quest for high utilisation. The result is the demoralisation of the academic workforce, a collapse of collegiality and impaired performance (Smith-Jackson and Klein 2009).

This scenario is likely to resonate with many academics. As researchers in this area, we have given talks, seminars and keynote lectures at various universities on the language of managerialism, and we have been struck at the lack of dissent towards our approach from audiences. Nor is this critique solely the provenance of humanities and social sciences; physicists, geneticists, psychologists, chemists are all represented on blogs and Twitter feeds which articulate and document resistance to managerialism. We have had little in the way of academic oppositional interrogation, and we look forward to generating more debate by publishing this book.

In 2014, Marina Warner left her university after ten years as a professor of creative writing in the department of literature, film and theatre studies. She wrote a strongly worded piece for the *London Review of Books*, entitled *Why I Quit*, which detailed the micro-management, the accumulating duties, unattainable targets and shifting criteria for satisfactory performance and promotion. Warner had had enough. The piece went viral on Twitter, and some months later, she was moved to respond:

> The correspondence reveals a deeper and more bitter scene in higher education than I had ever imagined. I had been naive, culpably unobservant as I went about my activities at [University name]. Students, lecturers, professors from one institution after another were howling in sympathy and rage; not one of them dissented or tried to justify the situation. I had thought that [University name] was a monstrous manifestation, but it turns out that its rulers' ideas are 'the new normal', as the Chinese government calls its present economic plan.
>
> (Warner 2015)

If Warner thought her experience was an isolated one, we are able to draw on a vast amount of testimony, and support with textual evidence that it is not. The discourse and practices of neoliberalism are well sedimented into the academy, and the purpose is to colonise a new kind of entrepreneurial, corporate academic. As we argued in the introduction to this volume, we view discourse as not merely something which is found in texts and contexts; it also structures those contexts and constrains behaviours and identities within them. We endorsed the view presented by Sealey (2014) that it is *discourse* which is central to the project of redefining of subjectivities. Certainly, it would appear from the amount of writing on the subject in the social media of academe, managerial discourse is the chief irritant. A key strategy has been an attempt to shift the discourse towards the new language of managerialism, marketisation and corporatisation. The way it circulates and imposes its discipline is to disguise itself as a necessary virtue which guarantees legitimacy in the outside world, and thereby, institutional survival (Davies and Bendix Petersen 2005: 78). The interplay between structure, culture, agency and semantics means that new formations of academic labour are relational. So, for example, when students are customers, the subjectivity of academics is shifted – they become service providers. And when students are products, academics are producers, or factory line workers, whose purpose is to uniformly mould students according to government specifications. In this way, academic identities are reconstituted within the discursive paradigms and value systems of their managers.

As administrators have mastered these discourses, they demand to be spoken to in their own language by academics who are required to justify their working practices on a frequent basis. As we have discussed in Chapter 4, in the last few decades since the 1990s, managers have imposed on academics an increasing number of methods of calibrating academic performance. These have ceased to have any institutional relevance, and indeed are costly and time-consuming to administer. Their function is entirely ideological, but the university is held in thrall to their delivery, with new processes of control justified with reference to international rankings, league tables and 'competitiveness' (Morrissey 2013: 800). The fact that they are sustained without effective opposition may be due to a characteristic of neoliberal discourse in that it disguises its own negative impact and so forestalls resistance (Davies and Bendix Petersen 2005: 85). As long as we are made to feel anxious about meeting our Performance Development and Contribution Review objectives, any critique is thwarted.

Another facet of managerial discourse is the relentless exclusion of the negative. Nothing may rain on the parade of formidables. Butler and Spoelstra (2014) comment on the regime of excellence which has taken hold as the organising principle of the contemporary university. Indeed, as Butler and Spoelstra argue, excellence is more often assumed to be reflected in externally located indicators such as citation indices and journal rankings, rather than the intrinsic value or rigour of research. The science critics of this discourse add insights from their evidence-driven disciplines (see the blogs of David Colquohoun, Philip Moriarty, Ben Goldacre amongst others). How can one do science when one is judged only by positive results and by 'impact'? After all, that is why they are called experiments, and by their very nature, outcome and potential impact remain unknown at the time of execution. The scientist who is deterred from risk to save their career, ironically, sacrifices their science. They become, as Colquhoun (2007) says, spiv scientists. *Excellence*, however, is a leitmotif of the neoliberal academy, and is one of the SDS we analyse next as well as in the preceding case studies in this book.

Case study 8: staff training documents

In this case study, we present a discursive analysis of data taken from a set of managerial training courses at X University. The aim is to explore and exemplify how neoliberal governmentality works within universities to effect the reconstitution of subjectivities as 'corporatised'. Such training courses, and the materials and documents used within them circulate widely in most university environments.

Before presenting the analysis, it is important to discuss some issues about the context from which these documents were located. Deem and Brehony (2005: 227) examine the process of 'learning to do new managerialism'. They cite an ESRC study conducted in 1998–2000, which found that many managers at the time had no management training. This is now changing with the arrival of the Leadership Foundation for Higher Education, which provides guidance and consultancy on management training for UK (and Swedish and Kazakh) universities. The management training courses at X University are located within that framework, and emerged at a particular historical moment around 2010–14. Our assumption is that these courses reflect the priority of the management team of a typical post-1992 university at that time.

All of these courses were delivered by the university's own Centre for Professional Learning and Development and were attended by one of the authors in the period 2010–14.

'Leading High Performance Teams' was designed to support employees across the university who had line management responsibilities. The course was detailed and drew on theories of management: teams, change, strategy, leadership, values. It was taught in three modules, consisting of two full days of activities, led by a facilitator. The associated learning packs, slides and documents provide the data. The discourse analysis also draws on the author's contemporaneous notes.

'Change Management' was a companion module to 'Leading High Performance Teams', and the associated training pack provided the data. This module was aimed at senior university staff who were deemed to be in a position to implement change.

The 'Succession Planning' data set was collected in 2012 and the course was aimed at senior staff in one university who might be 'fast-tracked' towards 'leadership roles'. The initiative was supported by the Leadership Foundation for Higher Education and other groups such as the Efficiency Exchange, a partner of Universities UK, JISC and HEFCE. A justification for succession planning appears on the Efficiency Exchange website:

> There are certain themes that have framed discussion and action around pay and reward in the higher education sector over the past five years or so. One of these is rising staff costs in a context of public funding restraint and another, the move to a competitive student funding system that has called for more entrepreneurial and market-responsive behaviours. In this context, the intensely competitive global environment for HE means that attracting and retaining top talent poses a critical challenge for institutions throughout the sector.
> (www.efficiencyexchange.ac.uk/6245/hes-got-talent-managing-the-sectors-workforce/#)

This short paragraph exposes the corporate ideology behind the discourse. Aside from what appear to be a series of non-sequiturs, there is clear linkage between 'talent' and 'entrepreneurial and market-responsive behaviours', and if these desirable behaviours can be moulded, it is appropriate that enhanced pay and reward follow. And so the academic is inducted into another simulacrum of business – there is a new managerial officer class within universities, and most academics will be excluded.

'PDCR' is X University's appraisal system. Annually, each employee is required to meet with their line manager to review the employee's self-assessment of their objectives, competencies and development needs. This data set is comprised of the university's PDCR policy and procedure documents, together with the 'competency framework'. The rationale of

PDCR is to make sure that all X University's employees' objectives are in alignment with the strategic plan. One of the possible outcomes of the meeting is that the employee may be recommended for a performance related pay award. It lies in tandem with the university's performance management process, which ostensibly is designed to diagnose under-performance. Most recently, though, professors at X University have been asked to submit to PDCR at six-month intervals. These are what Morrissey (2013: 806) has called anticipatory performance management practices which look less like the monitoring of under-performance than an insistence on constant improvement, reminiscent of Japanese 'kaizen' of the 1980s.[1]

'Gold Standard Customer Service' is an in-house training aimed at all university staff who are 'customer-facing'. The course offers a credential benchmarked to the OCR Level 2 Certificate in Customer Service and linked to the university's competency framework. It covers communicating effectively with customers, using customer service language and following the rules to customer service. The initial taught session was complemented by three online modules. The qualification was gained by submitting two short assignments.

A brief summary of the documents comprising the data set for this chapter is included in Table 6.1.

Corpus analysis

In the keyword analysis, it was helpful to conduct an analysis of all of the documents taken as a whole set, as well as separate analyses of keywords for each document sub-set. This facilitated the identification of prominent discourses in each document set as well as across the whole corpus. For all of the lists, the top 50 keywords are included (with the exception of the 'Gold Standard Customer Service' sub-set, which was too small to yield 50 words). Table 6.2 shows the keywords for the entire corpus of training course documents.

Table 6.2 shows that *change*, *team* and *PDCR* are key across the corpus. This suggests that there is a preoccupation with change, teamwork and reviewing staff 'performance' in the documents. As expected, these words appear as key in the sub-corpora (shown in Tables 6.3–6.7). The list also suggests a necessity of constantly keeping staff members 'under review'. This is signalled through the relatively high keyness of words such as *performance*, *review*, *feedback*, *objectives* and *competencies*.

Words which might explicitly identify the context as a university one (or as anything related to education and learning) appear only occasionally – *university* appears as the 27th keyword in the 'PDCR' sub-corpora. *Attainment* appears as the 34th keyword in this same sub-corpora. *Academic* only occurs in the 'Succession planning' sub-corpora and appears fairly low down (28th) in the list. Whilst *learning* does appear in a number

Table 6.1 Description of training documents data

Title of training course from which documents are taken	*Individual documents within set*	*Overview of content, audience and purpose of document set*
Change management	Overview document 'Six Change Models' information pack Introductory emails from vice-chancellor	A companion module to 'Leading High Performance Teams'. Introduces theories of institutional change.
Gold standard customer service	Module assignment instructions and tutor feedback x 3 Reflection activity	A training program aimed at all employees in the university. Introduces ideas about customer service and how to improve it.
Leading high performing teams (LHPT)	LHPT PowerPoint presentation 'Leadership and Management in Higher Education' information pack 'Team Development and coaching for Performance in Higher Education' information pack 'Change Management in Higher Education' information pack 'Culture Web' handout SEDA delegate handbook	A six-day training program, delivered in 3 x 2 day modules. Designed to support employees who are in middle management positions, e.g. team leaders, deans. Introduces theories of teams, leadership, change and coaching.
PDCR	Reflective diary handout 'Guidance for Line Managers and Participants' handout University's competency framework handout 'PDCR Staff Guidelines' information pack 'PDCR Policy and Procedure' information pack 'PDCR for Managers' PowerPoint presentation	Annual contractual performance review for all staff. Individual meetings with the line manager, based around employee's own assessment of objectives, competencies and development needs. These flow from the university's strategic plan, and the process is formalised by in policy and procedure document.

Title of training course from which documents are taken	*Individual documents within set*	*Overview of content, audience and purpose of document set*
Succession planning	Introductory emails Introduction handout 'Succession Planning' participant briefing pack 'Succession Planning' PowerPoint presentation	Training aimed at senior staff to identify their suitability for management roles at the dean and academic team leader levels. Assessment pack, includes psychometric testing and other assessment 'tools'.

Table 6.2 Keywords – training documents (whole corpus)

1. PDCR	2. team	3. change	4. [University name]	5. feedback
6. performance	7. coaching	8. objectives	9. competencies	10. reviewer
11. competency	12. process	13. review	14. learning	15. leadership
16. organisation	17. role	18. organisational	19. staff	20. development
21. contribution	22. manager	23. vision	24. key	25. succession
26. effective	27. reviewee	28. assessor	29. individual	30. personal
31. meeting	32. behaviours	33. behaviour	34. assessment	35. SEDA
36. roles	37. focus	38. appropriate	39. leader	40. teams
41. self	42. leaders	43. skills	44. management	45. outcomes
46. planning	47. work	48. exceptional	49. needs	50. job

Table 6.3 Keywords – 'change management' sub-set

1. change	2. Kotter	3. [University name]	4. denial	5. vision
6. tool	7. room	8. management	9. people	10. embed
11. stage	12. model	13. process	14. key	15. McKinsey
16. systems	17. processes	18. Lewin	19. need	20. support
21. dungeon	22. identify	23. projects	24. ensure	25. denigration
26. revitalisation	27. organisational	28. leadership	29. create	30. move
31. empower	32. staff	33. becomes	34. benefits	35. state
36. organisation	37. reinforce	38. models	39. renewal	40. project
41. sense	42. tools	43. feedback	44. resistance	45. communicate
46. leaders	47. wins	48. chaos	49. progress	50. initiatives

Table 6.4 Keywords – 'gold standard customer service' sub-set

1. [University name]	2. customer	3. service	4. course	5. session
6. gold	7. induction			

of the lists, closer inspection that *learning* usually refers to the learning of staff in organised training sessions (such as those in which the documents were used) rather than to the learning of students. In fact, *students* does not appear in any of the keyword lists. Other words which may signify meanings to do with education and learning are also entirely absent from all of the lists (e.g. *classes*, *teaching*, *knowledge*, *subject*) which, again, suggests that the content of the documents has more relevance to non-educational contexts and has not been adapted to the university environment. Instead, there is a proliferation of more vacuous terms such as *organisation* (rather than *university*) and staff (rather than *lecturers*, *administrators* and so on). In this way, we can start to see how the academic university context has arguably been 'colonised' by language and practices from other environments which may not be entirely suited to the purposes and practices of higher education.

Several of the keywords are suggestive of hierarchical structures. This is shown through the relatively high keyness of words which indicate status or position within a hierarchy such as *manager*, *assessor*, *reviewer*, *reviewee* and *leader*. Words which may indicate a less hierarchical organisation such as *peers*, *colleagues* and *mentors* do not appear in any of the lists. Keywords such as *process/es*, *systems* and *planning* also suggest a prioritising of practices which are linear, pre-planned, tightly controlled (by those in senior positions) and top-down rather than allowing the possibility of universities to be more organic, responsive and democratic.

The top-50 keywords across the whole corpus also reflect some of the main metaphorical uses of language which appear in the documents which are discussed later in this chapter. These include metaphors of sport (reflected in frequent and keywords such as *team*, *performance* and *coaching*) and tools/toolkit (*tool*).

Many of these observations about the keywords for the whole corpus also apply to each of the sub-corpora. Primarily for information, the keyword lists for each of the sub-corpora comprising the whole corpus are shown in Tables 6.3 to 6.7. Firstly, Table 6.3 shows the keywords for the 'Change Management' sub-set. As well as sharing similarities with the findings for the whole corpus, it is also noted that the keywords contain a preponderance of negative words to describe human emotion associated with change (*denial*, *denigration*, *resistance*) and some metaphors with negative connotations such as *dungeon*. Although there are positive words in the lists (*revitalisation*, *benefits*, *renewal*), these mostly occur lower down the order of keyness.

Table 6.4 contains keywords for the 'Gold Standard Customer Service' sub-corpora. This is a small sub-corpora, which means that only seven keywords are available. Therefore, the conclusions that can be drawn from this are limited. But the words suggest a retail-focussed environment, rather than an academic one. They also contribute to constructing customer service as something that is measured through the actions of

Table 6.5 Keywords – 'LHPT' sub-set

1. team	2. change	3. coaching	4. performance	5. feedback
6. leadership	7. [University name]	8. organisation	9. learning	10. competency
11. competencies	12. organisational	13. vision	14. behaviour	15. effective
16. SEDA	17. behaviours	18. leader	19. leaders	20. focus
21. development	22. individual	23. teams	24. appropriate	25. objectives
26. personal	27. style	28. skills	29. process	30. Belbin
31. self	32. values	33. learn	34. task	35. work
36. staff	37. goals	38. people	39. management	40. teamwork
41. outcomes	42. subordinates	43. reinforcement	44. action	45. key
46. needs	47. job	48. ideas	49. performing	50. role

Table 6.6 Keywords – 'PDCR' sub-set

1. PDCR	2. reviewer	3. objectives	4. contribution	5. review
6. meeting	7. competencies	8. reviewee	9. staff	10. performance
11. exceptional	12. role	13. development	14. feedback	15. manager
16. form	17. accelerated	18. competency	19. progression	20. [University name]
21. reviewees	22. achievement	23. procedure	24. personal	25. agreed
26. HR	27. university	28. learning	29. member	30. process
31. relevant	32. completed	33. following	34. attainment	35. recommendation
36. period	37. grades	38. evidence	39. application	40. plan
41. line	42. award	43. objective	44. required	45. job
46. website	47. CPLD	48. evidenced	49. employee	50. appropriate

Table 6.7 Keywords – 'succession planning' sub-set

1. [University name]	2. succession	3. process	4. assessor	5. assessment
6. feedback	7. planning	8. portal	9. SHL	10. role
11. key	12. criteria	13. roles	14. organisational	15. assessed
16. dean	17. line	18. talent	19. manager	20. phase
21. clarification	22. email	23. complete	24. stage	25. forum
26. start	27. completing	28. academic	29. potential	30. ATL
31. questionnaire	32. completion	33. pool	34. interview	35. individuals
36. mins	37. facilitated	38. associate	39. diagram	40. development
41. meeting	42. creation	43. self	44. raters	45. password
46. insight	47. capability	48. evidence	49. team	50. focussed

staff rather than through the achievements of students (e.g. *session* and *course* refer to those taken by staff, not students).

Several of the keywords (shown in Table 6.5) in the LHPT sub-corpora suggest meanings around sport and competition (e.g. *performance*, *coaching*, *goals*). As stated earlier, this is one of the key metaphors which is used in a sustained way throughout this sub-corpora and the corpus as a whole (and in other documents analysed throughout this book).

The keywords for the PDCR and Succession Planning data sets (Tables 6.6 and 6.7) reflect the findings from the whole corpus in that words such as *performance*, *award*, *reviewer*, *reviewee* and *manager* are suggestive of a discourse which prioritises hierarchy and competition.

Despite many of the documents being focussed on staff 'performance', the Succession Planning sub-set is the only one in which *talent* appears in the keyword lists (occurring at position 18). This means that 'talent' is notably absent from the other document sets and implies that it is something that is only recognised and valued in individuals which are being primed for promotion into managerial (rather than academic) positions within the university. This will be explored more in later sections in this chapter.

SDS analysis

Due to space constraints, we restricted the SDS analysis to what we considered to be one key SDS per data sub-set. In this part of the analysis, we consider how each SDS is conceptualised within the documents. We consider whether particular meanings of the SDS seem to be prioritised and whether they contain particular presuppositions. In the case of each data sub-set, we selected words which appeared in the keyword list for the relevant sub-set as well as basing our selection on words which seemed to function as strategically deployable within the documents. These presuppositions accrue significance and meaning as they are deployed within a particular institutional and political context.

'Change'

Analysis of the way that *change* behaves semantically in the documents reveals a number of underlying presuppositions. Firstly, the constant references to *change management* presuppose that change is something that must be managed and cannot simply be allowed to occur organically or naturally. This helps to create a discourse of change as something which must be 'controlled' by those in powerful positions within an institution (referred to in the documents as *change leaders*, *change masters* and *change agents*).

- The role of change <u>agents</u>.
- Mid-course work: the Change <u>Master</u> questionnaire.
- How do you rate yourself as a Change <u>Master</u> against the statements listed below?
- Change <u>Master</u> competency indicators.

Several of the uses of *change* presuppose that there will be resistance and 'barriers' to change and that change is something that will not be wanted by staff working in HEIs. This clearly is not the case. Academic staff are often the initiators of change (particularly in their subject areas). But this meaning of *change* is notably absent from the documents leaving a clear presupposition that change is 'top down' and can only be initiated and directed by those in the most powerful positions within an institution. A discourse is created that any change that is desired by those in less powerful positions must be suppressed and controlled by those higher up.

Parker (2014) documents a convincing case study of such a model, describing change management at its most strident as:

> a project which attempts to ensure that all parts of an organization 'share' values. Or, to put it a different way, to ensure that there is no disagreement with the corporate line, and that academics and students know their places and their 'best interests' [. . .]. Apparent resistance to change was often characterised as a problem of communication, and unhappiness discounted as 'inevitable in times of rapid change' (2014: 283–285).

This is confirmed in our data, as change is presented as a problem of making sure the management view prevails. In the following examples, the grammatical form of the sentence is imperative. This does two things: it indicates an addressee, presumably a manager, and it functions as a command, thereby erasing the possibility of discussion and negotiation.

- Develop a sense of urgency around the need for change. This may help you spark the initial motivation to get things moving.
- Convince people that change is necessary.
- Understand and address people's doubts and concerns about the change.

Words such as *risks*, *barriers* and *obstacles* co-occur several times in relation to *change*.

- Identify factors that act as barriers to the change and minimise or remove them.
- Recognise barriers to change and their impact on staff.
- Create strategies for overcoming resistance to change.

Examples such as these function to semantically construct *change* as perceived negatively by employees. In conjunction with the idea that change is something that has to be managed (including using *toolkits* from *consultancies and specialist organisations*), change is presented as something which will inevitably be complicated and difficult, but paradoxically, there is a presupposition that change is inevitably a good thing. It is strategically deployed in this way so that it appears that change *must* be managed by an elite team of *leaders* or *specialists*. This takes the ownership and initiative for change away from academic staff and moves it to managers who are then empowered with directing the change; it also legitimises the overriding of staff wishes. By analysing these meanings of change in the document, it becomes clear that 'managing change' is really about giving power to certain individuals who can then 'manage people'. In the documents on 'Change Management' and 'Leading High Performance Teams', for example, potential staff responses to change are only referred to in terms of negative emotions such as *denial*, *anxiety*, *resentment* and *apathy* ahead of the possibility of there being any positive response.

- Denial is often accompanied by an increase in energy level once the initial shock has subsided. For some people this will manifest itself in strong denial behaviours e.g. being very vocal about why the change is unnecessary/unfair etc.
- Managing stress induced by change.
- These phases can be described as Denial, Anxiety or Resentment, Apathy, Exploring Opportunities and Welcoming the Future. Staff may need to pass through each phase before they are able to accept the change and its consequences.
- Some people find the change process threatening. It can impact not just on their job, but also their family life. Because of this they could experience depression, frustration, or anxiety.

In Janssen's model of change which is included in the 'Six Change Models' document, it is presumed that all change will always be followed by complacency, denial, denigration, confusion, chaos and paralysis before it can be accepted. This psychological model presupposes that the responsibility for responding to change always lies within the individual so 'managing change' is all about managing people's emotions whilst superseding their wishes. Psychological models of change and responses to change predominate in all of the documents (especially models based in cognitive psychology). No alternative paradigms are presented such as social or political models of change. The word *negotiate* does not feature amongst the keywords in the data set. We notice as well, there is much overlap between the messages about change which are conveyed in the 'Change Management' and 'Leading High Performance Teams' documents, suggesting that the concept of change management is ideationally linked to team leadership.

In this model, all change is seen as revolutionary and self-evidently a good thing, often presented as 'shaking things up'. However, change is decontextualised from any previous history. Parker comments on the strange process of legitimation:

> [I]t was necessary to ensure that the past was not available as a valid position from which to criticize the present. In other words, the past needs to be articulated as a problem, as something that needs to be escaped from.
>
> (2014: 287)

Resistance from those with institutional memory (who are often in a position to identify the futility of the change, or its circularity) is framed in terms of their self-interest and intransigence. Those who leave are recast as not sharing the vice-chancellor's vision. The discourse creates binary options of compliance or exit, entrepreneur or whiner hankering for the 'good old days'. Indeed, as Parker points out, the very fact of staff leaving, retiring or falling ill with stress is often, in this managerial fiction of change, defended by the institution as evidence that change is both necessary and effective (2014: 288).

A final strong ideological assumption underlying the uses and meanings of *change* in the documents is that all change will ultimately be successful. What is notably absent from the texts is an acknowledgement that many change initiatives in HEIs fail due to lack of support or general inappropriacy, and we know from our experiences of working within such top-down structures that acknowledgement of failure will be discouraged. Many of us will recognise Canaan's observation (citing Thorpe 2008: 107) that we are impelled to go through permanent revolution so that no practices ever fully establish themselves or achieve legitimacy (Canaan 2010: 59). Despite reservations that covertly may be held, the discourse is relentlessly positive; there are never any 'problems', only 'challenges' and problems are solved, challenges are overcome, ruthlessly, just like resistance. The ideology created in the text prevents academics from interrogating the legitimacy of change being imposed – to technology, to working conditions, to 'performance management' or to redundancy criteria. The document asserts,

- In this final stage the individual reaches a new equilibrium. The change has been incorporated into the way they operate. The new becomes familiar.

There is no acknowledgement here that this chain of events may not unfold – what if the change is never incorporated and what if the new never becomes acceptable? These possibilities construe marked absences around the meaning potential of 'change' in the documents. One of the absences is the possibility of academics participating in democratic structures to agree change. Docherty (2014c) writes, 'Everything, including dissent, is managed and circumscribed to keep existing authority in power. Institutionally, it's called "change management" '. And to ensure compliance, there is the following directive:

- Align internal systems and processes including reward systems.

Even if the change is ill-advised or damaging, resistance is designed out of this 'future-proofed' scenario where all systems reward those who demonstrate amenability as the institution moves right along into 'business as usual'.

Indeed, if resistance fails, and the employee finds themselves stressed or their work impeded by change, then there are institutional means by which the institution attempts to manage the dissatisfied self. We see Continuing Professional Development courses in anger management, dealing with difficult people and stress management. The institution can manage your cognitive processes as well: giving and receiving feedback; motivation; setting objectives; developing yourself and others. It can nurture new identities – e.g. effective team member development, introduction to leadership and the role of the manager. All obstacles are flattened before the project of corporate managerialism.

'Customers/customer service'

The very prominence of a document set focusing on 'customer service' points to a construction of higher education as consumerised and transactional. At several points throughout the documents (and especially in the 'Gold Standard Customer Service' sub-set), academic staff are discursively constructed as a source of information. The assumption here is that academic staff possess information which is 'handed over' to students in exchange for their fees. Indeed, the whole notion of 'accessing' courses suggests that they are behind a paywall, and the notion of 'other services' locates higher education within the domain of a service industry. Indeed Mautner (2005), in a study of the semantic prosodies of 'the entrepreneurial university', finds that the university is predominantly 'cast in a 'serving role', *meeting* and *responding* to needs, rather than actively shaping them' (2005: 105). As we have discussed in Chapter 2, the possible meaning of students themselves as the creators of information is erased. Instead, students are constructed as passive and predictable consumers and/or as manufactured products of the university.

- Whilst academic study may not conform to the traditional consumer/provided model of customer service, many people (including students and their parents) would argue that students are indeed customers,

> spending thousands of pounds each year on accessing academic courses as well as other services provided by [university name].

There is also a presupposition that students are not individuals. It is implied that they will all behave and respond in the same way to particular practices. Therefore, if academic staff 'follow the rules' (a phrase used a number of times in the 'Gold Standard Customer Service' documents), they will deliver effective customer service regardless of who they are dealing with and in what context. Student behaviour is discursively constructed as uniform, predictable and therefore controllable.

- Follow the rules to deliver customer service
- Describe the steps of the customer service-related procedure you followed in this situation

A further presupposition underlying the uses of *customer/s* and *customer service* is that providing students with a good experience has little or nothing to do with learning or academic subject knowledge, or with the development of academic skills. A list of 'customer service roles and activities' presented in the documents are as follows:

- Identifying the needs of students
- Providing accessible information for students
- Informing students of other relevant agencies which can support them
- Answering students' questions
- Giving students feedback

What is presented as important is for academic staff to have 'customer service skills', and more recently these have started to appear on 'person descriptions' for academic posts. The importance of academic subject knowledge is entirely absent. The implication here is that having previous work experience in retail is perhaps better preparation for being an academic than, say, earning a PhD or publishing within the subject area.

Furthermore, it is presupposed that academic staff do not already have 'customer service skills' – they need to be instructed and 'trained' in how to do it. Also, these skills must displace more traditional academic skills of academic support, advisement and mentoring of students. This instruction in customer service cannot come from their peers – it can only be delivered by 'specialists' whose services are employed by those in senior positions within the university. For example, CPLD employed external 'consultants' to deliver the 'Gold Standard Customer Service' course at the university from where the documents are taken. It is beyond the brief of this volume to comment in detail on the expansion of these areas of the administrative arm of universities, but it is extensively documented elsewhere (Morgan 2015a; Sandler Clarke 2014; Williams 2013) and it marks the preoccupation with branding and public relations of the consumer-oriented university.

'Performance/high performance'

One of the major presuppositions that underlies use of *performance/performing* (and *high performance/performing*) in the documents is that there are standard 'key indicators' of performance which are invariable. It is presumed that management will decide what these indicators are, and that academic staff performance can be objectively measured using them. What is unclear throughout the documents is what these measurable 'standards' of performance actually are and who defines them. In the LHPT documents, the 'performance indicators' are implicit and subjective (e.g. *satisfactory*, *outstanding*, *above/below standard*) rather than being objectively measurable.

- A person who is performing below standard.
- People who are working at or above standard may develop resentment toward the leader's controlling behaviour.
- These people are highly developed and can be trusted to perform the task in a responsible and outstanding fashion.
- A person whose performance is satisfactory but not outstanding.
- The developments for a high performer may be promotion focussed and for a remedial or disciplinary case focuses on the here and now.

The semantic instability of such words means that staff will never be 'performing' perfectly, and it will always be possible to claim that there are 'areas for improvement'. 'Exceptional' job performance very often masquerades as 'expected job performance', because, as Davies and Bendix Petersen (2005: 89) note 'workers are compelled never to rest', and the worker becomes 'busier and busier . . . unable to see quite what it is that drives them' (2005: 89). In addition, the assessment of an individual or team performance is always top-down. Staff in lower positions within the hierarchy rarely have opportunity to make judgements about their managers' performance. This results in a very hierarchical model within which performance management is susceptible to the whims of those in the most senior positions.

Additionally, the discourse fails to take into account the multiplying tasks assigned to academics. Inevitably, because of unattainable expectations, most will fall short of some criteria. Technology, though, has offered newly observable 'metrics' which may not coincide with actual performance or competence as an academic, but which stand as convenient proxies because of their calculability. These are often referred to as 'deliverables' by HE managers. For example, 'key deliverables' in the LHPT documents is defined as 'high-level statements of the areas of responsibility through which the role is trying to deliver value'. Another example from the same document is the following:

- A good place to start to identify if there is a development need is to look at the competencies and the competency levels required doing the tasks/activities of a particular key deliverable.

The very notion of 'performance' also presupposes the idea that academic work is 'just for show' and is transient. Objectives and goals are presented as good and as leading to better 'performance'. The possibility of other models of work and learning are erased with objective and target-focussed models repeatedly presented as the only option. An alternative view is that targets and objectives close down potential valuable opportunities for learning and development as they do not allow space for initiative, productive divergence or 'surprise' (see Stern 2013 for a discussion of the value of surprise in education).

Furthermore, when you take into account the terms by which satisfactory performance are measured – or even what is acknowledged as work at all, the colonising nature of the discourse becomes apparent. For example, to be considered to be performing research (coded as 'research active') means satisfying the arbitrary criteria laid down by the REF (see Chapter 4). A scholar may be writing, researching and publishing, but if this is done without grant money, or perhaps in unfashionable journals, then this may not meet institutional criteria of research, and will be ignored.

The LHPT documents characterise successful 'leadership performance' as entrepreneurial, visionary, empowering, exemplary and rewarding.

- Entrepreneurial – challenging the business paradigm
- Visionary – communicating the essence of your dreams
- Empowering – enabling others to act
- Exemplary – modelling the way to practice what you preach
- Rewarding – encouraging the heart

Thus, the discursive construction of what constitutes effective team leadership and performance is highly restricted and very much tied to a neoliberal model of higher education:

- Our discussions on outstanding leaders have identified a number of common principles. These reflect the following five primary leadership 'traits' [. . .] the fundamental practices that enable leaders to get extraordinary things done.

Performance is also often presented using metaphors related to sport (discussed more in the following section). For example, *performance* co-occurs with other words and phrases in the semantic field of sport including *coaching*, *teams*, *team players*, *skills*, *techniques*, *tactics*, *game*, *win-win*, *goals*, *targets* and *slip through the net*.

- Manage upwards and provide hard data to support how well your team is doing against targets.
- Have off-site meetings[2] with the department and discuss the performance of current year and future goals/targets.
- Team working involves individual players.
- Schedule regular retreats to build team spirit and commitment to goals. Strive for win: win solutions.
- List the strengths and limitations of team members and play to their strengths.

The presupposition here is that performance is always competitive. *Teams* are encouraged and expected to compete against each other rather than the relationship being mutual and collegial. Mention is also made of *star performers*, *high performers* and *a remedial or disciplinary case*.

- What separates their 'star performers' from other staff?
- So the developments for a high performer may be promotion focussed and for a remedial or disciplinary case focuses on the here and now.

Such examples again contribute to a discourse of higher education as competitive and hierarchised. However, it is important to note that in other parts of the document, collegiality and inclusivity *is* prioritised, therefore, to a certain extent, competing discourses are present.

- Working co-operatively with others within your area or cross faculty to optimise the collective contribution or delivery of a common goal.
- the emphasis will be on cooperation, teamwork and goal-setting.

Performance is also presented in economic terms. For example, performance is described in terms of *delivering the goods*. This must be substantiated, as quoted earlier, with 'hard data'. Indeed, the rapidly accelerating use of metrics as proxies for performance means that any 'performance' must be concretised with 'deliverables'.

- The achieving group are most prevalent during the performing phase: Proactivity – making it happen, breaching barriers and delivering the goods.

In this way, judgement of performance aligns with management insistence that academic work consists of delineable 'tasks', rather than an autonomous and coherent blend of research, scholarship and teaching. Preferably, these should have been sanctioned during a PDCR (appraisal) meeting. Indeed, one academic who was asked to name an objective for the coming year offered her forthcoming book. This, she was told, was not an objective; it was a task. This, we feel, is a supreme example of the way a centrally defining and venerated academic endeavour is discursively dismissed by the power structures of the neoliberal academy.

Performance is also construed as something that can be 'managed' with a presupposition that teams can *only* perform if they have a leader to manage them. Staff also need to be given periodic 'feedback' on their performance (from a leader). The implication of this is that staff are constantly being assessed and are under review all the time. There is a presupposition that staff will not (or cannot) evaluate themselves. The reality is, of course, that many academics reflect on and evaluate every class they teach. The discursive construction of performance in the documents presupposes no autonomy on the part of academic staff. There is also mention that staff can be 'coached' (by someone else) to perform well.[3]

- Coaching for performance in higher education.
- Applying coaching processes to improve performance.
- The task of the coach is to help the person being coached find their own motivation, define their own goals and discover from within their own experiences and abilities how improved performance is possible for them, and then help them to produce it.
- Coaching is the 'missing link' that turns theoretical knowledge acquired in training into continuously improved performance in practice.

Coaching can be seen as the mechanism by which institutions seek to shape the underperforming in the mould of the high achieving. Most universities encourage senior managers to avail of coaching, and many make it available to academics and administrators. Mäkinen (2015) summarises the assumptions thus: 'It thus begins to seem that change always starts within the individual self – and also that if there is a need for change it is the self that is at fault'. This is one method by which the institution avoids asking difficult questions of itself – about governance, organisation, marginalisation and wider issues of structural inequality and centralisation of power. It is also the way in which individualisation is enacted. Whilst maintaining discourse about 'high performing teams', it is also made clear that responsibility, and 'performance' is located with individuals.

One more anomaly emerges from the discourse of performance and its measurement – at X university, academic teams were a creation of management. Their significance lay solely as administrative units, but in other ways, they were superfluous to the ways academics organised their actual work. Management-constructed teams would often comprise a group of people who might not necessarily identify any joint enterprise. On the other hand, there were functioning teams such as REF research units, degree courses, research collaborations which could all cross the administratively imposed structures. In the case of research units and collaborations, these would often be organised across disciplines, institutions and even national boundaries. In reality, teams would form organically; they might be temporary and multiple. The ostensive teams proposed by the university management were viewed as managerial fictions, and so the question arises, in the terms of the institution's performance review, whether imaginary entities can be assigned objectives as they were required to do so in the PDCR procedure.

'Competency'

The term *competency* features as a key part of the PDCR procedure. The term is used specifically at X University to denote nine behaviours split into three overarching groups: Working with Others (teamwork, customer focus and communicating and influencing), Delivering Results (making informed decisions, organisation and delivery, adaptability) and Focusing on the Future (entrepreneurial and commercial focus, creativity and innovation, leading and coaching). Each has a series of descriptors corresponding to supposed levels of attainment which they claim 'reflect behaviour patterns which distinguish highly effective performance in a role from average or poor performance. They have been developed to support the University's objectives as outlined in its Strategic Plan'. With the possible exception of entrepreneurial and commercial focus, and with some shifts of emphasis, we might expect that these qualities could be assumed to be an incontrovertible part of the academic role and require no measurement. There are, as we have pointed out already in Chapter 4, many activities which academics perform which are not measurable either qualitatively or quantitatively. Nevertheless, these competencies are designated on every person descriptor for posts at the university.

Competency, the documents tell us, must be distinguished from competence. This latter term refers to the level at which the behaviours are being performed, as indicated by the extent to which goals are achieved. However, a key anomaly in the policy and framework is that the policy sets out to measure the 'performance' of teams, but the 'competency' of individuals. There seems to be an assumption, therefore, that these competencies are the provenance of the individual, whereas 'performance' is more dynamic and collegial (within teams). However, the documents presuppose that punitive measures can be taken against individuals for poor performance, particularly in the university's 'Improving Performance Policy', which is clearly designed to be used with individuals, not teams or team leaders. Therefore, there is tension and inconsistency here – if the university aspires to have 'high performing teams', then it would logically follow that it should measure the performance of *teams*, not the performance of *individuals* within teams.

The outlined competencies are believed to underlie performance. In the documents, they are presented as measurable with the use of a predesigned 'framework' of descriptors. The framework is linear and binary in that it is presented in terms of positive and negative behaviours. The framework appears to be more retail-focussed (e.g. through reference to *customers*), rather than education-focussed, as the following illustrates:

- Show empathy for the customer.
- Treat each transaction on its own merits.
- Strive to exceed customer expectations.
- Vary your style with the customer appropriately.
- Customer focus: Provides the best quality services to internal and external customers.
- Anticipate the needs of customers, seeking evidence of demand from the market(s) and from stakeholders.

Examples of work 'targets' included in the LHPT documents are as follows:

- Volumes – calls taken, vouchers processed, files dealt with etc.
- Monetary – sales made, costs reduced etc.
- Time – deadlines met, average time for a call etc.

Clearly, there is a mismatch between these examples and much of the actual work that takes place in an academic environment. Academic staff are never required to make sales, process vouchers and are rarely required to interact with students over the telephone. Words such as *vouchers*, *sales* and *costs* belong in a retail environment, rather than an environment of learning. The examples therefore presume a working environment which is transactional and economic rather than scholarly. It is difficult to see how such examples could be applied in the university workplace.

What counts as 'competence' is actually rather limited and, in many ways, non-specialised in that the same competencies could equally be applied to non-educational settings. Agreeing and complying with change is seen as an indicator of competence, regardless of an individual's wisdom or acuity of judgement. Resisting change is presented as a 'negative behaviour'. Academic staff having an 'entrepreneurial and commercial' focus also appears as a competency. *Entrepreneurial* is an insidious SDS and, like other 'hooray words' (Whyte 2003) is never fully defined in terms of denoted meaning, only connoted meaning (Mautner 2005: 101). In sum, competency is presented as having nothing to do with knowledge, learning or interpersonal skills (although lip service is paid to this in that it is mentioned that they will be assessed 'elsewhere'). One wonders if the authors of this document seriously believe that the qualities of imagination, tenacity and intellectual range that underpin research can be 'upskilled' via a 'competency tool', or indeed by 'talent management'.

It is also interesting to observe that the term *talent* is only mentioned in relation to succession planning (e.g. in the phrase *talent forum*).

- Identify and agree additional input to talent forum
- The purpose of the talent forum feedback meeting is to share with you your personal outcomes from the talent forum
- Future focussed on action and talent development

Talent is seen as an innate skill which cannot be measured, whereas individuals and teams can be trained to be 'competent' and to 'perform'. Talent is only referred to in terms of an individual's potential ability to be a manager. The documents on succession planning state that such planning applies to the management posts of dean, associate dean and academic team leader. There is no suggestion anywhere that succession planning could be applied to academic leaders such as professors.

In sum, analysis of some of the key SDS is helpful for uncovering the underlying presuppositions of the words. These presuppositions are a key linguistic means through which ideologies of neoliberal governmentality and academic corporatisation are discursively achieved in the documents.

Critical metaphor analysis

Throughout the documents, a number of metaphors are repeatedly used in relation to some of the SDS discussed in the previous section (*change*, *performance*, *high performance* and *leader/leadership*). There are also recurring patterns around the use of particular metaphors to describe the university work environment in more general terms. Each of the most frequently occurring metaphorical source domains (journey, sport, war, tool/toolkit, building and construction, nature) will be discussed next with reference to examples from the texts.

Firstly, a frequently used metaphor throughout the documents is that of a journey. The target domain of these metaphors is mostly work, study, learning or career. Through using the journey metaphor to describe an individual's engagement with work and/or study, they are constructed as linear and measurable and predictable. For example, in the succession planning model, individuals are assessed as being *red* (not ready), *amber* (ready within two years) or *green* (ready). These designations may be awarded even in the absence of any actual vacancies. Universities are often characterised by the medium to long-term tenure of deanships and heads of department. But this incorporation of business discourse and practice has little to do with reality; it is more consistent with the focus in the previous section on modifying the behaviours of academics. We view this in terms of an analysis provided by Bendix Petersen and Davies (2010) that in academia, one is never allowed to arrive – one must always be on a journey of improvement. Examples include the following:

- Renewal is not the end of the journey
- reflecting on what has happened and their journey to this point
- Course milestones
- Goes extra mile to provide a quality customer service
- Agree review checkpoints if appropriate
- Manage upwards and provide hard data to support how well your team is doing against targets

The use of the journey metaphor to describe work erases other possibilities such as presenting work and study as cyclical and dynamic (qualities which are, of course, more difficult to measure).

Work is also presented using the formulaic militaristic metaphors of war and sport throughout the texts. The frequent occurrence of such metaphors means that working in a university is constructed as competitive and is never described in any other terms (Docherty 2014a: 84–89). The use of war and sport metaphors also presents a zero-sum scenario of victory or failure. As in the other case studies, the density of this lexicon is quite extraordinary. Examples include the following:

- How do we kick it [change] off?
- Kotter argues that many change projects fail because victory is declared too early
- Quick wins are only the beginning of what needs to be done
- Establish short-term goals
- Team involvement in goal definition
- emphasises the need for keeping in the win-win area
- Targets will be set by the line manager and/or the management of the area and must support the goals of the department
- how to motivate survivors of a savage round of downsizing
- When people feel they are under attack, one response is to become defensive. This might result in territory battles
- The use of specific tactics can also smooth the change process
- I quickly spot, and take advantage of, weaknesses in competitors

- Such individuals are not overtly self-protective or inclined to wage turf wars
- Negotiates 'win-win' outcomes
- Meeting financial and delivery targets
- What might you do to sabotage your own efforts to reach this goal?
- Coaching is about helping someone to get the best performance out of themselves – the potential for which was already there. Coaching is about releasing that potential
- Coach and guide them in areas in which they are weak or are making mistakes . . . If appropriate, encourage them to seek formal training or qualifications
- Coaches others in the team

Examples such as these fit with a dominant neoliberal discourse of universities as competitive, not collaborative. The target is to win, or, even better, to *win-win*. And a discourse is created in which it is acceptable (or even encouraged and celebrated) to exploit 'weaknesses' in an implied competitor or opponent. This discourse is, again, normalised and institutionalised as a commendable activity.

The metaphor of tools or a 'toolkit' is used on numerous occasions throughout the documents to describe sets of management behaviours. This is a word with a high enough frequency in this corpus to stand out as one of the most prominent keywords. As Morrish (2014) points out, there are a great many 'tools' in the managerial lexicon:

> We have: a Managing Academic Workloads tool (renders 'workloads' auditable but makes a lot of actual work invisible); a Change Management tool; a Research Development tool; an Auditing tool; a Benchmarking tool; a Competency Development tool (customer focus, team working, leading and 'coaching'); and a Smart Working tool.

Examples include the following:

- [University name] Change Management tool
- In 2010 [university name] developed a change management tool to be used across the university
- you can browse through the tools which are listed in alphabetical order
- Uses change as a tool for staff retention and development
- They are very much part of the Change Management toolkit of many consultancies and specialist organisations

Such examples imply that management behaviours around *change* are practical and facilitative in that *tools* are meant to make things easier and are always required for some tasks. Tools are also impersonal 'objects'. Therefore, in using them as a metaphor for management behaviour, it takes the focus away from the behaviour of *people* (i.e. the managers). In this sense, the metaphor functions to disguise or remove agency from human beings. Tools are objective and neutral and give the impression of being governed by algorithms.

The target domains of 'resources' and 'human characteristics and behaviours' are both often metaphorically conceptualised in terms of building or construction in the documents. The use of related verbs such as *build* encompasses meanings of structure and accretional growth. Examples from the documents include the following:

- Change management learning room
- The learning room is still under construction
- building commitment to change
- it might include major structural changes
- The key elements of the process of rebuilding self-esteem
- We will build organisational confidence

Finally, two sets of metaphors relating to the field of nature and science are used on a number of occasions in the texts. Firstly, metaphors of 'growth' and 'life cycles' are used to refer to teams, specifically the length of time a team of people will work together.

- The team life cycle
- energise and spark the team throughout its life cycle
- A leader will put the team together and clearly impact upon morale during the lifespan of the team
- The grow model
- Start new 'root' sheet when loop goes full-circle

Such examples imply that a 'team' will have a 'natural' end. Any break-up of a team through management imposition of redundancy, reorganisation and so on is presented as being part of a 'natural' process. This is important because it is difficult to oppose things which are 'natural' rather than artificial. The metaphor is useful for managers because it implies that all teams (in practical terms within a university, this refers to departments and faculties) are temporary and have an inevitable end point. The other science metaphor that is used is that of a *catalyst* to describe 'leaders'.

- High performance teams value leaders who provide appropriate direction by acting as a catalyst for change and continuous improvement.
- He sees his role as that of a catalyst.

In the natural scientific source domain, catalysts make things happen. Things are static without catalysts. In ascribing this metaphor to the target domain of leaders, the implication is that nothing will be achieved, and staff will not do things unless there is a leader/catalyst. Catalysts are natural and necessary; therefore, leaders and hierarchical structures are conceptualised as natural and necessary. Non-leaders are implied to be 'inert' and requiring a catalyst to create a reaction. The science/nature metaphors, therefore, work together to make 'leaders' essential and 'teams' expendable.

Discussion

The effect on academics – moulding ideal corporate subject

The analysis of data in this chapter has brought to light a number of recurring themes. This section will reflect on what the overall analysis reveals about the ways in which the discourse serves to colonise the corporate academic.

It is clear that the administrative architecture of the university has been reconfigured to resemble the domain of business and enterprise, particularly retail. Education is now positioned, not as an immaterial process, but as an auditable, monetised investment. It is apparent that the discourse of university management reflects that stance, and that they view it as desirable for academic identities to be brought into line. In the paradigm of academic capitalism (Slaughter and Leslie 1997) and the neoliberal university, the academic must be remade as a competitive entrepreneurial self, as the university is presumed to be governed by the rules of the market. Competition and 'winning' is revealed by the frequent use of sports metaphors. Similarly, the university is organised as a simulacrum of business. In our documents, the concerns of management and leadership – change, hierarchy, efficiency and performance – have supplanted concerns with teaching and research, academic integrity and freedom, and indeed the freedom to take risks and fail. Indeed, if these latter concerns are mentioned at all, it is only to bring them into the dirigiste purview of the former. When we interrogate the presuppositions encoded within the succession planning data set, we find that it is not enough, clearly, for academics to harbour a sense of themselves as scholars collectively developing the future of their discipline; the only goal to be accorded prestige is to embrace the aspiration to manage. If their aspirations should not be focussed in this area, the institution can provide coaching in the desired behaviours. This exceeds mere audit culture; it is the forcible citation of a discourse which inaugurates a new kind of subject. The exertion of this type of biopower requires the academic to undergo what Bendix Petersen and Davies describe as 'a kind of dressage; shaping the individualised, vulnerable, competitive, useful subjects into the generic workers who will facilitate the flow of capital' (2010: 102).

The focus on individualism, outputs and 'working smart' all coalesce to chide the academic into ever increasing 'productivity'. Managerial discourse, and the policies of 'performance management', function as a regulatory regime that circumscribes the 'mode of being' of academics (Morrissey 2013). The parameters of 'performance' are drawn so rigidly that they circumscribe what counts as academic labour, meaning that much of what academics do is rendered invisible and uncounted. Much of what is submitted to TRAC represents a severe undercount of hours, since the system only allows for the reporting of the contractual 37 hours of work. If your 'workload tool' does not have a spreadsheet column for mentoring a colleague, supporting a student with mental health difficulties, writing references, reading and commenting on a younger scholar's work – then who are we to claim it as work at all? It cannot be measured, audited or ranked. For example, it is impossible within the limits prescribed by the 'workload tool' to complain that you are overloaded. An analysis of workplace stress is refused by your 'failure to manage workload' and justifies your surrender to the 'Smart Working tool'. Any complaint about the intensification of work is met by bureaucratic structures which in an instant render your overwork invisible. An example, frequently cited in our workplaces, would be the way in which stress resulting from work overload and compulsory overtime is individualised as 'unable to manage workload'. The academic is positioned as culpable, and failure to cope is attributed to failure of the individual to make the right 'choices'. As Gill (2009) relates, new lecturers are liable to be sent on training courses aimed at constructing the ideal employee (e.g. 'time management', 'speed reading', 'prioritising goals') and which require each individual to work on the self to better manage proliferating workloads, as if there were a technical fix. The message is just make the choice to 'work smarter'. The desired product is the academic who works as ceaselessly as the Energizer Bunny (Morrish 2000: 232).

In a highly circulated piece, Gill (2009) brought the strategy of reflexivity to bear on her own experience of a neoliberal university as the context within which she is expected to do research. She describes the sense of overload, panic, stress, shame and guilt elicited by the incessant demands of the university and the feelings of failure when one does not meet those demands. And we have previously discussed the importance of recognising the differently gendered effects of the neoliberal concerns with competitiveness, efficiency and increasing productivity.

In many ways we see in these snapshots of academic life the society of control outlined by Deleuze (1990). Foucauldian (sequential) disciplinary regimes give way to societies of control where citizens find that they are never finished with any process (Morrish 2011). Just as one hurdle is surmounted, another, higher one presents itself, with the end point always at the far horizon. This analysis is consistent with our findings in the metaphor analysis of *journeys*, *milestones* and *checkpoints*. These are societies where control is exercised on a continuous basis, and the individual never quite arrives at the promised reward. Gatekeeping measures such as the imposition of perpetual training, or multiple-staged applications for research leave must be endured, even to participate. Even those who now attain professorial rank are subject to this regime of never quite 'becoming'. In several UK universities, the intrusive gaze of Human Resources has recently fallen on alleged 'underperforming professors'. In any sane university, this would be recognised as pure incongruity; since Human Resources decide the ever-ascending criteria for promotion to this level, they might be trusted to not betray their own judgement. However, as well as undergoing performance reviews as frequently as newly appointed probationers, professors must now meet exacting criteria for 'quality' of publications. No accrual of reputation can be permitted; the criteria must be met every year, not just over the course of a distinguished career. In this way, any prestige associated with the rank of professor must be considered temporary, as is their tenure, since perceived failure to meet the criteria invites 'performance management' procedures. Professors, then, have been made to join the expanding precariat of the academy.

The training which normalises a sense of impermanence and insecurity can start at the very beginning of an academic career. In 2015, one Russell Group university in the UK set up its own 'internal outsourcing' unit to recruit hourly paid teachers and researchers (www.teachhigher.com). Couched in the usual disingenuous justifications of 'transparency', 'consistency' and 'fairness', this new 'academic services department' ensures that only the most compliant apprentices to corporate citizenship will gain enough experience to qualify for full-time academic posts in the UK. To be eligible for these assignments means relinquishing rights to join industrial action or be able to join national pay bargaining. The 'consistency' vaunted by this university means, of course, a consistently low rate of pay. The very name of the unit *Teach Higher* is a cynical attempt to echo the progressive *Aim Higher*, the government's scheme (now closed) for widening participation amongst under-represented groups, such as those from economically deprived backgrounds, ethnic minorities and the disabled. *Teach Higher* will no doubt spawn franchises in one more move towards the casualisation of academic labour which we have already seen advancing in the US and in Australia. A large number of blogs have emerged in relation to the precariousness and exploitation of this spread.[4]

The effect of this neoliberal governmentality is to force the subject to comply with their own oppression. What academics find offensive is that there can be no rejection of the new subjectivity. Our professional lives are dominated by the need to provide discursive evidence that we are compliant with the managerial regime in the form of performance management reviews, teaching evaluations, student satisfactions surveys, REFs and so on. Failure to enter into the discourse results in illocutionary silencing (Sauntson 2013), since one has become literally unintelligible to the managerial mind. By locating critique outside the range of the sayable, our resistance is blunted.

It is an environment where the academic is made to feel responsible for their own oppression and stress, whilst at the same time feeling privileged and undeserving of better. An individual academic's value is calculated according to arbitrary criteria such as submission to the REF, and exhibition of 'competency' in alignment with the university's strategic plan. As Morrisey (2013: 805) identifies:

> The fear for many is that the limits and possibilities of academic productiveness today (and, by extension, the broader values and functions of higher education) are being overly determined by primarily economic delineations of productivity, which miss out on broader civic, political and social educational values.

The discourse of productivity and 'REF-able' research locks the individual into a distinctively neoliberal subject formation – indeed, the ideal corporate subject. Davies (2005: 1–2) reminds us that 'in speaking ourselves into existence as academics, within neoliberal discourse, we are vulnerable to it and to its indifference to us and our thought' and that to critique them requires collective work. She argues that the limiting force of neoliberal discourse is violent in its effect – 'it is the language in which the auditor is king. It is a language that destroys social responsibility and critique, that invites a mindless, consumer-oriented individualism to flourish, and kills off conscience' (2005: 6).

All the while, a new league of educrats drives the agenda of change, situated within a neoliberal topography of the management and manipulation of crises (Harvey 2005: 162). Anyone who works in a university in the UK will recognise constant reorganisation, restructuring, respecification, review – and all must be completed to unrealistic timescales. Frequently, faculty are admonished to prioritise the reform, with strict timetables for submission of paperwork which will never be consulted or be of any use for teaching, learning or research.

As scholars who study managerial discourse, our colleagues often ask us, 'Why do they do this?' In other words, why do managers use a discourse which would seem to alienate academics and divorce them from their scholarly inclinations and abilities which are clearly beneficial to society. One answer could be, as Deem and Brehony suggest, that manager-academics are those who are more attuned to institutional power structures. Critically, they assert that university managers do not constitute a separate class, but must still embrace certain ideologies and values of 'new managerialism' and that the presence of manager-academics has exacerbated a divide between that group and those academics not in managerial roles (2005: 231).

Another answer to 'why do they do it?' draws on the logic that it is precisely because a fiction has been constituted, that management has to work so hard to maintain it through discourse. A similar situation is documented by Carlen (2008) in which a new prison had recently modified the goals that staff were being asked to attain. Staff knew these goals were unachievable, but all understood they were required to act as if they were unproblematic. Furthermore, there was a requirement to provide auditable evidence that the goals were being achieved. Despite widespread knowledge that 'everybody knows' and recognises the unreality, the demands of the imaginary were allowed to displace any possibility of managing the reality effectively. I imagine most of us labouring in academia are fully able to empathise with this situation. We have learned to defer to what Krugman (2012) calls Zombie ideas: 'Policy ideas that keep being killed by evidence, but nonetheless shamble relentlessly forward, essentially because they suit a political agenda'.

Our situation recalls Baudrillard and his thesis of a postmodern boundary warping of reality and unreality which he terms 'hyperreality'. However, our frustration lies in the fact that we have no difficulty in recognising where the boundary between the real and the simulation is. As Docherty (2011) argues, academics are very aware that the official university culture of transparency and access to information is a perverse parody. Nevertheless, we largely placate the gods of audit culture, and in any remaining time, retreat to what Docherty (2011) calls the 'clandestine university' within. We recognise the purely ideological function of the management discourse, and conduct much of our authentic work in secret opposition to it.

An answer that we would propose is perhaps more provocative; we contend that those who pursue management roles are in the grip of a cult. Their identification with others in that tier, and their search for community, demands that they police the borders of the in-group whilst compelling subordinates to cite their norms. The distinguishing features of a cult are that those on the inside reject that designation, whilst there is firm agreement by those outside the cult. Judging from the response to our work so far, we confidently expect that most senior management teams would conform to this criterion.

Let us now consider the consequences of these developments in universities. We largely have a situation where those who manage in the academy do not, in any important sense, share its values. There is little sympathy between managers (a term unknown ten years ago in universities) and the academics they purport to lead. Heads of schools/departments are rewarded for delivering the vice-chancellor's 'vision' rather than responding to the aspirations of their staff and students. Particularly in post-1992 universities, we have seen the reproduction of a cadre of managers who perceive themselves as a new kind of officer class. Even more pernicious is that academics have been formed into a compliant, flexible workforce which has been obliged to internalise managerial values to the extent that they present no impediment to their own destruction (Docherty 2014b). All challenges and counter-arguments have been evacuated. We have all been forced to drink the neoliberal Kool-Aid. The metaphor is perhaps most vivid if we remind ourselves of its original referent. The Kool-Aid refers to the lethally poisoned drink that Reverend Jim Jones forced his followers to drink in the 1978 Jonestown Massacre; the phrase suggests that one has 'mindlessly adopted the dogma of a group or leader without fully understanding the ramifications or implications'.[5] It is a kind of kettling of the mind. On a daily basis we cite a discourse which is not even consistent with the values of public service, let alone academia.

Nothing has been gained by deference to the corporate mirage. As universities have worked to justify themselves in commercialised and marketised terms, so affirmation has shrunk further from their grasp. Universities are perceived by government as inefficient, featherbedded repositories of aloof intellectuals. As much as we have attempted to justify our research in economic terms, our courses may be closed anyway. Never mind the expertise, artefacts, collections and archives that have been amassed – these may all be disposed of if the discipline fails the test of consumer choice. All it takes is a successful TV drama to make courses in forensics or midwifery surge in popularity. And so the nation's scholarly resources are locked into a suspended sentence whose enforcement is at the behest of the nation's 17-year-olds. It is a barbarous approach to intellectual stewardship which has seen the reckless squandering of some of the nation's academic jewels. Instead of defending the role of universities in a democratic society, we have been sucked further and further into this zero-sum game where the parameters of usefulness shift on a monthly basis. Politicians from all quarters have charged universities with failing to address social inequality, failing to turn out employable graduates, failing to teach economically relevant courses, failing to prevent student radicalisation, failing to prevent illegal immigration, failing to give value for money, failing to tackle sexual assault on campus. Day after day, we learn that universities are repeatedly failing. Indeed, only 38% of MPs think that universities spend money efficiently, according to a recent report.[6] Who can forget the last minute imposition of 'impact' in the last REF? This was a clear message that research and 'outputs' are no longer enough to earn government favour; there must be economic benefit attached to each and every pound charged against UK academic research.

None of us has done enough to stand against this violent philistinism that destroys institutions, democracy and social justice. We are all cowards and collaborators to some degree. Canaan (2010: 58) asks, 'Why do we all just keep going along with it?' and suggests that the answer is because the carrot of self-actualisation is dangled before academics and their compliance is ensured with the stick of regulation. At a micro level, it mirrors the coercion that universities should have resisted decades ago. What we learn is that we don't transform institutions by assimilating to structures which are alien and repressive. It is time to defend humanistic values from strategic assault. At least we have a critique, and we must sustain it. This critique must take place explicitly, through fora such as publications and conference presentations, but also 'off stage' in staff-rooms, bathrooms and classrooms.

Managerial denial

Since we began writing this book, performance management has come under scrutiny by the press, academics and the UCU. As previously discussed, the death of Professor Stefan Grimm in 2014 shocked the academic community. Grimm took his own life after being threatened with performance management procedures when he was deemed not to have brought in 'prestigious' grant money. His obituary on the Imperial College website reads:

> Over the past 20 years, his work to this scientific field includes 50 publications in top-ranked journals, two books, more than 3000 citations and 5 patents on innovative strategies for screening novel genes involved in cell death pathways and new anti-cancer genes. Professor Stefan Grimm chaired and co-organized international conferences and served as reviewer for research-funding organizations and many international scientific journals. Recently, Stefan was elected as fellow of the Society of Biology.
>
> (http://www3.imperial.ac.uk/newsandeventspggrp/imperialcollege/newssummary/news_14-1-2015-17-40-44)

This hardly looks like the profile of an 'underperforming professor'. His crime, though, was that he prioritised science rather than the accumulation of capital. It took seven months for Professor Alice Gast, the President of Imperial College, to make a public statement on Stefan Grimm's death. In an interview on the BBC Radio 4 Today Programme, on 17 April 2015, she had this to say about the case:

> Professors are under pressures. They have a lot on their plates. Professors are really like small business owners. They have their own teaching to perform. They have their own research and they have their research funding to look after. They work with teams of post-docs and post graduate students. Then some of them work on translational work and develop entrepreneurial and new companies and spin outs. It's a very highly competitive world out there. The

> collaborative nature and the way in which we're moving towards highly collaborative work I think helps because one starts to recognise that you can't do it all alone. You need a team. You build a team with the very best colleagues. You have not only that interplay between the different backgrounds and disciplines but you get the new ideas that are generated by bringing diverse people together.
> (http://markcarrigan.net/2015/04/17/president-of-imperial-college-london-professors-are-really-like-small-business-owners/)

There has been a shockingly rapid move from entrepreneurship as metaphor, to a state in which it is both literal and mandatory. It features as a 'key competency' in academic job descriptions, and there is now an expectation that professors will earn their own salaries and research expenses. In the PDCR documents, reference is made on more than one occasion to 'stretching objectives' which are purported to sit in between an individual's 'comfort zone' and the 'panic zone'. 'Stretching objectives' are presented as desirable but objectives which place individuals in their comfort or panic zones are not. It is not clear what they expect the effect to be on professors of unattainable targets, constant surveillance and audit, and the knowledge that any dip in 'performance' may see their contracts terminated.

But there is another disturbing presupposition in this discourse of comfort zones. To be asked to go beyond one's comfort zone makes the patronising assumption that one's life is normally comfortable. It certainly reveals that those charged with auditing and defining these comfort zones are privileged in this way. It is a discourse which permits no acknowledgement that the employee may find teaching or research extremely stressful, at least some of the time. Their domestic circumstances may add additional stress – illness of a child, the loss of a partner's job, death of a parent – these may all lower the threshold of discomfort at work. The managerial class, who can at least assuage some of their discomfort with a larger salary, should check their privilege and 'think outside the box' they have just casually ticked.

Alternatives

Morrissey (2013: 800) notes that performance indicators are all cast in the mould of neoliberal priorities and asks if there are any other ways to manifest accountability and productiveness. He argues that in order to resist this distorting of academic priorities, it is vital to contest 'neoliberal and bureaucratic delineations of research and educational productivity – a regime of truth, in a sense, about academic performance' (2013: 807). We might, for example, find a way to recognise those activities which are collegial and valuable, but perhaps do not meet SMART criteria. Candidates for reward might be mentoring, reading others' work, listening to colleagues' frustrations, recruiting students, emailing students, turning up at graduation and many more instances of academic homemaking. Academia 3.0 badly needs a manifesto for academic citizenship to counteract the project of corporate colonisation. We need to spell out for the next generation of scholars how university life can be different, collegial and rewarding before their subjectivity is subsumed by the new hegemony of neoliberal governmentality.

Even within the management tier there may be an appetite for change. Janet Beer, the newly appointed vice-chancellor of the University of Liverpool, bemoans a masculinist narrative of heroism in the job descriptions and ethos of vice-chancellors.[7] Given the analysis we have conducted, showing a discourse of sports metaphors, competition and the rule of hierarchies, her complaint appears to be well founded. She accuses universities of overlooking other attributes which also sustain good leadership, such as 'consensus-building and collaborative and partnership working at all levels. Job specifications, she continued, can often emphasise qualities that aren't necessarily about leadership in a well-balanced way'.

Beer and Gast may occupy different poles of a rather narrow spectrum of university leadership philosophies. There are, though, small, meagre signs that the cult of managerial autocracy may be waning. In a 2012 speech, Jon Baldwin (deputy vice-chancellor of Murdoch University, Western Australia) noted that decision making at top-ranked universities was overseen by a self-governing community of scholars. By contrast, at Murdoch, the academy as a collective had been marginalised, and 'the embrace of corporate culture was almost total and the very idea of the university was threatened. In leadership and governance terms, the academic voice had to be rediscovered'.[8] The answer to how to resist corporatisation of academia may lie in turns towards collective governance. We note that such partial democratic moves are not incompatible with 'successful' universities: each of the world's top-ten universities have some form of staff governance.

What we cannot risk is an intensification of the state of affairs we reveal in this chapter. Docherty (2014c), who sharpened his critique under conditions of suspension from his university in 2014, writes, 'We are perilously close to a position where the unquestioned power of management is declaring war on the academic community, the university, itself; civil war in academia'. In the final chapter, we hope to suggest that critique and resistance are still possible in Neoliberal U, but that will demand a sophisticated understanding of the significance of discourse.

Notes

1. Kaizen is a Sino Japanese term denoting a philosophy of continuous improvement. In UK manufacturing, this approach was introduced by Toyota where it works in concert with 'lean' concepts of efficiency. All employees are equally

responsible for finding elements of the process of manufacturing which are not working and can be improved. (Toyota internal document, *The Toyota Way*, April 2001)

2. The rationale for having 'off-site meetings' is never discussed.
3. Coaching is an approach which has come under criticism, along with similar approaches such as neuro-linguistic programming. These are considered unscientific and have little scientific data to support their claims.
4. See, for example, Adjunct Nation www.adjunctnation.com/; Adjunct Project http://adjunctproject.com/; Canadian Association of Precarious Academic Workers (CAPAW) http://capaw.weebly.com/; https://ucuanticas.wordpress.com/; Australia Actual casuals https://actualcasuals.wordpress.com/
5. http://en.wikipedia.org/wiki/Kool-Aid#In_popular_culture
6. http://blogs.staffs.ac.uk/mikehamlyn/category/he-policy/
7. www.timeshighereducation.co.uk/news/janet-beer-on-leadership-diversity-dont-hold-out-for-a-hero/2019009.article
8. www.timeshighereducation.co.uk/world-university-rankings/news/a-return-of-the-academy-to-its-roots.

References

Baldry, C. and Barnes, A. 2012. The open-plan academy: Space, control and the undermining of professional identity. *Work, Employment and Society* 26 (2): 228–245.

Bendix Petersen, E. and Davies, B. 2010. In/difference in the neoliberalised university. *Learning and Teaching: The International Journal of Higher Education in the Social Sciences* 3 (2): 92–109.

Butler, N. and Spoelstra, S. 2014. The regime of excellence and the erosion of ethos in critical management studies. *British Journal of Management* 25: 538–550.

Canaan, J. 2010. Analysing a 'neoliberal moment' in English higher education today. *Learning and Teaching: The International Journal of Higher Education in the Social Sciences* 3 (2): 55–72.

Carlen, P. ed. 2008. *Imaginary Penalties*. London: Willan Publishing.

Colquhoun, D. 2007. How should universities be run to get the best out of people? www.dcscience.net/2007/08/03/how-should-universities-be-run-to-get-the-best-out-of-people/ (Accessed 13 April 2015).

Davies, B. 2003. Death to critique and dissent? The policies and practices of new managerialism and of 'evidence-based practice'. *Gender and Education* 15 (1): 91–103.

Davies, B. 2005. The (im)possibility of intellectual work in neoliberal regimes. *Discourse: Studies in the Cultural Politics of Education* 26 (1): 1–14.

Davies, B. and Bendix Peterson, E. 2005. Neo-liberal discourse in the academy: The forestalling of (collective) resistance. *Learning and Teaching: The International Journal of Higher Education in the Social Sciences* 2 (2): 77–98.

Deem, R. and Brehony, K. 2005. Management as ideology: The case of 'new managerialsim' in higher education. *Oxford Review of Education* 31 (2): 217–335.

Deleuze, G. 1990. *Postscript on the Societies of Control*. Cambridge, MA: MIT Press. 3–7.

Docherty, T. 2011. The unseen academy. *Times Higher Education*. www.timeshighereducation.com/features/the-unseen-academy/418076.article (Accessed 5 May 2015).

Docherty, T. 2014a. *Universities at War*. London: Sage.
Docherty, T. 2014b. Paper presented at *The REF and the State of Higher Education Today*. Institute for Contemporary Arts, London (Accessed 8 December 2014).
Docherty, T. 2014c. Thomas Docherty on academic freedom. *Times Higher Education*, 4 December. www.timeshighereducation.com/features/thomas-docherty-on-academic-freedom/2017268.article (Accessed 28 September 2018).
Foucault, M. 2008. *The Birth of Biopolitics: Lectures Given at the Collège de France 1978–1979*. (Trans. G. Burchell) Basingstoke: Palgrave Macmillan.
Gill, R. 2009. Breaking the silence: The hidden injuries of neo-liberal academia. In R. Flood and R. Gill, eds. *Secrecy and Silence in the Research Process: Feminist Reflections*. London: Routledge.
Harvey, D. 2005. *A Brief History of Neoliberalism*. Oxford: Oxford University Press.
Krugman, P. 2012. The ultimate zombie idea. *New York Times*. http://krugman.blogs.nytimes.com/2012/11/03/the-ultimate-zombie-idea/
Mäkinen, K. 2015. Working life coaching and the individualiztion of class. *The Sociological Review*. 18 February. www.thesociologicalreview.com/information/blog/working-life-coaching-and-the-individualization-of-class.html?utm_content=buffer92f81&utm_medium=social&utm_source=twitter.com&utm_campaign=buffer
Mautner, G. 2005. The entrepreneurial university: A discursive profile of a higher education buzzword. *Critical Discourse Studies* 2 (2): 95–120.
Morgan, J. 2015a. Warwick rebranding sparks petition. www.timeshighereducation.co.uk/news/warwick-rebranding-sparks-petition/2019888.article. (Accessed 27 April 2015).
Morrish, L. 2000. A feminist's response to the technologization of discourse. *The European Journal of Women's Studies* 7: 229–238.
Morrish, L. 2011. Con-Dem-Nation and the attack on academic cultures. *Campaign for the Public University*, November 2nd. http://publicuniversity.org.uk/2011/11/02/con-dem-nation-and-the-attack-on-academic-cultures/
Morrish, L. 2014. Institutional discourse and the cult(ure) of managerialism. *Discover Society*. www.discoversociety.org/2014/05/06/institutional-discourse-and-the-culture-of-managerialism/ (Accessed 27 April 2015).
Morrissey, J. 2013. Governing the academic subject: Foucault, governmentality and the performing university. *Oxford Review of Education* 39 (6): 797–810.
Parker, M. 2014. University, Ltd: Changing a business school. *Organization* 21 (2): 281–292.
Sandler, Clarke, J. 2014. Marketing spend up, but applications fail to follow suit. *Times Higher Education*. www.timeshighereducation.co.uk/news/marketing-spend-up-but-applications-fail-to-follow-suit/2012107.article 20 March 2014 (Accessed 27 April 2015).
Sauntson, H. 2013. Sexual diversity and illocutionary silencing in the English National Curriculum. Sex Education: Sexuality, Society and Learning 13 (4): 395–408.
Sauntson, H. 2013. Sexual diversity and illocutionary silencing in the *English National Curriculum, Sex Education* 13 (4): 395–408.
Sealey, A. 2014. The neoliberal university: Agency and responsibility. Paper presented at *Neoliberalism, Education and Applied Linguistics Symposium*, Institute of Education, June.
Slaughter, S. and Leslie, L. 1997. *Academic Capitalism: Politics, Policies and the Entrepreneurial University*. Baltimore: Johns Hopkins University Press.

Smith-Jackson, T. and Klein, K. 2009. Open-plan offices: Task performance and mental workload. *Journal of Environmental Psychology* 29 (2): 279–289.
Stern, J. 2013. Surprise in schools: Martin Buber and dialogic schooling. *Forum* 55 (1): 45–58.
Thorpe, C. 2008. Capitalism, audit and the demise of the humanistic academy. *Workplace* 15: 103–125.
Warner, M. 2015. Learning my lesson. *London Review of Books* 37 (6): 8–14.
Whyte, J. 2003. *Bad Thoughts*. London: Corvo.
Williams, J. 2013. *Consuming Higher Education: Why Learning Can't Be Bought*. London: Bloomsbury.

7 Conclusions

Possibilities for contesting the discourse

Summary of key findings

In this concluding chapter, we consider the extent to which academics may resist internalising a subjectivity which is subordinated to the neoliberal university, even whilst being compelled to cites its norms in the ways shown in the preceding chapters. Key findings from the linguistic analyses conducted throughout the book are as follows:

- The keywords and their frequent collocations in the documents examined all reveal an underlying neoliberal ideology;
- There are a preponderance of SDS throughout all of the documents examined. Our analysis suggests that these have been co-opted for managerial purposes on the force of their polysemicity. The SDS analysis reveals semantic slippage between managerial and academic discourses – this is damaging in that academics consequently find themselves struggling to find self-worth by measuring achievement in ever-changing and obscure terms set by the institution.
- Key recycled metaphors in most of the documents examined are sport, war, (knowledge as) building and, to a slightly lesser extent, machines and nature/plants. The discursive effect of these repeated metaphors is to construct the university as hostile, threatening, competitive, and always vulnerable. Within the university, knowledge is constructed as inorganic, linear and manufactured.
- SU websites deploy multimodal choices which construct students as both consumers and products/commodities of the university and which render them complicit in the colonisation of the corporate academic.
- University mission statements and diversity statements make routine use of evaluative language which reflects a preoccupation with self-promotion and corporate branding. The combined corpus and APPRAISAL analysis of these texts, though, reveals a paradox in that the formulaic nature of university mission and diversity statements betrays a rather undifferentiated approach to the mission of higher

education institutions. The analysis also demonstrates how the statements reflect the current obligation for universities to reflect corporate rather than academic values – a feature which is consonant with the way universities have been compelled to recast themselves in the mould of neoliberal ideology.
- In some of the documents, there are occasionally areas where resistant discourses can be found, but these are relatively rare.

In sum, the combined analysis from all of the preceding data-focussed chapters indicates a massive reorientation of universities away from their previous mission as serving the public good, as repositories of knowledge, as a refuge from the discipline of the market and capitalism, as governed by the pursuit of knowledge for its own sake. The discourse is more than just a reflection of these changes – we argue that it is constitutive of ideological change, and of a new kind of neoliberal, self-managing, subordinate subject. At the time of writing, the neoliberal surge in higher education shows no signs of slowing down. In a study of neoliberal practices in universities spanning the UK, Australia and New Zealand, Wright and Shore (2017) list seven major trends which characterise neoliberal reform in universities: state disinvestment in universities; new regimes for promoting competitiveness; the rise of audit culture; administrative bloat at the expense of academic decline; the rise of the 'administeriat'; the rise of the 'entrepreneurial university'; and higher education as private investment versus public good. In our work, we have observed how these trends are manifested through the language that is habitually deployed in texts which circulate and have currency in the HE context. Wright and Shore speculate that the seven trends could spell the end of the public university. Furthermore, they propose that the decline of public universities is part of a larger political agenda that threatens to fundamentally transform the public sector more broadly (in which organisations which have previously served public interests become privatised for-profit organisations). Indeed, we see similar neoliberal practices becoming increasingly dominant in schools and the NHS in the UK.

In Chapter 1, we explained how critical university studies has emerged from academics organising around concerns about funding, corporatisation, marketisation, academic capitalism, audit culture, academic governance and citizenship. Despite the overwhelming pervasive presence of neoliberal discourse and governmentality through the HE sector, our work has shown that there remain crucial areas in which such discourses can be contested. In Chapter 3, for example, we found that the frequent claims of uniqueness in the mission statements were undermined by a concurrent discursive uniformity. However, there was also evidence that counter-hegemonic/non-neoliberal discourses have not been entirely erased suggesting that neoliberal rhetoric does not sit entirely comfortably or without challenge. A key strategy for contestation is to expose the ideological underpinnings of managerialist and neoliberal discourse, and critical applied linguistics provides us with the tools for doing so.

Sealey (2014) argues that in order to form academic critiques, language is the agent in the redefining of subjectivities. New formations of academic labour are relational – when students are customers, academics are service providers. Discourse can channel resistance, but it requires a huge sensitivity to linguistic choices. Throughout this book, we have argued that managerialism is largely achieved and sustained through discourse. By submitting real-world data to a range of rigorous linguistic analyses, we have demonstrated that there has been a calculated shift of discourse in order to restructure the values, perceptions and behaviours of academics, but we have also shown that this discursive restructuring is open to contestation.

Significantly, though, the power of discourse is manifestly not lost on the governing structures of the HE sector in the UK where 'big data' and 'metric power' (Beer 2016) are deployed, not just in a search for learning analytics, but in an attempt to orient students towards those behaviours and choices which are judged to correlate with 'success'. In a powerful analysis, Williamson (2018) describes how the QAA has used 'unsolicited student feedback' from social media platforms in order to obviate the potential for institutional gaming through formal instruments such as the NSS or TEF. This social media mining or 'scraping' offers a route to 'sentiment analysis', and we wonder whether this approach may prevail in the near future, since projects designed to assess learning gain, such as Assessment of Learning Outcomes in Higher Education (AHELO), have been temporarily shelved (McKie 2018).

Perhaps, though, a necessary sensitivity to discursive changes, and to their significance, has been overlooked for too long by academics. Whilst academics in Spain, France, Canada, Turkey, Hungary and New York have protested over issues such as tuition fees, marketisation, casualisation and university autonomy from government, there has been little visible direct political action in the UK apart from the 2018 strikes over proposed pension reforms. It is remarkable that there has been so little work from a discourse point of view, in terms of critique of the academy. This is where we feel our work will take the project of challenging the neoliberal tide in HE forward.

However, as Parker (2014) recounts, techniques for silencing dissent have become more refined and powerful in the last few years. In his narrative of a particular form of change management in a business school, he documents the following strategies for blunting critique: shutdown of collective responses to managerial communication (no more 'reply to all' emails); school meetings redesigned to give out information and discourage questioning; disbanding of committees; problems redefined not as issues of structure, policy or behaviour, but as issues of communication; failure attributed to underperforming academics; re-writing history so that even evidence of good performance is over-ridden and appropriated as more justification for change; mass resignations, early retirements and sickness offered as evidence that change is both necessary and having a (positive) and much-needed effect.

In a similar way, Gabriel (2012) recounts recovery from what he terms 'institutional miasma'. Using the analogy of Greek tragedy whereby the institution is seen to be in the grip of disease, disorder and fear that corrupts the moral fabric of a social unit (2012: 1145), Gabriel describes how the process of culture change and removal of supposed 'dead wood' ends up reinforcing institutional toxicity rather than cleansing it (2012: 1144). Miasma overwhelms and shuts down resistance; it neutralises institutional narrative and makes sense of the journey from the past to the present. People who resist are made to disappear, often under unjust and inhumane circumstances. Gabriel recounts how remaining employees are left with a sense of uncleanliness. Miasma is deeply contagious – 'it undermines people from within; people lose their confidence and self esteem, moral integrity evaporates and a moral and psychological corruption sets in' (2012: 1147).

Parker's and Gabriel's descriptions will be familiar to many. Consequently, it is all the more important that our work should disturb some of those in management, both those who consciously or carelessly might wreak such misery amongst their colleagues, and amongst those who wonder how to break out of the institutional abuse. We are aware that many managers feel despondent and trapped by the authoritarian structures which deny them, also, strategies of resistance. We are aware that many feel themselves coerced into taking a stance they are unwilling to endorse. Many of them admit their peer groups have disappeared. Whatever happened to the monthly heads of departments meetings? Disbanding of these important structures has allowed dictatorial management techniques to take root. A dismantling of collegial structures which facilitated democratic decision making and real communication is justified as 'modernisation of management'. And open debate has been replaced by 'consultation exercises' (Parker 2014: 291).

It is important to speak out and ensure new, alternative narratives are legitimised, validated and given opportunities to take root. There is some promise in McMillan-Cottom's (2017: 10) observation that 'despite our shift to understanding higher education as a personal good, we have held on to the narrative of all education being inherently good and moral'. This message requires reinforcement, and we hope this book will enable the faculty voice to be raised more persistently and more audibly.

Ways forward?

If we are to advance critical university studies, it is important, as Morrissey (2013) argues, to be *critical for something* in order to insist on enacting alternative values and subjectivities (2013: 4). Wright and Shore

(2017) contend that, despite the many critiques of the demise of the public university, there have been relatively few attempts to propose any serious alternatives to the current neoliberal regime. They do, however, note that plans are taking shape in the UK for the development of a group of 'cooperative universities' (see also Hall 2018; Hall and Winn 2018). A cooperative model involves flat rather than hierarchical structures in which each faculty is a cooperative nested within a wider university cooperative. They also consider the development of a 'trust university' model as well as 'free universities'. Since the enactment of the latest legislation in the UK, the Higher Education and Research Act 2017, the government has facilitated the emergence of new 'providers' which they intend will provide competition for traditional universities. There is now an expedited route towards both degree-awarding powers and conferment of university title. However, HERA also offers new possibilities for reimagining the university in democratic as well as purely marketised formations.

In laying out a language-focussed analysis to expose the new anti-democratic and managed ethos of universities we believe we can also offer some concrete proposals for framing alternative discourses which may reflect the values of alternative university models. In critical metaphor analysis, Lakoff (2003: 4) has argued strongly that the 'analytic act is a political act'. The critical linguistic analyses presented throughout this book comprise a political act – that of aligning us with a set of values based around academic freedom, the creation and development of genuinely useful knowledge, the co-creation of that knowledge with students, collegiality and mutual cooperation between universities, and social justice. Lakoff goes on to state, 'Being able to articulate what is going on can change what is going on – at least in the long run' (Lakoff 2003: 4). We hope that this is precisely what we have achieved in this book from a linguistic perspective – through exposing the various ways in which neoliberal discourse is operationalised through the repeated use of a formulaic set of SDS, metaphors, evaluative features of language and keywords which prioritise neoliberal ideologies.

Following this exposure, a next step is to offer some discursive alternatives. How could a different set of values and ideologies be conveyed through the language used in the kinds of documents examined throughout this book? In order to address this question, we offer the following recommendations for those with responsibility for writing these kinds of texts (SU websites, recruitment materials, mission statements, diversity statements, REF and TEF documents, performance management documents, staff training documents).

- Multimodal texts can place emphasis on academic values and real student representation, rather than serving the economic needs of private companies (through advertising), producing stealth audits of academic staff 'performance', commodifying students and serving the interests of university managers rather than students themselves. Re-emphasise clubs and societies. Remove competitions and 'award ceremonies' relating to academic staff. Encourage students to find other ways of showing appreciation for their teaching staff which do not invoke ostensive competition and evaluation. Critical thinking can be enhanced by subjecting these processes to evidence-based analysis, such as a consideration of the way in which women, ethnic minorities, older and LGBT+ academics are under-appreciated in student surveys.

- Minimise the use of SDS in documents. If the use of certain SDS are deemed unavoidable, then their meaning should be clarified within the context of the document in question. There should additionally be channels through which students and academic staff are able to challenge university leaders on the use of SDS and to demand semantic clarity and consistency where necessary. In more than one chapter, we take issue particularly with 'excellence' and instead offer alternative such as 'soundness' or 'capacity' (Moore *et al* 2017).
- Carefully consider how evaluative language is used in documents. Consider what the evaluative language reveals about what is being valued, why and by whom? Are the values and ideologies conveyed through this language in line with those of students and academic staff?
- Minimise the use of metaphors that carry with them cognitive schemas associated with threat, competitiveness and hostility. Replace these metaphors with those which can map alternative meanings.

Alternative metaphors: how might they sound?

As an illustration of how the recommendations previously outlined can be put into practice, we consider how the language of higher education might sound if alternative metaphors are used. Lakoff and Johnson (1980) assert that because metaphors are one of the most basic mechanisms humans have for understanding experience, they have the power to create new meanings and therefore define new realities. Similarly, Charteris-Black highlights that, because metaphor can influence the way we perceive a certain social reality, then 'it is a potent and potentially powerful weapon' (2004: 23). Critical metaphor analysis can create possibilities for new ways of thinking and creating new types of discourse. The introduction of new metaphors into the discourse of higher education may, at first, sound unusual. This is because the recycled metaphors identified throughout this book have become naturalised into the discourse and this is precisely what affords them their power to create a version of reality which is perceived as the only possible reality. Indeed, there may well be places in which we have used them ourselves in this book and the literature of critical university studies is also pervaded with the imagery of war and siege (Taberner 2018: 134). For example, we could consider the replacement of war and sports metaphors in higher education documents with a more organic alternative, such as the conceptual metaphor of plants and nature. This source domain immediately removes the hostility, violence and competitiveness cognitively associated with the source domain of war and sport.

The introduction of a UNIVERSITY AS A PLANT metaphor might begin to construct an ideology of collegiality and unity where all of the different parts are needed to create a functional whole and which carries with it a cognitive typology which is organic, nurturing, part of a larger holistic ecosystem, and which serves an essential natural function. Another alternative may be to try replacing the KNOWLEDGE AS BUILDING metaphor with something more natural and organic, such as KNOWLEDGE AS PLANTS/NATURE or KNOWLEDGE AS FOOD/NUTRIENT. The cognitive schemas carried from these new source domains into the target domains of university and knowledge would then be focussed on ideas and feeling, such as *growth*, *life cycles*, *branches/branching*, *roots*, *incubating*, *bedrocks*, *climate*, *environment*, *blossoming*, *thriving*, *hatching*, *nurturing*, *nourishing*, and so on. In the examples that follow, we present the original text containing a sport, war or building metaphor in the first line, with an illustrative alternative metaphor presented immediately underneath each example in *italics*:

- and outstanding track record in collaborative research and process training
  thriving collaborative research and process training culture
- Engaging with research builds skills such as critical thinking and analysis
  Engaging with research nourishes and grows skills such as critical thinking and analysis
- The first year builds a foundation in core areas [. . .] In your second year, you build on this knowledge
  The first year plants the roots of knowledge in core areas [. . .] In your second year, you grow this knowledge
- We are proud of our reputation for providing a high-quality student experience underpinned by inspirational teaching
  We are proud of our reputation for providing a high-quality student experience rooted in inspirational teaching
- offers a high-quality springboard into coaching sport from community to the elite level

Offers high quality incubation into coaching sport from community to the elite level.

Even when no obvious metaphorical alternative presents itself, neoliberal values can still be evacuated from the discourse by removing the sport metaphor. For example:

- will give you the best possible chance of achieving your career goals.
  Will give you the best possible chance of achieving your career <u>aspirations</u>.
- This Foundation degree has been designed to ensure that graduates are equipped to tackle this challenge [. . .]
  This Foundation degree has been designed to ensure that graduates <u>are fully able to</u> undertake this challenge.

Because we are unaccustomed to language being used in this way, some of these examples may sound unusual or 'unnatural'. But if they begin to be used more, they will, over time, become naturalised in the way that the current recycled set of metaphors in higher education have become normalised. This suggested use of alternative metaphors could, over time, contribute to the construction of a different social reality in higher education.

Other recommendations

It is not just language, of course, which has worked to undermine the values held by large numbers of academics. There are now disciplinary mechanisms which have coerced academics into becoming neoliberal subjects and rendered them, literally, accountable. Not the least of these has been a transformation of the labour market such that many posts in universities are now filled by employees on 'casual' or insecure contracts. We have not dwelt much on this in the book, but it is nevertheless a significant cause of stress in the working lives of many academic employees. Over the past decade, stress has mounted and autonomy decreased, and Hall argues that academics have become alienated from their labour as it is subsumed ever more by the service of capital (Hall 2018). The whole architecture of performance management, mandating targets often outside of academics' control, such as research grant 'capture', has led to widespread incapacitation of individual workers due to mental health breakdown. It is hard to defend the descent of the university into 'anxiety machine' (Hall and Bowles 2016) when confronted on a daily basis with the consequences of this regime (Morrish 2017).

In addition, we are heartened to see structures which have arisen to monitor implementation of recommendations from the report on responsible metrics. In the foreword of *The Metric Tide*, Wilsdon *et al* (2015: iii) remarks:

> At their worst, metrics can contribute to what Rowan Williams, the former Archbishop of Canterbury, calls a 'new barbarity' in our

universities and we hope to see the spread of responsible use of metrics in promotions and hiring of academics.

The report finds that 'there is legitimate concern that some quantitative indicators can be gamed or can lead to unintended consequences; journal impact factors and citation counts are two prominent examples'. The report calls for more reflexivity, transparency in the use of metrics, and, notably, there is a call for humility in recognising their limitations: 'recognising that quantitative evaluation should support – but not supplant – qualitative, expert assessment' (2015: x).

There is a global campaign to promote adoption of similar values enshrined in the San Francisco DORA which requires signatories to 'eliminate the use of journal-based metrics, such as Journal Impact Factors, in funding, appointment, and promotion considerations'; and address 'the need to assess research on its own merits rather than on the basis of the journal in which the research is published'. Another statement is contained in the Leiden Manifesto for Research Metrics (Hicks *et al* 2015), which offers ten principles for the measurement of research performance, including a recognition that quantitative evaluation should support, not supplant qualitative, expert assessment. It also recommends that excellence in locally relevant research should be protected, and that excellence in research should not be equated with English language publication.

These attempts try to ensure that metrics are used responsibly and in ways which recognise different disciplinary norms in publication and citation practices. They also signal a future in which work is valued in terms of its intrinsic and social worth, not its value as a financialised commodity. To date, very few UK universities have signed DORA (DORA) and the movement to challenge metrics-based performance management continues (Morrish and the Analogue University Writing Collective 2017). We welcome these initiatives to confront and overturn the distortions occasioned by audit culture whereby research themes and indeed the very definition of research becomes not just constrained, but actually determined by its eligibility for the REF (Morrish and Sauntson 2016).

We look forward to a new era in which the autonomy of academics is recognised by universities, the citizenry and governments. In New Zealand, it is enshrined in law (Section 162 (4) (a) (v) of the Education Amendment Act, New Zealand) that universities are to be characterised by an acceptance of 'the role of critic and conscience of society'. In addition, teaching and innovation depend upon the safeguard of academic freedom. This means that academics have an ethical responsibility towards knowledge, its curation, advancement and dissemination, not just to an employer. As Morrissey (2013: 6) points out, this distinction captures the difference between 'responsibility' and the neoliberal concept of 'responsibilisation' which has been so successfully mobilised by NPM-influenced university managers.

The essential contribution of critical applied linguistics

We contend that the work of re-writing the language of higher education is a specialised skill which can be improved and enriched by the contribution of applied linguists whose job it is to understand language and its discursive effects. As we envisage an alternative, inclusive and democratic future for universities, higher education documents could be audited by applied linguists specialising in CDA to ensure that whatever ideological positions are advanced enjoy the support of the widest constituency of scholars. Indeed, critical applied linguists are ideally placed to advise on all of the earlier suggestions and recommendations. They have the specialist knowledge, for example, to conduct corpus analyses of any draft documents to see if the keywords and collocations encapsulate the desired message. Critical applied linguists are also able to identify SDS and recycled metaphors which may not accurately reflect the values held by academic staff and students.

Importantly, those working in the field of critical applied linguistics are teachers as well as researchers. Through their teaching, they are able to develop students' awareness of how language operates in student-facing documents such as SU websites and mission and diversity statements. Indeed, this is already happening, and discourse analysis based on these kinds of documents now features in many linguistics and media and communication studies courses in the UK and elsewhere around the world.

Students, as well as academic staff, must be educated in critical thinking to play a key role in resisting neoliberal discourse. This book has revealed that the language of higher education documents constructs students not only as consumers but also as depersonalised products/commodities of the university. In our own professional experience, we observe that many of our students reject this and the consequences that flow from this characterisation. Many are resistant to compulsory exercises every six months in which they are required to reflect on their 'employability skills' and to complete 'training needs analysis' forms. We also routinely observe undergraduate students electing not to attend sessions which have no academic content and instead focus on generic 'skills' and 'employability'. Attendance at sessions which implicitly embed skills development into academic content (a feature of university courses which goes back for centuries) are, by contrast, well attended. Despite nominating 'getting a good job' as one of their primary motivations for entering a university course, students appear less inspired by the notion of employability or expectations of graduate earnings, than with their actual academic accomplishments. Our students appear personally invested in how their degree will help them to pursue careers and projects which serve the public interest, a mission shared with many academics. It is refreshing to witness their idealism in an era in which global capitalism is 'casting off its increasingly inconvenient liberal humanist ideological shell' (Thorpe 2008: 104).

Nevertheless, liberal ideals continue to be cited by the government agency charged with regulating universities, even as government policy results in a clear contradiction in practice. At the time of writing, the newly established OfS has produced a set of 'public interest governance principles' with the purpose of regulating the ethical conduct of higher education providers in the UK. The very first principle is academic freedom, suggesting that this is something that the OfS values highly. This principle states:

> Academic staff at an English higher education provider have freedom within the law
>
> - to question and test received wisdom; and
> - to put forward new ideas and controversial or unpopular opinions without placing themselves in jeopardy of losing their jobs or privileges they may have at the provider.
>
> (Office for Students 2018 www.officeforstudents.org.uk/advice-and-guidance/regulation/public-interest-governance-principles/)

In the same document, the OfS also places importance on 'accountability', demanding that HEIs operate 'openly, honestly, accountably and with integrity and demonstrates the values appropriate to be recognised as an English higher education provider'. Unlike New Zealand, however, they omit a statement which would articulate those values unambiguously.

Over several decades, the cult of managerialism has attempted to undermine the legitimacy of other forms of authority, including that of evidence and expertise. As academics, we support that legitimacy together with the upholding of principles of academic freedom and autonomy that enable it. We have attempted, throughout this book, to show how the two principles of academic freedom and autonomy are inextricably linked and how essential they are if we are to restore vitality and reward to a troubled profession. It is disconcerting to see in our analysis of documents how overshadowed those values have become when subordinated by university managers to values of 'branding', reputation, competition, accumulation of profit, and metric-driven accountability. As we pointed out in 2016, 'Where there is deliberately diminished professional autonomy, the academic will feel themselves unfree in deciding what to research' (Morrish and Sauntson 2016: 49). Furthermore, the culture of performance management, overwork, anxiety and surveillance has proved utterly counter-productive. It has led to a precipitous decline in the mental health of academics whereby 55% of the 6,439 UK academics interviewed in one study cited in the *THE* say they had experienced symptoms including depression, sleeping problems and cognitive impairment (Grove 2018).

Academic staff and students are united in their belief that the current toxic environment of universities – not just in the UK, but globally – needs to change. Academics must be able to speak out as their consciences dictate when they see the academy falling short of its traditional mission. We end with an urgent plea for managers, academics, administrative staff and students to work together to ensure that values of democracy, cooperation, integrity, freedom, truth and humanity are cherished by 21st-century universities.

References

Beer, D. 2016. *Metric Power*. Basingstoke: Palgrave Macmillan.

Charteris-Black, J. 2004. *Corpus Approaches to Critical Metaphor Analysis*. Basingstoke: Palgrave Macmillan.

DORA. *San Francisco Declaration on Research Assessment*. https://sfdora.org/ (Accessed 17 July 2018).

Gabriel, Y. 2012. Organizations in a state of darkness: Towards a theory of institutional miasma. *Organisation Studies* 33 (9): 1137–1152.

Grove, J. 2018. Half of UK academics 'suffer stress-linked mental health problems'. *Times Higher Education*. www.timeshighereducation.com/news/half-uk-academics-suffer-stress-linked-mental-health-problems (Accessed 17 July 2018).

Hall, R. 2018. *The Alienated Academic. The Struggle for Autonomy Inside the University*. Basingstoke: Palgrave Macmillan.

Hall, R. and Bowles, K. 2016. Re-engineering higher education: The subsumption of academic labour and the exploitation of anxiety. *Workplace: A Journal for Academic Labour* 28: 30–47.

Hall, R. and Winn, J. eds. 2018. *Mass Intellectuality and Democratic Leadership in Higher Education*. London: Bloomsbury.

Lakoff, G. 2003. Metaphor and war, again. www.alternet.org/story/15414/metaphor_and_war%2C_again (Accessed 20 June 2018).

Lakoff, G. and Johnson, M. 1980. *Metaphors We Live By*. Chicago, IL: University of Chicago Press.

Hicks, D., Wouters, P., Waltman, L., de Rijcke, S. and Rafols, I. 2015. The Leiden manifesto for research metrics. *Nature* 23: 429–431.

McKie, A. 2018. Standardised tests measuring learning gain fail to make the grade. September 13. www.timeshighereducation.com/news/standardised-tests-measuring-learning-gain-fail-make-grade (Accessed 30 September 2018).

McMillan-Cottom, T. 2017. *Lower Ed. The Troubling Rise of For-Profit Colleges in the New Economy*. New York: The New Press.

Moore, S., Neylon, C., Eve, M.P., O'Donnell, D.P. and Pattinson, D. 2017. 'Excellence R Us': University research and the fetishisation of excellence. *Palgrave Communications* 3. Article number 16105.

Morrish, L. 2017. Stress fractures: One year on. *Academic Irregularities* blog. https://academicirregularities.wordpress.com/2017/03/14/stress-fractures-one-year-on/ (Accessed 16 July 2018).

Morrish, L. and The Analogue University Writing Collective. 2017. Academic identities in the managed university: Neoliberalism and resistance at Newcastle University. *Australian Universities' Review* 59 (2).

Morrish, L. and Sauntson, H. 2016. Performance management and the stifling of academic freedom and knowledge production. *Journal of Historical Sociology* 29 (1): 42–64.

Morrissey, J. 2013. Regimes of performance: Practices of the normalised self in the neoliberal university. *British Journal of Sociology of Education* 36 (4): 614–634.

New Zealand Legislation, Education Act. 1989. www.legislation.govt.nz/act/public/1989/0080/latest/DLM183668.html (Accessed 17 July 2018).

Parker, M. 2014. University, Ltd: Changing a business school. *Organization* 21 (2): 281–292.

Sealey, A. 2014. The neoliberal university: Agency and responsibility. Paper presented at *Neoliberalism, Education and Applied Linguistics Symposium*, Institute of Education, June.

Taberner, A. 2018. The marketisation of the English higher education sector and its impact on academic staff and the nature of their work. *International Journal of Organizational Analysis* 26 (1): 129–152.

Thorpe, C. 2008. Capitalism, audit and the demise of the humanistic academy. *Workplace* 15: 103–125.

Williamson, B. 2018. The mutating metric machinery of higher education. *Code Acts in Education* blog. 26 September 26. https://codeactsineducation.wordpress.com/2018/09/26/metric-machinery-of-higher-education/ (Accessed 30 September 2018).

Wilsdon, J. et al. 2015. *The Metric Tide: Report of the Independent Review of the Role of Metrics in Research Assessment and Management*. London: HEFCE. www.hefce.ac.uk/media/HEFCE,2014/Content/Pubs/Independentresearch/2015/The,Metric,Tide/2015_metric_tide.pdf (Accessed 17 July 2018).

Wright, S. and Shore, C. eds. 2017. *Death of the Public University? Uncertain Futures for Higher Education in the Knowledge Economy*. Oxford: Berghahn.

Glossary of terms

CAL	Critical Applied Linguistics
CDA	Critical Discourse Analysis
CMA	Competition and Markets Authority
DLHE	Destinations of Leavers from Higher Education
HEA	Higher Education Academy
HEFCE	Higher Education Funding Council for England
HEI	Higher Education Institution
HEPI	Higher Education Policy Institute
HERA	Higher Education and Research Act
HESA	Higher Education Statistics Agency
JISC	Joint Information Systems Committee
MCDA	Multimodal Critical Discourse Analysis
NM	New Managerialism
NPM	New Public Management
NSS	National Student Survey
NUS	National Union of Students
OfS	Office for Students
QAA	Quality Assurance Agency (for Higher Education)
REF	Research Excellence Framework
SDS	Strategically Deployable Shifter
SKE	Success as a Knowledge Economy
STEM	Science, Technology, Engineering and Mathematics
SU	Students' Union
TEF	Teaching Excellence Framework
THE	Times Higher Education
UA	University Alliance
UOA	Unit of Assessment

Index

Note: Page numbers in *italics* refers to figures.